RICHARD BURTON

ALSO BY PAUL FERRIS

NOVELS
A Changed Man
Then We Fall
A Family Affair
The Destroyer
The Dam
Very Personal Problems
The Cure
The Detective
Talk to me about England

REPORTING
The City
The Church of England
The Doctors
The Nameless: Abortion in Britain Today
Men and Money: Financial Europe Today
The New Militants: Crisis in the Trade Unions

BIOGRAPHY
The House of Northcliffe: the Harmsworths of Fleet Street
Dylan Thomas

Richard Burton

BY PAUL FERRIS

Weidenfeld and Nicolson
London

Contents

Illustrations

Introduction

ACTORS are tempting subjects for biographers, but the nature of their trade makes them difficult to see plainly. One becomes irritated, forgetting that they make a living from deception. Richard Burton, born Richard Jenkins, was elusive in the flesh as well. I pursued enquiries for three years, off and on, but always through relatives, friends, colleagues, film, tape and printed text. Letters to him went unanswered. He had a fresh wife and was reported to be a soberer, wiser man. A new Burton would presumably have little interest in helping a stranger excavate the old Burton's past.

In 1977, at the start, I took an aide out to dinner, affecting a friendliness I didn't quite feel, and was told that 'Richard is not terribly keen on anyone doing his biography, but he's writing to you next week.' I heard no more. A year later I had a message from the head of a recording company, who, after trying for years, had persuaded Burton to select and read some poems. He told me that at the studio Burton had asked about his would-be biographer and said he would be in touch. Nothing came of that, either. After a few more letters I stopped trying and got on with the book.

The many people whose help I acknowledge are listed below. Some were unwilling to be identified; they appear, if at all, as 'Anon' in the main text or Notes. I am indebted in particular to members of Burton's family who, usually after misgivings, talked to me at length. The sisters in order of seniority are Cecilia James, Hilda Owen and Catherine Thomas, ladies with smiles and strong characters; they were the key witnesses to the distant past. Two brothers, Will and David, were kind and helpful, too. So was the actress Siân Owen, Burton's niece. In a category of his own comes Philip Burton, a man of many talents who has had to bear the cross of being known as 'Richard Burton's adoptive father', though in fact he was never strictly that. Now in his seventies, and long since an American citizen, he was once a schoolmaster in South Wales. He took the adolescent Jenkins under his wing, gave him his name and pushed him in the right direction.

Without wanting to be invidious, it might be useful to list a few of the more important people, from my point of view, who declined to talk about Richard Burton: some with friendly letters, some with silence. There is no reason why any of them should have said yes. But the absence of a name can be as important as its presence. Too many accounts of the famous pretend to know more than they do. I would rather go to the other extreme.

Conspicuous by their absence, then, are Claire Bloom, Alexander Cohen, Princess Elizabeth of Yugoslavia, Sir John Gielgud, Hugh Griffith (who said no before he died), Joseph Losey, James Mason, Vincente Minnelli, Mike Nichols, Rachel Roberts (who has also died), Daphne Rye and Jean Simmons. Burton's close circle of aides, advisers and others on payrolls past and present did not seem likely to yield its secrets, or even to tell me what day of the week it was, and in most cases I didn't bother to try; when I did, the results were as expected. There seemed no point in approaching Elizabeth Warner, formerly Taylor, who has been discreet about her years with Burton. Susan Hunt, Burton's third wife, was as unapproachable as he, and said to be even less keen on seeing his past raked over.

Sybil Christopher, the Welsh woman who was Burton's first wife, now lives in America. After Burton himself, she was the one I most wanted to meet. I tried by letter to convince her that we could confine our conversation to her, and leave Burton out of it, but she believed no more than I that this was practicable. It was just as well that we shouldn't meet, she wrote back, adding mischievously that the Welsh were inclined to fabricate, and she might confuse me. I thank her for taking the trouble to write.

I am grateful to the following: Vivian Allen, Jim Backus, Romany Bain, Lady (Ellen) Baker, Terence Baker, Nina Bawden, Keith Baxter, Alan Bridges, Jack Brodsky, Peter Bull, Lord Bullock, Sir Alec Cairncross, Phyllis Calvert, Mrs Campbell (South Wales Miners' Library), Cecil Clarke, Douglas Cleverdon, Joan Collins, Sir John Colville, George Cukor, Cliff David, Jenkyn David, Hubert Davies, Mrs Morfydd Davies, John Dolan, Paddy Donnell, Lynne Dorsey, Dillwyn Dummer, Philip Dunne, Sydney Edwards, Clifford Evans, Elwyn Evans, Mrs Janet Evans, Roger Falk, Anton Felton, Richard Findlater, Robin French, Christopher Fry, Trevor George, Peter Glenville, Jack Gold, Harold Griffiths, Sir Alec Guinness, Leslie Halliwell, Robert Hardy, Kathleen Harrison, Frank Hauser, John Heyman, Donald Houston, Tom Howell, John Vivian Hughes, Emyr Humphreys, Waris Hussein, Brinley Jenkins, Mair

Jenkins, Mrs Katharine A. Johnston, Elliott Kastner, Jacqueline Kavanagh, Ed Knappman, Elizabeth Knappman, Henry Koster, Eric Lamborn, Richard Leech, David Lewin, Gerry Lewis, Richard Lewis, Euan Lloyd, Dr David Luke, Andrew V. McLaglen, Brenda Maddox, Tom Mainwaring, Jack Meelan, Doc Merman, Ivan Moffat, Evan Morgan, Colin Morris, Glynne Morse, Jack Nicholas, Barry Norman, Philip Oakes, John Osborne, C.J. Parsons, Denys Parsons, John Perry, Daniel Petrie, Anthony Quayle, Dr J. Russell Rees, Phil Samuel, Shirley Seaton, Vincent Sherman, Jonathan Silverlight, Audrey Smith, Betty Smith, Lady Soames, Victor Spinetti, Anthony Storey, Eleanor Summerfield, Elizabeth Sweeting, Brian Tashara, Harry Tatelman, Dennis Van Thal, Bryn Thomas, Mrs Kate Turnbull, Harley Usill, Aled Vaughan, Jack Le Vien, Alexander Walker, Hal Wallis, Francis Warner, David Williams, D.B. Williams, Emlyn Williams, Noel Willman, Herbert Wise, Robert Wise, Audrey Wood.

My thanks are also due to: The BBC, including the Written Archives at Caversham, the Recorded Programmes and Script Libraries, the Cardiff Registry, the New York office; the British Film Institute; the *Observer* library; the *Western Mail*, Cardiff; the Theatre Collection at the Lincoln Center, New York City; the Enthoven theatre collection, London; the University College of Los Angeles; the University of Southern California; the Academy of Motion Picture Arts and Sciences, Los Angeles; David Frost's New York office; CBS; NBC; *Harpers and Queen*, *Woman's Own* and *McCall's*, all for photocopies supplied; and to the copyright holders listed in the notes for permission to quote copyright material.

CHAPTER ONE

Jenkins, Arise

MANY wondrous stories have been told about the childhood of Richard Burton. He was poor, hard, cunning, bold, alone and very Welsh. He knocked down his enemies with his bare fists and made his friends roar with laughter. He was charming; singular; a devil. Giant figures loom up in the narrative, a coalminer father who drank like a fish, a coalminer grandfather who died careering downhill in a wheelchair. Before them came other shadowy sons of the earth, sweating their guts out to provide wealth for the English and their 'bare-shouldered remote beauties in many mansions', as Burton once described them, long after he had found bare-shouldered beauties of his own.

For someone as famous as Burton has been in his time, it would be almost indecent not to detect some drama in his origins. Besides, he was a film star in the days before film stars ceased to be magical creatures. Studio publicists turned out potted biographies that hinted at his wild Celtic nature. Newspapers gobbled them up. Burton gave interviews and improved on the facts out of devilment, nostalgia or simply boredom. His past became larger than life. It was hardly surprising, since his present, too, in the years of his rampant relationship with Elizabeth Taylor, came to look like a press agent's invention. The film industry thrives on exaggeration, and the Welsh are among the least straightforward of people; it is a deadly mixture.

The mining valley of the River Afan where Richard Burton was born is in the western half of the coalfield. Straggling between the hills is the township of Cwmavon, literally 'the valley of the Avon', or Afan, which in turn means 'river'. The twisted landscapes of slag and slate roofs were never so oppressive there as they were to the east, in deeper and more infamous valleys like the Rhondda. Today all the valleys are shells; Cwmavon no longer has pits, copperworks or any reason for being there except its brief industrial heyday. Above Cwmavon, where the valley begins to shrink, is the village of Pontrhydyfen, some of it low down, most of it high up. A brick viaduct for the railway, now disused, crosses road and river. A grander set of stone arches nearby was built early in the last century to carry an aqueduct, long since converted to a road bridge. A pair of small dwellings stands in its shadow, beside the Afan; the right-hand house is Burton's birthplace. Once or twice a plaque announcing this fact has been fixed to the wall, only to vanish at night.

His family name was Jenkins; the change to Burton came later, when a schoolmaster of that name took him under his wing. The Jenkinses of Wales are a numerous tribe, tens of thousands strong. This particular strand of them is first recorded at Colwinston, a village in the Vale of Glamorgan. The Vale, easily entered by invaders from the east, and peppered with English place names, bulges out from the extreme south of Wales, between the coal valleys and the sea. Miles Jenkins, a 'servant in husbandry', is marrying Mary Arthur, a farmer's daughter, in 1838; perhaps he worked on the farm and won her father's approval. His father was another Miles, a cattle dealer. The great-great-grandson of the cattle dealer, four generations on, was Richard Burton.

At some time in the next two or three decades the family or a part of it left the Vale and moved to Pontrhydyfen in the hills fifteen miles away, with its new mines and ironworks. Miles had become a miller and so kept his links with the land; but his son Thomas, born about 1848, who married in 1875, was a coalminer. From now on they were urban people, bound to the iron wheels. Thomas married a local girl, Margaret Walters, a joiner's daughter. Neither could write, and the marriage certificate has their marks, not their signatures. This Thomas was to be the crippled grandfather who supposedly crashed to his death in a wheelchair, shouting the name of a racehorse he thought he was riding at the time. That he was crippled in a mining accident and used a wheelchair seems to be true. As for his spectacular exit, shouting 'Gee up, Black Sambo!', it sounds like another of the tall tales, rich in black comedy, that the hardships and bleakness of the mining valleys produced as a by-product to help an oppressed population keep its spirits up. There is a powerful South Wales tradition, male rather than female, of leg-pulling and blarney, irreverent and tinged with violence. It is still there like an afterglow; the wicked anecdotes that delighted Hollywood when Burton began telling them to Americans in the early 1950s are part of a local culture that sprang out of dirt, ugliness, poverty and the rain blowing in from the sea.

All through the nineteenth century industrial communities grew up in the valleys where formerly there were hamlets and farms. Pontrhydyfen's aqueduct was built to serve blast furnaces nearby; shallow pits were sunk into coal seams with names like Jonah, Sulphury and Golden Rider. Pontrhydyfen is at a junction in the valley, pinched between the hills. 'Pont' is Welsh for 'bridge', 'rhyd' is a ford. 'Fen' may be the same word as 'wain' or cart. In that case the name means, roughly, 'Cartersford Bridge'. Rural life persisted nearby. A mile away at Efail Fach, the Little Forge, was the water mill where Miles was probably the miller. When she was a child, Burton's eldest sister Cecilia, born in 1905, used to visit an aunt and uncle who lived at the mill cottage. In the kitchen was a Welsh dresser, the traditional sideboard with shelves for plates, sign of a good solid home.

Thomas and Margaret seem to have had only one child who lived to be an adult. He was born in 1876, when they had been married eight months, and was given the names Richard Walter after Margaret's father, the joiner, who was Richard Walters. He came to be known as Dic. He too was a coalminer and married a local girl, Edith Maud Thomas; Dic and Edith were to be Richard Burton's parents. On his wedding day, Christmas Eve 1900, the bridegroom was twenty-four, a stocky, handsome man with moustache and fringe of black hair over his brow. Burton has described him as 'a man of extraordinary eloquence, tremendous passion, great violence. He looked very like me: that is, he was pockmarked and devious and smiled a great deal when he was in trouble.' There are other versions, but this one will do for the moment.

The marriage was not welcomed by the bride's parents. Edith was only seventeen – the marriage certificate shows eighteen, but her birthday was not for another month. It is said that they did not want her to marry an only child, who was likely to be spoilt and 'difficult'; there was a story that Dic's mother used to carry him to school when he was small. Edith had been born in Swansea, the manufacturing town on the coast ten miles away. The birth certificate shows her sex as 'Boy'. The General Register Office can only suggest that the registrar in Swansea was drunk.

Edith's mother, Jane, who notified the birth, signed the register with her mark, not her name. The family later moved to the Afan valley, where her father was a sampler in a copperworks, known locally as 'Harry Sampler', an aloof and anglicized figure. In one family memory the Thomases appear as 'very select – people called them "the lords"'. Edith was a handsome girl with fair, curly hair, taller than the man she was marrying; she worked as a barmaid at the Miners Arms in Pontrhydyfen, and this is the address she was married from. Both signed the register, the first of Richard Burton's ancestors to be literate. Dic liked to read; the house had a bookcase.

Their married life in the village followed a common enough pattern for the place and time. The father was indulged in his pleasures, especially drinking, but the mother, despite her youth, was the real authority. Edith scrubbed, washed, polished, baked, brewed, prayed and provided the point of steel around which the household revolved. Babies came regularly: Thomas Henry in 1901, Cecilia in 1905, Ifor in 1906, two Margaret Hannahs who both died in infancy, William in 1911 – six births while she was still in her twenties, and the family had not yet reached the halfway mark. In ways that now seem as remote as candlelight she found time to eke out the housekeeping by washing neighbours' clothes and papering their parlours. She brewed small beer from hops and nettles, selling it in the village to be drunk at Sunday lunch. She made trays of sweets and sold those, too. In the children's memories their own table was well supplied. They owned a pig or two, shared with neighbours who had a sty, and salty bacon hung in the kitchen. Dic was a good man with a rabbit snare. The children roamed the hills (or 'mountains' as the Welsh are apt to call anything over a few hundred feet) gathering blackberries and whinberries for the 'ten plates of tart' that Edith would bake at weekends. The family continued to grow – David was born in 1914, Verdun in 1916, Hilda in 1918, Catherine in 1921, Edith in 1922. Before she was forty, Edith Maud had nine children living. Two were still to come.

Much of this information is from Hilda, now Hilda Owen, who lives with her husband in one of a row of nineteenth-century houses in the upper part of Pontrhydyfen. She has been there all her married life. At first she rented the house, but Richard bought it for her years ago. Mrs Owen is plump, busy, methodical and attractive. When she turned her head, the first time I was there, looking out of the window to see if the rain had stopped, the resemblance to her brother was evident. She rattled teacups and asked if I would like a piece of cake. Mr Owen, a carpenter, appeared briefly in a doorway, smiled and vanished again.

It had taken me some time to approach her. While I still thought there was a chance that Richard Burton might talk to me himself, I kept away from his close family. I had spoken to a journalist who published a series of articles towards the end of the 1950s, in which Burton seemed to have unbuttoned himself and spoken freely. But the journalist told me that the articles had been written from the cuttings of other articles. They contained no original material. It was not for want of trying, he said. He managed to get on to the film set of *Look Back in Anger* where Burton was working, and asked him for an interview; Burton said he would talk to him if he had the time. The journalist hung about for three days, at the end of which, in desperation, he went to Burton's dressing-room and said politely that he could wait no longer. 'I said to him, "If it's all right with you, I'll go and talk to your relations." He came close and said, "If you go near any of my people, I'll tear you limb from limb." I retreated hastily.'

Eventually it became obvious that Burton was going to be unavailable whatever I did or didn't do, and I began to write letters and make telephone calls to the family. David Jenkins, eleven years older than Richard, is a retired police inspector, living in a suburb of Swansea. A hand-delivered letter failed to reach him because he had moved. I telephoned Hilda, who was dubious and on the point of saying no. After much persuasion, and when she had spoken to David and others, she said yes. I half expected that someone would telephone Richard in America, where he was playing in *Camelot*, twenty years after he first appeared in it. But this was to misunderstand the relationship between Burton and his relatives. They keep in touch by letter and telephone, but Richard and his life are too remote and impregnable to need protecting. What concerned Hilda was that I might be another of the strangers with tape recorders who go away and write that Richard was brought up in terrible poverty or that their father was a roaring drunkard. The fact that I was Welsh and born in Swansea, though not resident there for almost thirty years, will have helped. At least I could pronounce 'Pontrhydyfen' and knew that whinberries are what the English call bilberries. I made no secret to his relatives of the silence in which Burton had wrapped himself as far as I was concerned. I told them I was writing his biography and that he wouldn't lift a finger to help, even to say that he was not going to help. Hilda shrugged her shoulders and said he was no great letter writer. Her brother Will was staying. He smiled and nodded.

Welsh was spoken at home when Hilda, Will and the rest were children; so was English, the language of progress. On Sundays Edith took the children to chapel, where she sang in the choir, but Dic had better things to do. Reputedly a man who liked to read his Bible, he kept chapel for funerals. His grandfather, Miles, had been married in the Anglican church in his Vale of Glamorgan village. But his father, Thomas, and Dic himself had made do with a civil marriage at Neath register office, down the road. Many miners had no time for religion. Long shifts bent double in icy water, breathing dust and bad air, hacking awkwardly at narrow coal seams for a pittance, bred iconoclasm. Dic was a strong, fierce workman who could earn good money when he felt like it. The children called him 'Daddy Ni' – 'Our Daddy'. To the village, which needed nicknames because Joneses and Jenkinses were so common, he was 'Dic Bach y Saer' – 'Little Dick the Carpenter', although that was not his trade. His maternal grandfather was Richard Walters the joiner; perhaps as a child the grandson was seen about the village with the carpenter, a chip off the old block.

Dic's weakness was drink; that, and a certain cockiness and bravado, echo in Richard Burton's anecdotes and occasional writings about a time before he was born, when a younger Dic and his handsome Edith walked the earth. The day Dic came home from a spree with Paris, a mangy greyhound or whippet that was going to make their fortune, became a little legend. '"Boys," he bellowed, "our troubles are over."' In Burton's written version it is Christmas week. The family collapse with laughter, and the father, ashamed of himself when sober, vanishes on another drinking bout, until a son tracks him down in a distant pub ('"And it's the *gwas y gwr drwg* in you, the servant of the Devil in you, that is driving us all mad."') He returns to the village, works an extra shift to give them money for Christmas, but ends up badly burned in an explosion. The story contains fragments that Burton heard as a child from older brothers and sisters. There was a real dog, but Dic wasn't allowed to bring it through the door. At that time they lived higher up, near the aqueduct, the 'Big Bridge', in a tiny house now demolished. Cecilia, the eldest daughter, put her foot down; Paris stayed in the steep back garden.

I heard this story, and others, from Cecilia herself, one afternoon in the sitting-room of her bungalow in north London. She was the sister who brought Richard up, and has always been the closest to him. Her husband, Elfed James, once a coalminer, is dead. Her daughters have grown-up families of their own, and the bungalow stands in the garden of the house where the daughters live. It is on the edge of London; the trees were full of birds. Mrs James is the Welshest of them all, happier to speak and write her own language. She seems to belong in another time, a world of blackleaded grates, regular chapel and the men handing over their pay packets at the end of the week. But the spotless rooms are full of sun and bright fabrics. A photograph of Dic and Edith at the time of their marriage hangs near the door into the kitchen, coloured by hand. It is the only picture from the period that seems to have survived; the poor don't have photograph albums. Mrs James, too, had doubts about talking to me. She had woken up in the night worrying, she told me afterwards, and nearly rang to stop me coming.

When I arrived I found another sister there, Catherine or Cassie, also widowed in recent years. She had spent much of her life in London, working in a medical laboratory; like me, she was Welsh with added layers of Englishness. Cassie was a foil for Cissie, who recalled elderly female relatives of my own that I dimly remembered, women in small houses, wearing white aprons, making pots of tea and popping things in ovens. Dislike of strong drink was another feature of Mrs James that brought back my childhood. My paternal grandfather was supposed to have come home drunk on Saturday nights, which produced strong temperance reactions in the next generation. In the case of Mrs James it was her father, Dic Bach, who liked his drop. We reached the subject, unwillingly on her part, when I brought up the story of Paris the mangy dog. 'There was a terrible row between Father and I,' said Mrs James. 'I said, "If that dog is coming in here, I am walking out. There's too many children." I think that Rich heard the story because I was so nasty about this dog. "You can keep him, Dad," I said, "but it's got to be at the top of that garden. You feed him outside and you have a kennel for him." I could tell him what I liked. But nobody else could, you see. He said, "Right-ho" – he was a very quiet man. A very nice man, except that he liked his drink. Of course, I was against that, it's true. I'll say it, I've never touched a drop.'

'Never,' confirmed Cassie.

'I've been abroad with Rich, I can't tell you how many countries I've been, when there's champagne – "Come on," he says, "one mouthful – do you the world of good." I wouldn't say a word.'

The story came out of the terrible night Cissie and Ifor had to collect their father from the Colliers Arms at Efail Fach. This, too, is echoed in Burton's account. It didn't seem all that terrible. Ifor has been dead for years, but must have told Richard all the family yarns. 'Ifor and I were very close,' said Cissie. 'There was only thirteen months between us. You'd have liked my brother Ifor. And truthful, mind. You should have seen him picking Dad up, mad as a hatter. He was only about twenty, I think he was. Furious, he was. We got him under each arm to take him. It was dark, you see. Lights were very dim, then. I said, "Now, Dad," in Welsh, "don't you open your mouth, we don't want to show anybody that we are taking you home, right? Whatever you hear now on the road, don't you speak." We took him all the way, a mile, and he never opened his mouth. And that's all he would say, "I've got children in a thousand, good as gold."' This is what he says in Burton's story. Mrs James finished the real story. '"... good as gold". "I don't want any soap," I said. "No soft soap." We took him home. He shouldn't have a *bit* of food, then. I'd see to that. Straight to bed. And I think Mother was going to have a baby then. I was sorry for her, too, you know. But there wasn't a better man walking.'

It was true, said Cissie, that occasionally he would vanish for days at a time, drinking in Neath or Swansea, always returning with the same excuse: 'I met a friend.' His excursions meant rows at home, but he was good at coaxing himself back into favour. The drinking might stop for months. 'A lovely man,' say the daughters, shaking their heads at the memory of all that beer. Even the explosion that burned him is true. Their mother, says Hilda – or perhaps it was Cissie – 'cured him by pouring olive oil over him all the time'. Only his eyes and nostrils showed through the bandages, and 'you could hear him groaning from the road'. But he recovered and worked again. 'Our mother' is always on the edge of the stories and anecdotes, the 'beautiful mother' of Richard Burton's versions, the safe presence at the centre of the family that vanished when he was still a baby. There is a sense of loss behind the comic tales because they are about a world in a village that fell apart as the child was coming to know it. Perhaps this explains nothing about him; all childhoods are lost countries anyway. But it is not difficult to imagine some connection between the death of Burton's mother before he was two years old, with its effect on the family home, and his long search thereafter for the necessities of affection, fame and money.

Richard Burton was born in 1925, a year of unrest and bad omens in the coal industry; the General Strike lay ahead. He was Edith's tenth living child, and he was given his father's two names, Walter as well as Richard. She was then forty-two and had been bearing children for almost a quarter of a century. Earlier in the year they had moved from the house in Station Road, on the same level as the Big Bridge, to a slightly larger house just above the river level, downstream from the arches, No. 2 Dan-y-bont (literally, 'Under the bridge'). The birth was on 10 November. Family gossip suggests that from the start the child was everyone's darling, but this could be hindsight. Something else has stayed in Cecilia's memory, that he was unhappy if parted from his mother, even for a moment. He would 'cry and scream' if she was out of his sight, and she 'couldn't go to put clothes on the line without him holding her skirt'.

Tragedy followed with the birth of a further child. Pregnant again little more than a year after Richard was born, she had another boy on 25 October 1927, a Tuesday. Complications arose after the birth, though when Cecilia, who had married her coalminer, that summer and gone to live a few miles away on the coast, visited her mother the following Sunday, there seemed no particular cause for alarm: childbirth had made her ill often enough. On the Monday Cecilia came again. The bus brought her up the valley in the morning. As she got out she saw 'crowds of people on the Big Bridge' and thought the subdued voices and air of expectancy meant what they usually meant in a mining village, an accident underground. A woman came up to her and said, 'Your mother has just passed away.' The death certificate gave her true age, forty-four, 'wife of Richard Walter Jenkins, Coal Hewer'. Her body stayed in the house for the neighbours to pay their respects. In a later account by a journalist who visited Pontrhydyfen, Graham and Richard had to sleep in the same room as the coffin; Cecilia says this is nonsense, and is shocked at the impropriety.

The family reorganized themselves as best they could. Graham was to live with the eldest boy, Tom, a miner, who was married and lived in Cwmavon; Richard with Cecilia, who stayed in the village until the funeral, then took him home to Port Talbot. From then on, she insists, he never asked for his mother, and never cried for her.

Port Talbot, only four miles by road from Pontrhydyfen, is a small industrial town dominated by steelworks, clustered at the base of hills on the eastern side of Swansea Bay. Smoke of many colours hangs over the streets, merging with the rain clouds. Local philosophers shake their heads and call it 'Poor Albert'. This was where Richard Jenkins grew up, went to school and was a candidate for drudgery.

Elfed and Cissie lived on the edge of the town in one of a group of cottages, since demolished, on the outer slopes of Mynydd Margam, Margam Mountain. Town, works, rail sidings and docks were spread out below; beyond them was the bay, its farther side occupied by the larger town of Swansea, built along the coast with hilly suburbs behind. Dylan Thomas was writing schoolboy poems in one of those middle-class suburbs when Richard Jenkins was an infant. Looking east across the bay, Dylan would have seen Mynydd Margam as a blur in the industrial haze; Thomas-land and Jenkins-land were worlds apart. Richard was brought up to expect a mixture of hardship and rough pleasures, with the chance that a bright boy might elbow his way out of the working class. At first even that would have seemed unlikely. They were a very ordinary family. The Jenkinses of Pontrhydyfen had been a large, colourful clan, inclined to independence, even arrogance. Richard went back there frequently for weekends or holidays, shared a big bed with his sisters, and caught echoes of the old days. Brother Ifor, twenty-one when his mother died, emerged as the strong character. He was the one Richard looked up to. But the Jenkinses had lost their real centre; they married one by one, and eventually Daddy Ni went to live with Hilda, where he studied racing form and told his disapproving daughters, 'There's no harm in it, I only spend a shilling.' Richard's everyday family consisted of Elfed and Cissie, and they in turn were part of a tight web of local relationships. Elfed's parents, the elder Jameses, lived nearby. So did Elfed's sister, Margaret Ann, whose married name was Dummer, and who had a son, Dillwyn, of Richard's age. The Dummers and Jameses lived hand in glove. It was a Dummer/James rocking horse, an ancient beast handed down through the family, that was used to comfort Richard Jenkins when he first came to his new surroundings.

People of that generation who remember straitened circumstances and hard times will admit they were 'not well off' but not that they were poor. To be poor was to be disgraced. The poor wore boots without socks, bought sugar and bread 'on tick', and failed to polish the door knocker till it shone. It was vital to keep up appearances. 'There was little visible poverty in the school,' says one of Jenkins's earliest teachers. 'People were at great pains to disguise it.' Elfed and Cissie kept a clean, respectable home. She was an ardent duster and polisher; they were chapel-goers, and first met at a chapel eisteddfod in Port Talbot where

Cissie, who had a soprano voice, was singing. They were second cousins – their maternal grandmothers were sisters. Elfed didn't drink and was careful with money. After a while they moved down to the newly built Caradoc Street, where the houses are thicker on the hillside. A motorway built to bypass the town runs a few feet above its chimneypots. The slope, with its terraces of houses and a school, is known as 'The Side'.

From an early age there are sparse family reports that he was 'quite the little actor'. So there are with many personable children. A plump infant, he would 'stand on a stool and imitate preachers' (Hilda) and 'act with two candlesticks that were supposed to be the telephone, because we didn't have a telephone' (Cecilia). 'You could have eaten him,' they say. Cecilia doted on him, even when she had two babies of her own, and he on her. The Jameses and Dummers spoke English, like most families on The Side, but Richard and Cecilia used Welsh to one another; she was the Jenkins connection, his daily link with the past. He once said that his first memory was of 'running through snow, absolutely naked, being chased by my eldest sister'. In the best of his occasional writings, *A Christmas Story*, in which Burton recalls childhood with a feverish clarity that he has managed nowhere else in print, Cissie is the 'green-eyed, black-haired, Gipsy beauty' who had 'become my mother, and more mother to me than any mother could ever have been'. She is 'innocent and guileless and infinitely protectable', and 'I knew that I had a bounden duty to protect her above all other creatures. It wasn't until thirty years later, when I saw her in another woman, that I realised I had been searching for her all my life.' The woman he meant was Elizabeth Taylor.

The school on The Side, Eastern Infants, was near the house. Probably Jenkins went there at the age of five, but there is no record. At the end of the summer holidays in 1933, and before his eighth birthday, he transferred to the 'Boys' School', the senior department of Eastern, in a leaky building on the main road at the bottom of The Side. Tom Howell, his first teacher there, remembers a small boy 'wide-awake, big eyes, cow's-lick of hair, freckles, a voracious reader. Before long he had read everything in my cupboard.' The books were mostly Howell's own Sunday school prizes, improving works like *Lamb's Tales from Shakespeare* and *How Paul's Penny Became a Pound*. Classes were around the fifty mark but the children behaved themselves. Chapel, deprivation and their family histories all encouraged obedience to authority. Howell, a kindly man with a sharp eye, found it 'a good time to be teaching.

Respect for authority was an inborn quality, it didn't have to be beaten into anyone. It was innate – for headmaster, teacher, policeman.'

Eastern was the school where futures were decided. At the end of three or four years came the competitive entrance examination for the two local secondary or 'grammar' schools, the so-called 'scholarship'. The scholarship was solely in English and arithmetic. The handful who passed it went on to further education; the rest became clerks or labourers. The driving force at Eastern was the master who taught the scholarship class, Meredith Jones, now dead but widely remembered in the town as a mixture of slave-driver, wit, intellectual and bully that made him a skilful promoter of bright boys. Burton was later to hail him as the man who changed his life, 'a recognizable spiritual descendant of Geraldus Cambrensis and Shakespeare's Fluellen – passionate, fluent, something of a scholar, mock-belligerent, roughly gentle, of remarkable vitality and afraid of nobody'. Jones was not one of the meek. His voluble character, which struck some as bombastic, spoke directly to a boy who, in his own account later, was having his eyes opened to the power that lay waiting in words and attitudes. The appeal of Jones to Richard Jenkins identifies the kind of boy he was, intelligent enough to catch the other's interest, hard enough to enjoy his hardness. A contemporary at Eastern recalls how 'a boy, a rather big boy, did something wrong in class. He had to bend over and have one across the backside. Well, it was quite ludicrous – he was a very fat chap. We laughed. So Meredith caned everyone. We didn't all laugh but we all got caned. Another boy had a speech impediment. Meredith made him come out and recite "Twinkle twinkle little star" in front of the class. I thought that was terribly cruel.'

Tom Howell remembers him as 'hail-fellow-well-met, very fond of himself'. Jones's pupils (having passed through Howell's hands earlier) were dismissed as 'all rubbish, for the first two months they were in his class. Then all the geese became swans.' Young Jenkins was not put off by Jones's belligerence, mock or otherwise. He was not one of the weedy boys who must have existed even in that harsh climate, who hated the punches, the stinking school lavatories and the bruising bouts of rugby football, the national game. Meredith Jones was fanatically keen on sport in general and rugby in particular, and Richard was devoted to it. The boys would play in the paved school yard before the morning bell, with frost still on the ground. The touchline was the wall; a boy who was tackled might crash into it. Trevor George, school friend then, headmaster in an English village now, says it was 'part of the system in those days. My Dad used to say, if you can't take a tackle, you shouldn't be playing the game. Learn to grow up, be a man. You daren't do it today. You'd be taken to court.' 'We were the cream,' says Tom Mainwaring, another of the rugby boys. 'Meredith got the best out of us. I don't know what happened to the weeds. They watched us, I suppose.'

It was the middle of the 1930s. The worst of the Depression was over, but times were hard in a town like Port Talbot, and remained so until the war began in 1939. There was little money to spare for children, except to meet basic needs. Members of a family would share a bicycle as later they would share a car. Richard and Dillwyn Dummer shared a pair of skates, one each for careering down streets on The Side. As in most recollections of times past, pleasures were not costly. Children played kick-the-tin and allerbeleese, where rival gangs ran whooping through one another's dens. For ball games without a ball, copies of the *Football Echo* or other suitable newspapers were folded small and tied with string. Trevor George remembers how they all learned to swim at 'The Sidings', a series of saltwater pools where high tides could penetrate. It meant a walk along the railway line from Port Talbot, but was nearer than trekking across Margam Moors to the beach. There were expeditions around Mynydd Margam, past the Tumbling Field and the woods; miles of empty mountainous country lay to the north, with Pontrhydyfen out of sight behind the ridges. 'The whole of Margam Mountain was our domain,' says Dillwyn Dummer. 'We used to go camping behind the houses in gangs, twenty of us to a tent. We dug dens in the mountains and put branches over the top. Trouble? No. If you went to pick a couple of carrots out of a man's garden you were living dangerously.'

For a seat at the local cinema, a few pence sufficed. The Picturedrome, popularly known as the 'Cach', or Shithouse, had been a drill hall for the Territorials. The seats were laid out on a level floor in front of the screen, with a sloping section at the rear. On Saturdays children swarmed in for the 'tu'penny rush'. Parents who wanted to be rid of their brood for a few hours would give them the money to go 'over the Cach'. It was one way of clearing a small house with thin walls and enabling husband and wife to make love. Sunday school, bottling up the children for a safe hour or two in the afternoon, served the same purpose. Richard had the small boy's distaste for romantic movies. Sometimes he and Dillwyn would come home early from the Picturedrome. 'Bloody love, Auntie,' he would say to Mrs Dummer, 'bloody love.'

In March 1937, when he was eleven years old, it was time to sit the scholarship. The results were not announced until late in June. 'It was the be-all and end-all of everything,' says Tom Howell. 'If you didn't go to the grammar school you stayed till you were fourteen and went out into the workaday world. Richie would have left and become a butcher's boy, and where would he have gone eventually? Into the steelworks or somewhere like that.' Burton, praising Meredith Jones, wrote that without him 'I would not have gone to a great university and I would probably not have become an actor.' For the Jones strategy to succeed, his pinched and precocious pupils had to make themselves credible candidates for the educational ladder by passing the scholarship. Second chances were rare. About one boy in twelve went on to further education; many were not even entered for the examination. A page at random in the school records for 1937 shows the fate of twenty boys. Nine went to local butchers, grocers and other tradesmen; four to work on farms; one each to docks and tinplate works; one to a carpenter, one to a stone-mason; two to a private school at Bridgend; one to Port Talbot Secondary School.

That year ten boys at Eastern School passed the scholarship, not a bad score for Meredith Jones. Richard W. Jenkins was among them. Now all he had to do was apply himself to his studies for the next decade of his life, and before the end of the 1940s he would be something distinguished and agreeable, like a schoolmaster, which indeed is what happened to the cleverer boys among his friends. He was on his way to becoming the first educated Jenkins descended from Miles the cattle dealer.

CHAPTER TWO

The Other Burton

MANY of the children who went to secondary school were only ten years old. Jenkins was nearly twelve, and in addition was unusually self-assured. This is how people remember him at Port Talbot Secondary School, which he entered in September 1937. He showed no sign of being a distinguished pupil; rather, of being a difficult one. If he cared about anything it was sport, which was useful as far as it went, but a long way from satisfying a staff that expected high standards. School was a sanctuary from the bleak world on the doorstep, and the masters were there to see that children didn't waste their chances. Economically depressed areas like South Wales often had teachers who were better qualified than the job required; they found work where they could, and schools like Port Talbot's reaped the benefit.

The master in charge of rugby says that what Richard Jenkins lacked in flair he made up with enthusiasm. If it had not been for the war he might eventually have played for the Welsh Schools XV. He was in the cricket team and ran with the cross-country harriers. On school sports days he rushed from one event to another, doing high jumps and long jumps, throwing discus and javelin. He became known in other respects. He was developing bold features with fine, wide-spaced eyes, blue-green and burning with excitement: 'the face of a boxing poet', as the Welsh playwright Emlyn Williams saw it a few years later. He began to acquire a presence, a sense of himself that other boys couldn't fail to notice.

He could be comical but the jokes had an edge. Legends sworn to with differing degrees of certainty have accumulated among Jenkins's contemporaries. Accused by Reynolds, the headmaster, at morning assembly of forgetting his gas mask, which had to be taken everywhere on pain of punishment, the boy replied to the question 'Where was it, Jenkins?' by saying, 'Where was yours, sir?' He had noticed the headmaster coming to school without his container; a school friend, now a headmaster himself, says he saw the wonderful episode with his own eyes, and heard the mighty figure of 'Pop' Reynolds reduced to mumbling 'Dismiss, dismiss.' In another scene, witnessed by another former friend and present-day headmaster, the schoolboy joke of urinating from a train window was performed by Jenkins and a second boy. They had been playing rugby in one of the valleys; had been drinking beer illegally; found themselves in a non-corridor train for the journey home; and happened to relieve themselves as the train was going through a station. Jenkins's hysterical laughter is what the friend remembers best.

Exciting stories are told of how Jenkins persecuted a physical training master. Once, says a third friend, he 'went to the youngest form in the school and borrowed a tiny pair of shorts. He left his socks and suspenders on – he always wore sock suspenders for some peculiar reason – and he had his tie round his bare neck. He walked about four times up and down the gym with that peculiar walk that Olympic walkers use, leered at the master, said, "Right, are you happy now?" and went back to the changing room to finish his cigarette, which had been tucked behind his ear.' Could that have happened in a strictly run school forty years ago? On another occasion, when the same master was rummaging inside a vaulting box where sports equipment was kept, Jenkins 'slammed down the lid and sat on it'. Shouts and hammering came from inside. 'Then the headmaster walked in, demanding to know what the noise was about, and it went deadly quiet in the box. Poor thing!'

The former PT master now lives in another town. He says both stories are nonsense. Richard was 'a bit cocky' and 'I had to speak sternly to him once – I threw him out and let Reynolds deal with him.' The original informant sticks to his story about the box, but says that perhaps, after all, it was a joint effort by the class, with Richard as ringleader. And the tiny shorts episode? 'Funny, I can't get a picture of that in my mind. Did I see it happen or did I hear about it? It was such a long time ago and there are so many apocryphal tales that reality gets mixed up with fantasy.' It is difficult for anyone as famous as Burton to be remembered accurately over thirty or forty years, especially since his particular variety

of fame itself became a fantasy, shrouding the 'real' Burton, and before
him, the 'real' Jenkins.

Even the most important event of those early years at the school is
blurred. At some point Jenkins and the senior English master, Philip H.
Burton, became aware of one another. This account is not quite ready
for the stout, stern figure of P.H. Burton to come marching in. But before
he became surrogate father and magic uncle to Jenkins, the schoolmaster
was on the scene. Still in his thirties, a bachelor who lived in lodgings in
the town, he was one of those highly qualified teachers who were there
by ill-luck more than anything else. The theatre was his private passion;
he wrote radio scripts for the Welsh station of the BBC, and seemed to
float with a natural buoyancy beyond the grey confines of the town; his
eyes were always on London. Looking for young actors to take part
in a radio play he had written about Shakespeare's childhood, he
held auditions in the junior school. Among those who failed to be chosen
was Richard Jenkins. Philip Burton insists that he remembers nothing
about the incident: it was the actor who had to remind him, years
later.

When Jenkins was in his fourth year at the school, he did succeed in
catching the master's eye. The school play in January 1941 was George
Bernard Shaw's political comedy *The Apple Cart*, one of many ambitious
pieces that P.H. Burton staged, cheerfully confident that his boys and
girls – the school was co-educational – were capable of having decent
performances wrung from them. Jenkins, on a stage for the first time,
played an American, Mr Vanhattan, in a thick Welsh accent, overlaid
by the drawl familiar from films at the 'Cach'. Aged fifteen, it is just
possible that he already thought of bettering himself via the stage. P.H.
Burton talks about a diary that Richard kept when he was first at the
school. When the older man came to read it later on, it contained
respectful references that showed he had been noticed, long before he
taught the child. 'Don't forget', says the elder Burton, 'I was doing the
radio stuff. I was known locally because I had a good theatre company.
Was Richard interested in the theatre then? I'm not certain. If I was his
hero, and I was thought of as a theatre man, and he knew the adulation
that other boys were getting when they were in school plays ... I'm not
certain.'

The idea that young Jenkins had a master plan is implausible. On the
contrary, there is evidence that it was the elder Burton, bewitched by the
glories of the English theatre, who thrust the boy towards the stage once

he recognized the striking nature of his looks, voice and personality. Richard Burton spoke about it in 1961, in a comparatively early radio 'profile' for the BBC, which he always treated with respect, and which was more likely to hear the truth. He said he was 'not quite sure why I wanted to be an actor. It's all very clouded now, the images are blurred, but I think that originally I was striving in some way to acquire an education of almost any kind.' He once told a newspaper that 'I had a wild ambition to go out into the world and starve. I didn't know what I wanted to do. I liked talking so I thought of becoming a preacher. But it was pointed out to me that I had no religious feeling. So I gave up the idea' (1955). School was not proving a success in 1941, and Elfed, his coalminer brother-in-law, with two daughters to bring up as well, must have had unkind thoughts about higher education. There were rows in Caradoc Street. Relatives on the James side of the family, anxious to make a good case for Elfed without making a bad one for Richard, remark that 'it was hard to bring up a boy in those days', that 'there were three of them to rear', that 'Richard had to toe the line because there wasn't a lot to be had – you know what miners' money was.' Cissie, caught in the rows, says that Richard had 'gone to smoke cigarettes a lot', that he needed money for this and for girlfriends, that he borrowed from her and she borrowed from the housekeeping. 'How are you going to pay back, Rich?' she would say. 'Use a bit of common sense.'

In June, five months after *The Apple Cart*, he was due to try the next rung of the ladder, the school certificate examination. This had to be taken in at least five subjects. Without it there was no point in having been at the school. Cecilia says that he talked of leaving and she tried to dissuade him. Whatever happened, Elfed was not interested in prolonging the agony. His father was on the committee of the big Co-operative Stores on the main road. Smart boys were in demand; the war was on, the staff was depleted, and wages were one pound and eight shillings a week, enough to buy thirty packs of cheap cigarettes. Easter term ended on 4 April, and Jenkins, R.W., left school to go into the world of work; perhaps his end-of-term report had been the last straw. In the 1961 radio profile Burton said merely that 'something of a small family crisis demanded that I should leave school and go to work'.

The job was not congenial. The Co-op had many departments, Grocery and Fruit, Chemist and Footwear; Jenkins went to Outfitting, selling men's clothes. A haberdasher's assistant was not a manly post for the son of a miner.* Young Jenkins is said to have felt humiliated. In the semi-autobiographical *A Christmas Story* a character called Mad Dan says to the child, 'Shut your bloody trap and listen, or I'll have you apprenticed to a haberdasher.' Burton adds that 'this was a fate worse than death for a miner's son' and goes on to sing the praises of 'the lords of the coalface'. The feeling that he has been cut off from his working-class roots raises its head now and then in Burton's life, and although when heard on some distant film set it may sound like an affectation, behind it is an echo of an old regret. Coalminers, he wrote in a 1970 rugby reminiscence, were 'hard volumes of which I was the soft-cover paper-back edition'. In 1941 Men's Outfitting was irksome or worse. His sister Hilda, who lives now where she lived then in Pontrhydyfen, and whose snug house was one of Richard's regular ports of call, remembers his desperate 'I hate it, I hate it.' She will not go into details. Cissie shakes her head over it all. 'The manager would send him out on an errand, and the next thing was, he was having dinners in the houses. The Co-op said to us, he's never there. But he didn't tell me he was unhappy.'

The Co-op has produced a crop of stories about young Jenkins the comical haberdasher. Winking at friends and relatives, he sold them overcoats and trousers without collecting the wartime clothes coupons. Taking suits to be altered by tailors, he dawdled in their houses, reading books and drinking cups of tea, while back at the shop the manager tore his hair. Cissie says, 'Oh dear, he'd get cigarettes in the department and put them down in our name.' Friction with Elfed continued. 'He used to get cross with Rich at times,' she says. 'I used to spoil Rich, I know. I gave in. Then Elfed had to be strict on him, you see.' A school friend says that 'we felt he was a devil of a lad, but I think it was a bad patch for him. He wasn't going home for his dinner. He'd be popping across to the Talbot to have a few pints, even though he was under age. A funny thing, he was everyone's friend at that age, but I never remember him having one particular butty.' Twelve years later Burton hinted at the resentment he had felt, when he talked to a reporter in Hollywood. 'Cecilia's husband', said the article, 'died of silicosis when Richard was thirteen [he didn't die until 1980] and he went to work. In the slums where they lived, he was called "Wild Jenk" and was famous locally for both brawling and singing.'

* The actor Stanley Baker, another Welsh miner's son, and later a friend of Burton, had a brother, Freddie, who went to work in a shop. He couldn't stand the ridicule and fled to the pits, where he worked for twenty years and contracted pneumoconiosis, which killed him.

There are grains of truth. He liked boxing. He sang. Like others in the family he had a good voice, a treble before it broke, and in the Co-op days he went to eisteddfods and chapel festivals with Cecilia and Elfed, wearing his best suit and behaving himself. This was the 'Welsh' side of his life, singing or reciting to audiences who took their amateur performers seriously. His mother had sung in the chapel, and Cecilia carried on the tradition. Graham, his younger brother, won prizes as a boy soprano. Tom, Ifor and Verdun all sang in the Afan Glee Party. Hilda was later a well-known singer of *penillion*, an intricate system of lyrics. The local culture included a strong tradition of amateur dramatics. The writer Emyr Humphreys, when he was a producer for the BBC in Wales, directed a radio play with Richard Burton in the cast in 1958. 'I remember his brother Ifor sitting next to me in the control box when we were recording a scene between Richard, Emlyn Williams and Clifford Evans. He thought I was unduly enthusiastic about the result. "Heard better in our vestry many a time," he said to me in Welsh.' Inasmuch as he had anything to do with this native tradition, Richard Burton alias Jenkins used it, as many a Welsh emigrant has, as a means to an end. Welsh patriots can occasionally be heard regretting that Burton moved away from Wales in a professional sense so swiftly and completely. But it is fanciful to suppose that as an actor he could have done anything else in the 1940s, when ideas of Welsh nationhood, later revived, were in the doldrums.

Reports of Jenkins the Shop filtered back to his former teachers. Jack Nicholas at the Secondary School says that 'the Co-op manager nobbled me and asked, "What was he like in school? Because he's bloody hopeless here."' But Jenkins was not lost sight of. Meredith Jones, the teacher from Eastern School, knew that his promising ex-pupil had gone to a job without a future. Jones, his finger in many pies, had started a youth centre. Jenkins went there for table tennis, gymnastics, debates and the drama group. He attracted attention – dressing up, playing the fool, fighting comic boxing matches. He played a convict in *The Bishop's Candlesticks*, a one-act play based on an incident in *Les Misérables*. The idea took shape with Jones and others that he was too able a boy to be left in Men's Outfitters. Moves were made behind the scenes to have him readmitted to Port Talbot Secondary, an unheard-of development. The school governors were persuaded against the better judgment of the headmaster, and eighteen months after he left, Richard Jenkins was allowed to go back. The bare account conceals a more complex story that is difficult to unravel now. Those who knew Jenkins in Port Talbot assume that clever Phil Burton had a lot to do with wangling his return. The tactics were arranged elsewhere, between Meredith Jones, who knew everybody, and one of the school governors, a powerful local politician, Llewelyn Heycock. But it is taken for granted that it was Burton, soon to become the boy's benefactor and close companion, who strove to have him back at school.

P.H. Burton, however, denies this. He insists that it was 'Meredith who spotted Richard after he left school, and was getting a bad reputation at the Co-op'. In this version of events Jones conceived and carried through the plan, then approached P.H. Burton before the boy returned, and 'asked me to keep an eye on him because he might be a bad influence in the school. I knew that he was potentially wild.' It may be that P.H. Burton is unconsciously playing down his interest at that early stage, where the details are safely blurred, because he prefers not to seem too much of a Svengali-like figure,* manipulating the young Jenkins as, on a lesser scale, he had sought to manipulate other promising boys. It is unlikely that he was unaware of Richard Jenkins, who had acted in a school play and was now acting with the youth club. They had at least one other connection, the Air Training Corps, a wartime national cadet force. P.H. Burton commanded the Port Talbot squadron; Jones was one of his lieutenants, and Richard Jenkins one of the rank and file. In January 1942 – nine months before Jenkins returned to school – the BBC's Welsh studios made a radio documentary about the ATC called *Venture, Adventure* (the corps' motto). P.H. Burton wrote the script; one of the cadets taking part, selected by audition, was Richard Jenkins.

Jenkins can hardly have been a passive onlooker. According to P.H. Burton with his story of the childhood diary, the boy was aware of the master from his early days in the school. Richard Burton has been quoted as saying, 'He never discovered me, I discovered him.' Whatever the precise dispositions, the careers of troubled boy and scholarly bachelor were converging.

When Jenkins returned to school, on 5 October 1942, he was within a few weeks of his seventeenth birthday. Philip Burton was nearly

---

* In his autobiographical *Early Doors* Philip Burton wrote, 'There must be a thing called the Pygmalion complex; if there is, I have it. It's a deep urge to fulfil myself as an actor or a writer through another person. Perhaps I should be unkinder to myself and call it a Svengali complex. It is not satisfied just by teaching a class; there must be a close personal identification with the pupil.'

thirty-eight, a senior master who had long settled into the ways of schoolteaching. Among the staff he was regarded as learned, excellent at his job, mildly eccentric, a little apart from the rest. His home for years had been a house not far from the steelworks where a widow took in gentlemen lodgers. 'Ma' Smith cooked his meals, dusted his bedroom and watched over him. Her little rabbit pies were among his delights. 'Ma,' he would grin, 'I could write a poem about that pie.' He was an odd mixture of fun and austerity. His accent – an almost pure English, clear, weightless, touched at the edge with a Welshness about the vowels – helped to isolate him. His life out of school was busy with the amateur stage, his work for the BBC, and theatre trips to London and elsewhere. In 1939 he had taken a sabbatical, and, financed by a University of Wales scholarship, spent five months travelling around America and being astonished by it; in one of the talks he gave to the school on his return, perhaps heard by Richard Jenkins, he described meeting Dorothy Lamour and Eddie Cantor in Hollywood. He was not in the mould of his fellow lodgers, a bank clerk and an engineer; he was deeper and more mysterious, and Ma Smith thought that he lacked companionship. A daughter, Audrey Smith, recalls a woman teacher in the town who was 'very keen' on Phil Burton. 'Mother used to say, "Why don't you hit it off with her?" "Oh," he said, "I'm quite happy on my own." He used to tell Mother, "You know, a cultured person is never lonely."' Once, the schoolmistress visited Ma Smith's on a winter's evening, and had to return home along streets blacked out in case of air raids. As she was leaving, Mrs Smith took her lodger on one side and asked if he meant to accompany her. 'No,' he said cheerfully, 'I didn't ask her to call.' P.H. Burton himself says that he was madly in love with a girl, a waitress, when he was at university. But she died.

Although he seemed English rather than Welsh, he had been born and brought up only twenty miles away, in the coal mining town of Mountain Ash. His father, Harry Burton, was a rolling stone from Staffordshire, a miner who joined the coal rush to the valleys, the Celtic Klondike of the nineteenth century. His mother came from another family of English immigrants, and was already a widow with a son when she met Harry. Philip was a late child, born when she was forty-five, in 1904. The father was artistic and amiable; while he played his clarinet and violin, and drank as much beer as he could get, his dominant wife, barely literate, devoted herself to bringing up Philip as 'a spotless youth'. The words are his; he says it was not a happy childhood. Street games and rough boys were not tolerated. His upbringing was guarded, calculated to turn him in on himself. So were other things about his Anglo-Welsh childhood. Clever at his studies, he learned Welsh at school and could write it better than his fellow pupils. But it was a 'literary' Welsh, not a daily language; when he tried to speak it, boys laughed at him. Even the fact that his parents were Anglicans and 'church' helped to split him off from the working-class life of the town, which was Methodist and 'chapel'.

Feelings of cultural uncertainty are common enough in South Wales, where people argue about what it is to be 'really' Welsh. A lonely child in any case, Philip seems to have been edged into making his own private discoveries, and so came across the theatre, which he believed in at once. Perhaps the fact that it was English and cosmopolitan fed his imagination, solved his problems of identity and gave him his lifelong taste for the stage. The discovery, begun at the local Empire and the Workmen's Hall when travelling players visited the town, dictated the course of his life and deeply influenced Richard Burton's.

The quiet boy's education was managed somehow, despite the fact that when he was fourteen his father was killed in a fall of rock underground. He went to the University of Wales and emerged with a curious double honours degree in pure mathematics and history, not in the first class; he had spent too much time at the three Cardiff theatres of the day, and decided that English was his real subject. He thought, but not for long, of becoming an Anglican priest – he saw himself 'preaching dramatic sermons' – and slid into teaching because there seemed to be nothing else that would pay him a salary. In 1925, when he was still only twenty, he went to Port Talbot Secondary School to teach mathematics, about the time that Richard Jenkins was born in the village on the other side of Mynydd Margam. A schoolteacher's life was not what he wanted, but for twenty years it is how he earned his living. He lacked the courage to break away from the safe, required pattern. As a teacher he soon changed from mathematics to English and used his classes to develop and expound a passion for the language and its classic writers. A generation of middle-aged men and women in Port Talbot remembers him lecturing in faded rooms, his tongue like a whip on occasion but his face lit up; visit schools there today, and half the headmasters seem to have been his pupils.

The theatre is what he cared about most. He produced plays in the school and the town, sometimes acted in them, sometimes wrote them. Always aiming at London, he sent plays to West End managers, but they sent them back. A sub-career with the BBC, that ubiquitous patron, as freelance writer and occasionally director, began in the late 1930s. All this time his Pygmalion or Svengali complex was busy. A promising boy was raw material to help him realize his own dreams of excellence. His first successful protégé was Owen Jones, a handsome pupil at the school, who, coached and fussed over by P.H. Burton, won an open scholarship to RADA, the Royal Academy of Dramatic Art. Jones spent two seasons with the Old Vic in London and played Laertes to Laurence Olivier's Hamlet. Injured while serving with the RAF during the war, he died in 1943, just when Richard Jenkins was emerging as a more fiery apprentice.

Other boys came under the master's wing. Evan Morgan, later a radio actor, says that P.H. Burton 'guaranteed' to get him through RADA, but was thwarted by Morgan's parents, who declared it would be time enough to think about that when he had his teaching diploma. Another young actor at the school, who enjoyed a moment of fame in a wartime radio play, came from a chapel-going family who frowned on the theatre as a career. There is a local story that P.H. Burton told the parents he wanted to adopt the boy – the year would have been 1942 or 1943 – but was given a cool reception.

The roles that P.H. Burton wanted his protégés to fill on distant stages were the great heroic parts, Shakespeare's in particular; a film star was not in the same class. He wrote in *Early Doors* that 'the adulation of movie stars by film fans' is 'a very inferior substitute' for what a Henry Irving could draw nightly from a live audience. The filmgoers' reaction, he suggested, has 'little or nothing to do with the artistic merits of the artist. The life, as revealed or manufactured by the man paid to project and protect the public image of a star, is more important than the performance; the extravagance of the reported life is a matter of such envy that some measure of sharing it is provided by avid adulation.'

Such views, old-fashioned and austere, read ironically now in the light of what had happened to Richard Burton by the time he expressed them, in 1969. But in 1943 the idea that he might help create a film star would not have occurred to the teacher. He went to and from the school; ate Ma Smith's rabbit pies; longed for a son; drew closer to Richard Jenkins.

CHAPTER THREE

Difficult Roles

THE school governors had been swayed in Richard Jenkins's favour by promises that he would work hard, obtain his school certificate the following summer and become a teacher. There are one or two school-teachers now who say wryly that they went on to training college only because Richard talked about going there. It was the sensible thing for him to say. Any suggestion that he wanted to be an actor would have been unwise. His reputation was dangerously colourful. Girls at the school were set trembling by the return of such a manly youth, who close on seventeen, was two years older than most fifth formers. He had been out in the world and earned money for beer and cigarettes. But Jenkins, half an adult already in the working-class scheme of things, would hardly have gone back to desks, torn textbooks, inky fingers, schoolboy jokes and discipline unless he had decided or been convinced that it was worth his while to settle down and play the game of academic snakes and ladders. On his first day back in October 1942 he threw a gym shoe at someone and broke a window. Perhaps it was a gesture to make him feel better. During the school year he spent as an over-age fifth former 'Wild Jenk' was not especially wild. He was a diligent if eccentric pupil in the iron grip of P.H. Burton.

In the schoolmaster's memory it was the boy who made the overtures. 'He courted me,' says Burton. After heavy air raids along the South Wales coast in 1941 the school was patrolled at night by 'firewatchers', recruited from teachers and senior boys. Richard 'saw to it that he was on duty when I was, and we talked and talked. As he always does, which

I didn't realize at the time, he exaggerated his situation for sympathy.' They talked about the boy's home, and in particular his unhappy relationship with his brother-in-law, Elfed. Philip Burton knew there was going to be a room available at Ma Smith's because the bank clerk had been called up for military service. 'You don't mean it,' said the boy. 'Nobody ever means it.' There followed visits to Cissie and Elfed, and finally an agreement that Richard should be looked after by the schoolmaster.

All this can't have happened overnight. Yet Jenkins was living at Ma Smith's within five months of going back to school, and had been a regular visitor there even earlier. This is another reason for supposing that they were very much aware of one another before October 1942. 'I was fascinated by him,' says Philip Burton. 'I thought he had incredible potential and great need.' As for his own need, to 'fulfil myself through other people', in the case of Richard 'he became my son, and very emotionally so. He was an extension of me. He had qualities that I lacked. He had an obvious virility. He was more macho than I am. In some ways he was more direct. I was a much more private person than he.'

In the radio profile of 1961 Richard Burton said that at school the master was ' a kind of God in our eyes, and indeed he still is in mine'. In this account, too, the boy is seen approaching him, this time to 'suggest that I might become an actor. So one day after school, I believe it was a Monday, he had taught the last lesson, and after everybody had been dismissed, I lagged behind, and finally I plucked up the courage to go and talk to him.' The schoolmaster was not encouraging. Philip Burton remembers trying to dissuade young Jenkins from being an actor. Or was he only going through the motions of dissuasion? In retrospect it is as if they were playing a game with one another. 'Of course he knew the story of Owen Jones,' says P.H. Burton. 'Everyone knew it. I was the magician. I had the things he wanted.' This must be the key to what happened. The boy was sharp enough to recognize what the master could offer and strong-willed enough to over-ride any family doubts. He knew that Philip Burton could give him a background. The stories, jumbled up over the years, afford glimpses of the process. One day after school – another day – Jenkins asked Burton to teach him to sing a difficult solo, Sullivan's 'Orpheus with His Lute'. It was a time when Graham Jenkins was winning prizes with his voice, and Richard wanted to compete with his younger brother. With Philip Burton at the piano in the empty assembly hall he croaked away in what was left of his school-boy treble until the master collapsed with laughter and the boy stormed away shouting 'I'll show you some day!' But wouldn't Jenkins's voice have broken altogether by the time he was seventeen? Perhaps it happened years before.

In the 1961 radio profile Richard Burton spoke of seeking 'an education of almost any kind'. He knew he could go to RADA on a scholarship 'and acquire a knowledge of the world, at least, and spend two years in London. That may have been one side of my ambition. The other side was, I think, that I really thought I might be able to act well enough to make a living out of it, despite P.H. Burton's laughing refusal to entertain my ambitions. I was determined in some way to attract his attention, and I went back two or three days later ... I don't know exactly how many times I must have gone back and persisted, but eventually he took it upon himself to ask me home after tea, and began the first lesson. I may say it was the most painful and hard-working period of my entire life.'

This account in turn suggests that he went to Ma Smith's in order to be taught how to act. But even if he and Burton conspired to this end or secretly hoped it was what would happen, the schoolmaster had other things to do. Jenkins had to be coached for his school certificate, the badge of respectability. The boy had to be given some polish. Richard Burton said in 1968 that 'Phil virtually took me out of the gutter and taught me to speak English and all that.' In Port Talbot one still hears stories of how he couldn't use a knife and fork properly until he went to live with the schoolmaster. Cissie, proud of her home and the pains she took with Richard, dismisses them. No doubt he was rough-edged and awkward by genteel standards. His voice was an early challenge for the schoolmaster. Whatever future was envisaged for him, a thick Glamorgan accent was not the thing. In the front room of Ma Smith's, where P.H. Burton ate his tea by himself in front of the red-tiled grate, and in the evenings wrote or listened to the wireless, Jenkins was now to be found, being coached in algebra, in essay writing and in speaking less like a Welshman. In less than a year he would go some way to losing his accent altogether. To P.H. Burton there was never any question of encouraging him to continue with it. The fashion for 'regional' British actors in serious roles didn't arrive until well after the war. And the serious roles that the schoolmaster intended for his protégés were in classical plays. 'How acceptable would Hamlet with a Port Talbot accent be to the world at large?' asks Philip Burton, dismissing the idea. An accentless speech was his ideal, equally acceptable on both sides of the Atlantic. The vowels were to be controlled; he had no time for the old-fashioned style of upper-class English speech, the so-called 'Oxford accent' in which 'man' and 'men' sound like the same word. This was the mincing speech beloved of gentleman actors that used to make British films incomprehensible to American audiences. Consonants had to be precise. Jenkins was required to extract the full value from words like 'as-k-ed' and 'dep-th-s'.

To friends at school he was growing towards a different world. By March 1943 he had moved in to Ma Smith's; Philip Burton thinks he may formally have arrived on 1 March, St David's Day, which commemorates the Welsh patron saint, and 'is an anniversary of ours'. From now on 'he was my son to all intents and purposes. I was committed to him. He knew I was doing it out of love.' Later the protégé said it was hell. 'Poor fellow, it wasn't hell for me, it was excitement and achievement. I did feel very much his guardian and his father, and was proud of him, even in those days. It was a fine relationship. He has a good mind, you see, a stimulating mind. His questions were always exciting. I enjoyed the process.' As for his contemporaries, what impressed one of them in the fifth form was 'seeing his socks with "P.H. Burton" on them – here was Richie, actually wearing the great man's socks.'

In the school magazine he was 'Richie', an 'old stalwart', playing rugby for the senior xv, winning second prize in a verse speaking competition on St David's Day. He was aggressive; it was 'as if he was looking round for rivals all the time'. Once again people remember the way he mocked susceptible teachers. A girl in his class recalls 'a young teacher, just out of college. She'd ask a question, and Richie, having swotted it up, would recite chapters from the textbook. She didn't know how to cope with it. At the same time he used to flirt with her with his eyes.' With the Welsh teacher, Miss Griffiths (many of the male teachers were in the Army), he used different tactics. She was older and more motherly, so 'he played the motherless boy with her, and they got on well'. He was now quite tall, with heavy, brushed-back hair and the face hardening into a casual handsomeness. His poor complexion, with acne biting into the skin and leaving it faintly pockmarked, was noticeable; his back was affected, too. Apparently none of this made him less attractive to girls. 'They pursued him,' says P.H. Burton. One night the boy didn't come back; he arrived in time for breakfast, saying he had forgotten his door key, and that when he threw stones at the window, everyone must have been asleep. 'Typical of his romantic Welsh streak,' says the schoolmaster, 'he had spent the night in the cemetery.' P.H. Burton believed the boy's story that he had sat brooding in the darkness within earshot of the Ffrwd-gwyllt, the 'Wild Brook' that ran down from Mynydd Margam to the sea. Perhaps he had. His sexual adventures in Port Talbot sound fairly decorous. As a teenager his behaviour in that direction was 'cabined, cribbed, and confined', he told a journalist in 1972. He 'grew up in a far more circumscribed world, where kissing a girl at fifteen was tantamount to making her pregnant'. He seems to have been at least eighteen and in England before he slept with a girl.

From time to time he called on Cissie and Elfed. In Philip Burton's memory the visits were on Sunday mornings when 'he went to chapel with them. It was the only time he saw his family. Then he'd come back and have lunch with me.' In Cissie's memory 'he came straight from school to see me, for a long time. He wasn't happy there.' It was an odd situation, charged with emotion. To the Jenkinses, P.H. Burton was a distant figure, aloof, not one of them. He in turn had little to do with the family. Richard was his only concern, and he had to hurry if he was to make something of his pupil in the year or so that was all he had. He continued to use him in plays. In *Gallows Glorious* at the school, a piece about John Brown and the slaves, Jenkins had a small part. In *Youth at the Helm*, staged in the town to raise money for the Air Training Corps, his role as a business executive was more demanding. At one point he was alone on the stage, talking into five telephones at once, a scene that P.H. Burton rehearsed for days. 'I made him imagine the person at the other end. He had to keep the five clear in his mind, and use a different tone for each character.' The schoolmaster knew that acting itself could be learned only through stage experience. He kept his actors under strict discipline, working them hard, drilling words and gestures into them. It was 'gate', not 'gairt', 'go', not 'gor'. A simple act like picking up an object had to be performed almost by numbers. A visitor to one of his rehearsals was seen to count the boys and mutter, 'Twenty-eight bloody little Burtons.'

In his private sessions with Jenkins, during long walks or in the front room at Ma Smith's, much of P.H. Burton's time was spent on his pupil's voice. It was 'raspy and uncontrolled and had no range'. They acted out scenes in the front parlour; sometimes the Smiths thought they were quarrelling. 'Breath control' had to be learnt. An old actor had told

P.H. Burton that no one could play Shakespeare until he could recite the six verses of the First Psalm on a single breath, from 'Blessed is the man' to 'the way of the ungodly shall perish'. The psalm was often heard. So was the Chorus of Shakespeare's *Henry V* ('O! for a Muse of fire'), where 'character is not involved, and it's merely a question of holding the attention of the audience with the rhythm of the blank verse'. His pupil had 'a natural feeling for poetry from the word go. I never gave him that. I never even had to help him get it.' He has a story that Jenkins rushed in to Ma Smith's after chapel one Sunday, waving a copy of a newspaper, the *Sunday Referee*, containing a poem by 'a young man then unknown to me'. The poet was Dylan Thomas; the poem, 'The force that through the green fuse drives the flower'. The date would have to be October 1933, when Jenkins was seven, which makes nonsense of the story. But Jenkins was sensitive to language; there was a vague feeling that if he was not to be an actor he might be a writer. Although his energies flowed naturally into performing before people's eyes, in later years he was to hanker after a writer's life, more private and demanding. 'Acting?' he said in an aside to a reporter. 'We all do that.' On a film location, full of drink, he was heard declaring that 'the only thing in life is language, not love, not anything else', while Elizabeth Taylor wept.

In 1943 he was still a young man in search of a background. His family and its line of legendary coal hewers going back into the mists was not much use in that respect. Philip Burton's plan called for a good education. In the early summer, after three school terms of cramming, Jenkins sat for the school certificate of the Central Welsh Board. By the time the results were published at the start of September, other wheels had begun to turn. But for the moment that was incidental. The plan, which P.H. Burton used all his guile to promote in 1943, was to send Jenkins to a university, the more famous the better. The route was to be the Air Training Corps, in which Jenkins was an NCO and Burton the commandant. First, the exam results had to be satisfactory. When they appeared, Jenkins was one of sixty-two successful candidates from the school. He passed in seven subjects, two of them (English literature and mathematics) with a 'very good' rating; in Welsh his percentages in the two papers were fifty-seven and sixty-five. Overall the result was up to 'matriculation' standard, permitting entry to university if he could obtain a place. At that time it was not easy for a boy like Richard Jenkins to go to a distant university. To reach Oxford or Cambridge, which were expensive and geared to middle-class needs, the only feasible method was for him to win a scholarship or special entry of some kind. This is where 499 Squadron of the ATC came in useful. Philip Burton and his fellow officers had made it into a show squadron, often paraded for air force occasions. When places in the university 'short course' scheme were allocated, the Port Talbot squadron was well placed to put forward candidates. As a short course entrant Jenkins would spend his first six months in the RAF at Oxford or Cambridge, doing both academic work and service training, before moving to an air force unit and a probable career in aircrew.

Behind the scenes the teacher had prepared the ground for his protégé. It was important that he be presented to the RAF authorities in the best possible light. War had not eliminated class distinctions in the services. If youths were to spend time at an ancient university, the authorities saw no point in wasting the privilege on bumpkins. It was suggested to P.H. Burton that his candidate would stand a better chance if instead of being known as Jenkins, coalminer's son, he was promoted to Burton, schoolmaster's son.

The document that spelt out the change is dated 17 December 1943. Philip Burton would have adopted his pupil if he could have done so, but the difference between their ages was twenty days short of twenty-one years, the minimum required by law at that time. This ruled out official adoption. Instead a legal agreement was drawn up between Philip Burton and the real father, making the eighteen-year-old 'infant', whose parent was 'in poor circumstances', the ward of the schoolmaster, 'child-less and in good circumstances', until Jenkins reached the age of twenty-one. The agreement declares that he has lived with Burton and has been in his custody for 'nine months or thereabouts'; that the parties (Philip Burton and Jenkins Sr) are agreed on adoption; that the adopter shall have 'uncontrolled custody and tuition', and will pay for him to be kept, clothed and educated; and that Richard Jenkins shall 'absolutely re-nounce and abandon the use of the surname of the parent and shall bear and use the surname of the adopter and shall be held out to the world and in all respects treated as if he were in fact the child of the adopter ...' One of the brothers took the document to the father for his signature. It was not until later that P.H. Burton met the old miner, and then it was only once, in Cardiff. Some of the family, never very keen on what had been happening, were even less keen to think that a Jenkins had become a something else. Having stolen his accent, the schoolmaster was now making off with his name. The boy himself must have had mixed feelings. Perhaps the speed with which he was estranged from his working-class roots in the interests of getting on in the world is what produced the bouts of nostalgia later on. Richard Burton said that he should have worked with his hands, and claimed to have a 'split personality about being an actor and also being a descendant of generations of Welsh miners' (1966). All his life there is a suggestion that he should have done something more manly than wear greasepaint and exhibit himself on stages. Actors, like shop assistants, were sissies in the boy's world of a steel town. Richard Burton has encouraged the legend of Richard Jenkins the street fighter, hard as nails, with a fist ready for anyone who crossed him; local people will tell you that he 'knocked down so-and-so', but when you talk to so-and-so he looks blank. Jenkins was aggressive, few more so, but his real weapon was his tongue. There were hundreds of tougher, harder young men in the Port Talbot of the 1940s.

By the time the wardship agreement was signed in December, Burton-alias-Jenkins* had begun his professional career. This was more than Philip Burton had planned for. The RAF and Oxford were still to come, with the short course due to begin in April 1944. But on 21 August 1943, a few weeks before the school certificate results were published, a news item appeared in a Cardiff newspaper to say that Emlyn Williams was seeking Welsh actors and actresses to fill 'small parts in his new play which will open in London in the autumn'. He also wanted 'a Welsh boy actor'. Williams was an actor as well as a playwright. It was too good a chance to miss. Philip Burton and his cadets were at an ATC summer camp at St Athan, an air force base near Cardiff, when the advertisement appeared. The Burtons, like dozens of others, sent in an application. Emlyn Williams was assailed by hopeful parents with sons who wanted to act. When the auditions were held in Cardiff the candidates included a well-built girl of sixteen, her hair in pigtails; her parent said she could easily impersonate a boy, adding by way of encouragement, 'There's a war on, isn't there, Mr Williams?' The hopeless applicants were screened out by Daphne Rye, casting director for H.M. Tennent, the powerful theatre management that was to present the play, a comedy called *The Druid's Rest*. It was she who picked out Richard Burton, buttoned up in his ATC uniform, and passed him on for Emlyn Williams to have a look at. She found him tense and insecure; despite or

* From now on he becomes 'Burton' in this account.

because of this he sat on the table where she was auditioning and made a pass at her.

He was too mature for the 'boy' part, a fey Welsh child in a village who starts a chain of events based on mistaken identity. The only feasible role, a small one with a single important scene, was as the boy's elder brother, Glan. Over lunch in Cardiff, Emlyn Williams discussed it with the Burtons. He was impressed by the schoolmaster, noting that he was neither an over-fond parent nor an embarrassing pedagogue, but a professional adviser who knew about the theatre. Richard Burton's most recent part had been in the school production of Shaw's *Pygmalion*, where P.H. Burton had cast him as Professor Higgins, the Englishman of culture and perfect pronunciation. That he should be asked to play a Welsh villager for his entry into the commercial theatre appealed to Williams, who delighted in telling people that when he asked Burton what his last part had been, 'he replied in a thick Welsh accent, "Professor *Hig*-gins"'. Williams noticed 'the rare gift of repose, and one even rarer – a paradoxical quality one longs to find in actors and rarely does, that of modest assurance'. Besides, there was the matter of his looks. Burton's head already had something of the quality that would make women – and men – gobble him up with their eyes. Williams found his appearance 'startling', his bold eyes set wide apart in a dramatic face: 'a clean adolescent leaf, waiting for a life to write on it'. The lunch was a success. Burton was told to attend the Haymarket Theatre in London for rehearsals, ready for the opening in the provinces. His schooldays were over.

The play, according to Richard Burton, was 'a half success'. It opened in Liverpool at the Royal Court Theatre in November; moved briskly from town to town (in Swansea in mid-December, the local newspaper reported loyally that Burton was 'an accomplished performer'); and arrived in the West End towards the end of January 1944, where a couple of London critics said kind things about him. *The Times* found him 'consistently droll' but mixed him up with another actor. The weekly *New Statesman* was lukewarm about the play ('mistaken identity is not the freshest of themes') but ended with the sentence, 'In a wretched part Richard Burton showed exceptional ability.' Burton has said that this changed his life. By the time the RAF claimed him and he went to Oxford for his short course in the spring, he had been in the play for four months. Living away from home for the first time, he was watched over by Emlyn Williams and his wife, and visited by his guardian and some of his brothers and sisters. Ifor, who was married but had no children of his own, was effectively the head of the family. The father, Little Dic the Carpenter, was losing his fire, and lived quietly with Hilda in Pontrhydyfen. It was Ifor who kept an especial eye on the brother who had gone to do such amazing things in England.

Burton's understudy was another miner's son, Stanley Baker,* who came from a poor family in the Rhondda Valley. Baker was a rougher version of the valley Welshman. He and Burton began a friendship that lasted, with ups and downs, until Baker died in 1976. Aged sixteen when they went on tour, Baker declared later that the pair of them were 'like wild animals let loose to enjoy the birds and the booze'. He recalled the goings-on in Cardiff, where the play was running at Christmas. 'Richard was making up to go on stage and we suddenly started fighting in the dressing-room. I was thrown back against the window, about four floors up and overlooking Queen Street. It was a windy night ... the whole window frame went smash ... Emlyn Williams read the riot act ... the very next day we did the same thing exactly. But you know how it was. Cardiff and all that and nobody to say "No".'

In Liverpool the month before, Burton is supposed to have had his first serious sexual liaison. There is a story of an usherette at the theatre, a journey in a tram – or perhaps it was a bus – a house with parents asleep upstairs, embraces in front of the fire, and as an epilogue, Burton's feet beginning to scorch in the hearth when they fall asleep. 'I thought I was in hell fire. I was sure it was a visitation for being wicked. But it was just my socks smoking.' The story occurs in different versions. On one occasion it was used by a Sunday newspaper with the girl's Christian name included. She wrote to the paper to complain that the story made her seem promiscuous, and she was not. People sometimes catch these glimpses of themselves whizzing past, artefacts of the Burton anecdote industry.

From *The Druid's Rest* at the St Martin's Theatre Burton went to Exeter College, Oxford, in spring 1944. He and his fellow cadets were not there as undergraduates but as visitors who might return after the war to take a degree, and in the meantime would be given a taste of university life and graces. Burton attended lectures in English literature, when he was not at service parades and classes; he had his first taste of

---

* Baker, like Burton, had a schoolmaster behind him, Glynne Morse. When Baker was thirteen, Morse took him to an audition which led to a part in a film. In 1943 Morse tried again, and Baker caught Emlyn Williams's eye at the *Druid's Rest* audition. Morse, too, found a son in his pupil, whom he naturally thought as talented as Burton. He and P.H. Burton never met.

flying in an RAF aircraft at Abingdon. By his own account later, his first reaction to Oxford was 'terror'. This didn't last long. Elsewhere he has said the word for him at Oxford was 'ruthless'. Fellow students fresh from public schools in England who greeted the Welshman at breakfast with inanities like 'How are you today, indeet to gootness?' received stony stares. An early admirer who began as something else was the actor Robert Hardy, whose early stage career was to be entwined with Burton's. The first time Hardy heard him speak was at a meeting of the Experimental Theatre Club. A production of Auden and Isherwood's *The Dog Beneath the Skin* had been proposed. There were doubts about who could direct it. Then Hardy saw 'this creature with a rugged, rather frightening face' stand up near the piano and begin to lecture them on the importance of experienced stage direction. 'If you want to do this play, I can get you the best director in Britain,' he said; as he sat down he added, 'who is my father.' Hardy, though impressed by the style, thought, 'My God, I'm not going to like the Experimental Theatre Club if it's full of people like that.' When they met soon after at the same chart table during a navigation exercise, Burton was 'ready to regard me as an effete public schoolboy'. But they were soon friendly and intent on exploring one another's interest in the theatre.

Burton's social reputation at Oxford has grown over the years; the stories, fuzzy at the edges, are mainly about the beer he drank, with a wink or two about women and other escapades. His drink doctored with crude alcohol, he falls down a flight of stairs and is taken to hospital. Climbing in over the railings after hours, he impales himself on a spike and groans melodramatically all next day. In London on leave he sings to a cinema queue for money and is chased away by the regular buskers. He is supposed to have been fond of fighting; Hardy never saw him hit anyone. Nina Bawden, the novelist, who went to Somerville College in 1943, met him at a dance and had a brief acquaintance. He called at the college one afternoon to take her out to tea, limping dramatically and announcing that he was in terrible pain. Miss Bawden was 'only moderately sympathetic', and the limp disappeared as they walked to the teashop. She thought he looked older than he was because of his pitted cheeks; there were boils on his neck, too. At some point he made a vague proposal of a weekend in London, where, he said, they could stay with, or at, the Emlyn Williamses. She was not interested, and thought it unlikely he knew such a famous man in any case.

Perhaps Burton's knack of impressing those who were receptive to his charms lay in his presence rather than his behaviour, in what he was rather than what he did; the anecdotes are about a boisterous drinker, but what his friend Robert Hardy recalls is something else, an imperious quality, deep and somehow menacing. 'In our friendship, back to the earliest days, he always struck me as a man of greatness. And one meets awfully few in life. One always went to a considerable degree in awe of him. He attracted the other hell-raisers, but they would fall into second place when he was about, because you didn't mess with him. There was great *danger*.' This is extravagant stuff, but it is not unconnected with remarks that others were to make about Burton as a theatre actor, when people tried to pin down the experience.

At Oxford that summer he found himself on another stage. Once again he was lucky. A prominent member of the college, Nevill Coghill, Fellow and Tutor in English Literature, had many theatrical interests. OUDS, the Oxford University Dramatic Society, was suspended during the war, but the 'Friends of OUDS' had replaced it for the duration, and Coghill was its director. His production that year was *Measure for Measure*. Here was a chance for Burton to let a small but important audience see him in the kind of play that his guardian had been nudging him towards. Coghill, when approached, said the play was already cast, but Burton asked that he might do something, if only attend rehearsals ('which I did, I may say, more assiduously than anyone else'). To impress Coghill he recited 'To be or not to be', and Coghill noted how Burton's 'melodious Welsh voice and way of speaking' became 'received standard English' when he began the soliloquy. 'The change was utterly convincing and instantaneous. Out came the most perfect rendering I had ever heard, except that given a short while before by John Gielgud in his Haymarket *Hamlet*. But it was not just an imitation of Gielgud.' Coghill seems to have fallen under the physical spell of Burton. He claimed to have written in the college files, 'This boy is a genius and will be a great actor. He is outstandingly handsome and robust, very masculine and with deep inward fire, and extremely reserved.'

At the rehearsals of *Measure for Measure* Burton understudied the leading part of Angelo. It had occurred to Coghill from the start that the newcomer would make a good Angelo – 'tragic, powerful, emotional, an angel, but a falling angel, who turns into a seducer almost against his will, and is caught in his sin, stricken with repentance, and ends the play on his knees'. The actor who had the part found difficulty in attending rehearsals. Burton said his chance came because the other man fell ill, which was (he added slyly) 'nothing to do with me, nothing to do with the Welsh and wizardry'. Whatever it was, the gods were looking after Burton. There is the hint of menace again. The leading man vanishes in a puff of smoke. Burton steps forward, word-perfect, green eyes blazing. It is a calm summer's evening for the open air performance. In the shadow of Christ Church the audience contains the famous Hugh Beaumont of H.M. Tennent, leading impresario, maker and breaker of reputations. His eyes dwell on Burton, he recognizes talent and beauty, in an instant a brilliant future is assured. No doubt it is a fanciful story. But he had been noticed.

At rehearsals Burton threw himself into the part. He summoned up his guardian from Wales, and P.H. Burton arrived at Oxford to go through the play's text with him, 'line by line. We scarcely took time to eat.' The schoolmaster thought the 'complicated, sex-driven puritan' a wonderful role for Richard. The performances are still remembered. Coghill used stone steps as a natural set. Burton's 'stillness' at crucial moments was singled out by Coghill in later reminiscence: 'His arms at his side, his fingers clenched, yet ever so slightly unclenching and clenching again – an almost invisible, yet overwhelming movement. His features motionless, like stone.' Robert Hardy, remembering it nearly forty years later, says that Burton's hands were inexpressive and his walk was more of a waddle. It was almost a miner's walk, a slight bandyness about the legs. 'My idols of the time', says Hardy, 'were Olivier, who was all grace and fire, and Gielgud, who was all grace. This creature was bandy. But equally there were moments of extraordinary power and command of the audience, a view into an unquiet soul. One didn't know then whether it was he or the character one was glimpsing. At Richard's best [Hardy is looking a few years ahead] it was an amalgam of the two. His strengths are profundity and threat. He is a great exponent of threat and danger, in acting and in life.'

The performances went smoothly enough. At one, Burton pushed a piece of stonework with his hand so fiercely that a fragment came loose and hit him in the eye. He was using the hand-against-stone gesture to solve the problem of saying 'Ha!'* because like many actors he found Shakespeare's exclamations awkward to deliver. Throughout, Burton was 'extraordinary' (P.H. Burton), 'a triumph' (Coghill), 'pretty, with a good voice and nothing else' (a student critic). Hugh Beaumont, who

* 'What's this? what's this? Is this her fault or mine?/The tempter or the tempted, who sins most?/Ha!'

had been invited by Coghill, was called many things in his lifetime – suave, secretive, dangerous to offend* – but few denied he had an eye for talent. In Burton's account he met the impresario at a party; was asked if he meant to become a professional actor; said that he wasn't certain but he might; and was told that, if he did, he must be sure to call on Beaumont when the war was over. Once again events turned out better than Philip Burton could have hoped. After the last performance he sat up for hours waiting patiently for his ward, who arrived at dawn with torn trousers after climbing over the college railings, perhaps the source of the 'impaled on a spike' vignette.

Well before the end of the year Burton had left Oxford. On the south coast, at Torquay, he went through the rigmarole of aptitude tests, physical and psychological, and was marked down for training as a navigator. In the trainees' hierarchy this was better than bomb aimer but not as good as pilot, which was Robert Hardy's classification. In January 1945 Philip Burton gave him the leading part of Morgan Evans in his radio production of *The Corn Is Green*, the play that Emlyn Williams based on his early life, and he had leave of absence to be at the Cardiff studios. His last posting before he went overseas for aircrew training was to Heaton Park, a sprawling air force camp outside Manchester, where recruits waited for their orders. Twice a day they paraded for blocks of men to be selected. In the early spring Hardy went to the United States, Burton to Canada, sailing in the old *Aquitania*. In Europe the war was coming to an end. Burton's theatre of action would be the Far East. For a while, now, he disappears from sight. Tales filter back to Wales. He has hitch-hiked to New York to look for friends of P.H. Burton. He is singing 'Calon Lân' and 'Was You Ever See Such a Funny Thing Before?' in Greenwich Village. He has broken his nose in a fight.

In August the atom bombs were used on Japan, and the fighting was over. Soon after, American dollar aid was ended, and the aircrew trainees, now a drain on British resources, were hurried back across the Atlantic. Burton, like thousands of others, was sent to an RAF station to pass the time until he was demobbed. He was to remain in this limbo for two years. But an actor's career was on the horizon.

* Another of the things was homosexual. 'Binkie' Beaumont was suspected by some of encouraging the London theatre's bias in that direction; see Kenneth Hurren, *Theatre Inside Out* (W.H. Allen, London, 1977). It is unlikely that non-homosexual actors were discriminated against, unless they were unwise enough to sneer openly at powerful homosexuals. In any case, it seems to have had little effect on the career of Burton, an enthusiastic heterosexual.

CHAPTER FOUR

An Actor's Life

AT RAF Docking in Norfolk, which had been a bomber airfield, the occupants were left to themselves. When they paraded it was only to be told there were no orders for the day. The parent unit was a few miles away, at Bircham Newton. Unwanted servicemen were a nuisance, but the logic of orderly demobilization meant a long wait for late arrivals. They sat around noxious stoves in Nissen huts, keeping warm with coke, twigs and smashed-up furniture. Robert Hardy, attached to a unit in London, went to visit Burton at Docking in the winter of 1945-6. They walked around the silent runways, talking (he says) about Shakespeare's *Henry IV*, which was in the Old Vic's repertoire for its first postwar season. Laurence Olivier, whose film of *Henry V* was attracting praise and large audiences, had chosen to take the lesser part of Hotspur, in which he emphasized the eager husband as well as the rough warrior. Hardy, who admits he has 'driven people insane about this for forty years', thought that 'the romantic Hotspur created by Olivier, inherited by him from other actors of the then recent past, devalued the centre of the play, which is Prince Hal'. He and Burton argued about the prince and how he should be seen to move towards kingship.

Burton's winter at Docking is supposed to have been another round of hi-jinks. Windows were smashed, local girls entertained, pheasants poached; the garrison lorded it over the countryside, and Burton moved into a manor house and became known as the Squire of Docking. This was fast work for young aircraftmen of nineteen and twenty who had been preceded in East Anglia by a long line of real-life bomber crews,

British and American. Robert Hardy heard about the adventures but was only a visitor. A Welshman who was stationed at Docking and lived in the same hut as Burton saw no roast pheasant and few hi-jinks. He and Burton were wing forwards with Bircham Newton rugby XV, meeting local teams, having beery evenings afterwards, singing their heads off. They were always hungry. RAF Docking had its airmen's mess but no canteen to sell sticky buns or bacon, beans and chips. Living off the land consisted of looking for mushrooms in the early morning or raiding root crops from farmers' fields. The mushrooms could be fried with margarine stolen at breakfast. Turnips and mangel-wurzels could be sliced up and toasted experimentally over the stove. The nearest town was the tiny resort of Hunstanton on the Wash, five or six miles away, and some evenings a party from Docking would trail down the country road on foot to the grey North Sea coastline and a couple of pubs. The height of devilment was banging on a baker's door at midnight as they walked back to camp and making him sell them bread as it came fresh from the ovens. On Saturday evenings the parent station sent over three-ton lorries to take them to a bigger town, King's Lynn. Here there were cafés selling Spam and chips. The ravenous aircraftmen would eat before moving on to beer, songs and any young women who seemed approachable. Burton's fine, deep singing voice is what his hut-mate remembers best.

By summer 1946 the end-of-war hiatus was over and men were being posted more rationally. Burton was sent to a smarter station, RAF Staverton in Gloucestershire. That summer he went with his guardian to Stratford-on-Avon, not far away, to see plays that included Marlowe's *Dr Faustus*. Philip Burton was no longer a teacher. He had left Port Talbot and the school, partly because he had been passed over for the headship (he was no good at playing local politics), partly because the BBC invited him to join the staff at Cardiff as a features producer when the war ended. Having used his ward in the radio production of *The Corn Is Green*, the Emlyn Williams play, he may have dropped his name in the right ears when BBC television, developing its small postwar service in London, decided to do its own version. Or Williams may have suggested him; Burton was accumulating friends in high places. As in the radio version, he had the part of Morgan Evans. Originally played on the stage by the author, it called for a young actor who could use Welsh here and there. This was the basis of the BBC's request to the commanding officer at Staverton in August; the letter said that No. 3025224 Aircraftman Second Class Burton was their last hope. Permission was given, and for the first two weeks of September Burton was rehearsing with the cast in London. Plays were transmitted live in those days, and there were two separate performances, on 15 and 20 September. The audience research report doesn't mention Burton.

In November he was in London again for the BBC, this time for a small part in Douglas Cleverdon's radio version of *In Parenthesis*, an allegory of Welsh soldiers in the First World War. Cleverdon has forgotten how he heard of the young actor, but Philip Burton was in the cast. So was Dylan Thomas, whose performance included the scream of a dying man that Burton wrote about nearly twenty years later ('... and we were all appalled, our pencils silent above the crossword puzzles, and invisible centuries-long astavistic hair rose on our backs').

From Gloucestershire he had been posted to Wiltshire, to the RAF hospital at Wroughton, where he worked as a clerk. A colleague, Alan Grainge, later a journalist, remembers him coming back from London and telling them about Thomas. Burton gave the impression of being reserved, contemptuous of his job, deeply aware of himself – 'as if he was appearing before an imaginary audience', wrote Grainge. 'Even working as a clerk he seemed to be rehearsing.' His imitations of Churchill were entertaining; he was an amusing fellow when the mood took him. At a local pub Grainge saw him jump on a table and start to declaim Shakespeare. He pressed two empty beer bottles against his eyes like binoculars, shouting 'It's land! Land, I tell you, we're saved!' Nor was he ever in trouble; as Grainge observed, he had too much to lose as a part-time actor who needed passes out of camp. Once he showed his savings book in the village post office. It recorded thirty-one pounds and fifteen shillings, equal to several months' pay. This is almost exactly the amount received for *The Corn Is Green*, where he was careful also to persuade the BBC to pay his rail and other expenses. Even five pounds and five shillings for *In Parenthesis* was nearly as much as one of his brothers earned for a week's coal-cutting.

In the spring of 1947 he was home in Cardiff to play a miner who digs his way to trapped workmates, in a P.H. Burton production called *The Rescuers*. 'Home' was now the house where his guardian (who technically ceased to be his guardian when he reached the age of twenty-one the previous November) had moved on joining the BBC. During a break in rehearsals, Burton went for a drink with another Port Talbot actor and borrowed five shillings. When they returned to the studios he asked

Philip Burton if he would please repay the actor. The producer looked stern and said, 'Pay your own debts.' He tried to write for the BBC, without success. A script, presumably a story or a 'talk', was sent back; in his covering letter, still in BBC files, he called himself an actor.

Meanwhile he had an actress for a girlfriend, Eleanor Summerfield. They had met in *The Corn Is Green*, and although she was four years older than Burton they were soon seeing each other regularly, or as regularly as her career and the RAF allowed. At first she was on tour with a play, and he used to meet her at weekends in provincial cities. Miss Summerfield, fair-haired and vivacious, was taken with him, half against her will; he was forceful, romantic, full of poetry learned by heart, with 'more fire in his belly than most young men of his age'. She noticed how quick he was to emphasize his origins. It was still unusual for an actor to flaunt a working-class background. 'He always used to say he was an inverted snob. It never made any kind of sense to me, but I suppose he meant that if you didn't come from the working class, you weren't any good.' Her father was something to do with catering at the Bank of England, and they lived in Willesden, a genteel London suburb. She took him there for Christmas 1946; he didn't take her to Wales. Soon they were much involved and unofficially engaged, although without a ring. Her mother didn't wish them to marry; nor did P.H. Burton, who wanted no chances taken with Richard's future. There was talk of him going back to Oxford to read for a degree, but it came to nothing. Eleanor Summerfield remembers him as moody and frustrated while his last months in the RAF dragged past. One night she took him backstage at a theatre club in London where she was appearing. He was 'a bit bloody-minded' with the cast; she thinks it was because he wanted to be one of them himself. They broke up not long after. He was 'perhaps a shade too stimulating for me, a bigger personality than I could cope with'.

One day Burton was in the RAF, the next, more or less, he was on the stage; if there was a period of uncertainty between the two, it has been discreetly covered up. Considering how many young actors were leaving the services and fighting their way into an overcrowded profession, he met few problems. He liked to boast about how easy it had been – 'Came out of the RAF Tuesday, into a play Wednesday, been a star ever since.' His progress was fast but in retrospect he had to make it faster. Freed from the RAF near the end of 1947, he made contact with his acquaintances at H.M. Tennent, Hugh Beaumont, who held a large slice of

London's acting in his gift, and Daphne Rye, who seems to have taken a particular liking to Burton. For a year's contract at ten pounds a week he had to be available as and when he was needed; the guaranteed income, a respectable living wage at the time, was offered by Tennent's to a handful of promising newcomers. His first play, which opened on 24 February 1948, was *Castle Anna*, a tale of landed gentry in Ireland, adapted from an Elizabeth Bowen novel. Daphne Rye was the director. Burton's part ('Mr Hicks, an officer stationed at Clonmore') was tiny. The play was staged outside the West End, at the Lyric Theatre in Hammersmith, by the 'Company of Four'. This belonged to a Tennent offshoot, and used money derived from a government tax on theatre seats that could be ploughed back into plays of 'artistic merit'. Unkind observers said, 'Company of Four, audience of two'. The play was politely reviewed and ran briefly, which is all it was meant to do; nobody noticed Burton.

To rivals in the company he was still a raw outsider. Richard Leech, a young middle-class Irishman who had qualified as a doctor before taking to the theatre, was another of Tennent's contract actors. Leech looks back on his years of friendship with Burton as a distant episode. In later times Burton's fame came between him and many of his former friends. Leech bears him no ill will. When they first met – in Daphne Rye's drawing-room, before *Castle Anna* was staged – Leech was already making a reputation. 'In he walked, this creature who apparently had some sort of contract but wasn't yet in a play, and I thought, "Ah, Welsh peasant, I don't think we need worry about *this*." ' Burton's Welshness took time to soften. He could be heard telling people at Tennent's that his demon was the poverty of Wales. Leech remembers him talking vociferously about the miseries of the Depression years, and how hard the miner's life was. The perspective had changed; Burton was looking back on a part of his life that was over. He spoke of money and the need to have a lot of it, saying, 'Christ, if I can't make a living at this in another year, I'll give up.' Leech listened with amazement as his new working-class friend said he was not in the least dedicated to acting, and that he had no intention of being penniless.

It is hard to believe that he was as indifferent to a career as he pretended; easier to see him already as a man experimenting with a mask. Work materialized around him. His indifference, natural or assumed, was not a disadvantage; rather it was to become part of his stock-in-trade as a proud figure standing apart, waiting for the world to come to him, and not waiting in vain. From *Castle Anna* he went on tour with another Tennent play, *Dark Summer*. That was of no consequence. Then Emlyn Williams offered him a goodish part in a film that he had written and was to direct for Alexander Korda, *The Last Days of Dolwyn*, with Anatole de Grunwald as producer. The British film industry was still busy with pictures for the home market.* This one turned out well, despite a surfeit of harps and shepherds, a comedy tinged with melodrama about a Welsh village that is to be flooded to make a reservoir for an English city. Emlyn Williams wrote himself the best part, the oily Welsh cosmopolitan who comes back to his native village to plan the deed. To tempt Edith Evans he included a sweetly obstinate old lady who refuses to leave. With Burton in mind he invented Gareth, her foster son who hates cities. Leech was surprised that his friend showed so little concern at having landed a part in a film. It was a 'fantastic break', but he seemed to take it in his stride. Burton – lean-cheeked, hair dark and glossy, voice melodious, Welsh accent thick but gentle – made a convincing attempt at the unconvincing part of Gareth, whether he was reading Mam 'The Lord Is My Shepherd' in Welsh or playing the tongue-tied lover. They filmed in London for much of the summer, and were on location in North Wales well into the autumn, delayed by bad weather.

Emlyn Williams had few problems with Burton's acting but found him unable to look sufficiently innocent in one mute scene. Gareth, outside a window of the big house, watches the unattainable girl he is in love with as she dances. A boy sings a Welsh folk song from a convenient thicket. A gramophone record of the song was played to help Burton with the atmosphere. All he had to do was appear bemused; instead he looked fierce. Between takes he said, 'God, I can get something out of this.' Williams told him to concentrate on the innocence, but 'it wasn't in his range, it wasn't in his nature. He did the rest of it marvellously, but that shot he couldn't do.' In repose, standing and staring, he produced some signal that was too strong for the part. The film was released the following year, 1949, and well reviewed. Burton was noticed, with a phrase here and there, an 'impeccable acting' and a 'very promising performance', together with a paragraph in the *News of the World*. This took a year off his true age of twenty-three, thanks to the studio

---

* It was also released in the USA, where *Variety* said that 'although the frequent use of the Welsh language and the constant Welsh dialect may prove a deterrent ... the production should have some appeal to the art house trade'.

handouts, which did the same, and spoke of 'the fire of great acting allied to good looks, a manly bearing ... and an innate tenderness that renders his love scenes so movingly real'. For the first time Burton had a taste of metropolitan praise. He said years later that he disliked the performance, which is what he eventually said of almost every film he made. Shown an extract from *Dolwyn* in a television interview in 1967, he called his contribution 'febrile' and 'a lamentable thing. Thank God I never have to live through that again, to live through those terrible years of puerility, of idiocy.'

Work on *Dolwyn* completed, Burton returned to H.M. Tennent and the plays of artistic merit. The Company of Four was performing Bernard Shaw's fantasy *Captain Brassbound's Conversion*. Flora Robson had the leading part, and Richard Leech was Brassbound; one critic wrote that his 'handsome, blustering charm' was sure to bring him offers of films. Burton had no part worth talking of. He slipped into the cast as an Arab, and shared his friend's dressing-room. Leech enjoyed his company, the stories about how much he had hated the Co-op in Port Talbot, how he adored Cissie, how the Jenkins ancestor who liked a bet had whizzed to his death in a wheelchair with Black Sambo's name on his lips. The two Richards were 'very hot, the two of us, the contract boys. We had more money than we knew what to do with. We were at all the parties. The champagne was flowing and we weren't paying for it. I don't remember him ever being drunk in those days, but he never stopped drinking. He used to play a lot of squash and tennis. And there were the ladies. But he was clever. He didn't talk about that much. And he was always careful not to get too involved.'

Some of those early friends remember his sexual prowess with respect. Others shake their heads and almost put fingers to lips, hinting that he was insatiable when young but that too many people's feelings are still liable to be hurt by indiscretions, even though it all happened more than thirty years ago. Burton himself has always given the impression that he is a devil for the ladies but that at the same time he thinks fidelity important. No doubt there are warring strains. But he was highly sexed, liked women and knew how to attract them. He was a good talker but he also listened to what they said; he was story teller and even clown when he felt like it, but behind the jokes was a darker presence that women responded to.

In *Brassbound* Burton made only one entrance, with a crowd of cloaked Arabs. He delighted in blackening the bridge of his nose, the sole bit of him that was visible. He understudied an actor with a speaking part, and when he had to take over one night, bluffed his way through, according to Leech. 'He didn't care. He had this outrageous arrogance and faith in his own personality. He really didn't know many of the words, but he smiled and they all loved him.' Was he unserious, indifferent or what? Half a lifetime later Leech still sounds unsure. Burton settled casually into an actor's life that was an apprenticeship of sorts but lacked the drudgery of small parts in provincial theatres, regarded as the natural way into the profession. Douglas Cleverdon used him again in a new BBC production of *In Parenthesis*, and he was cast in a second Anatole de Grunwald film, *Now Barabbas Was a Robber*. Adapted from William Douglas Home's play about prison life, it was thought to be authentically 'realistic' at the time, the kind of drama that television would be able to do better in twenty years. Burton was an Irish terrorist; Leech helped him with his accent.

While making *Dolwyn* in the autumn he met a Welsh drama student, Sybil Williams, who had talked her way into a tiny part in the film. She was only nineteen years old, a small, vivid girl from a family that would have been a rung or two up the social ladder from the Jenkinses. Her father had been an official in a coalmine, an under-manager, who had married for the second time when his wife died. Sybil was a child of the second marriage, born in one mining village in the Rhondda and brought up in another. Like Philip Burton, a close friend in later years, she found a taste for the theatre in 'amateur dramatics' in the valley. Her father died when she was still a child, and at the age of eighteen she went to live with a married sister in England, in Northampton. By this time she had decided to be an actress, and so went to London in search of a career. She was a drama student for a year. Then one day she wrote to Emlyn Williams, relying on her Welshness and perhaps on the fact that they were both members of the great tribe of Williamses. The famous man gave her a job. 'It was just a small part,' she said once, 'but obviously he was keen to use all the Welsh people he could find around London, and save himself the expense of transporting actors from Wales.' She was shrewd and cheerful, a happy woman radiating warmth and competence. 'Beautiful in a beaky sort of way with a darting dark eye,' according to Robert Hardy, who noted her 'good Welsh nose', she had silver hair that had begun to grey when she was a child. She and Burton were quickly attracted to one another. Perhaps she appealed to him because she was part of a Welsh tradition that he knew and understood, yet had marked herself out as a fellow escaper from the physical straitjacket of that tradition, its villages and chapels. 'I love her dearly,' he told a friend, late one night in his room, 'and she assumes that I will marry her. So I suppose I shall.' The friend, who knew Burton well and came to know and admire Sybil, concludes that 'she conquered him, so to speak, by innocence'.

It was not long before she was being taken to meet his family. She spoke little Welsh, just the smattering that every child picks up in the valleys, but she had the Welsh manner, at ease with people of her own kind, as if Williamses and Jenkinses were branches of a single South Wales family. 'She was so homely,' says Hilda Owen. 'She was down to earth, you know? Got to know people's names and ages. She was *Welsh*. But mind you, we all had a shock he was getting married.' No doubt they warmed to her as a steadying influence: a nice girl with a mind of her own was what Richard needed. Robert Hardy remembers 'an immediacy and a shine about her. Perhaps they were not equals but they were wonderfully matched. She was always generous, always funny. She would do terrible, hilarious imitations', and he imitates her imitation dialogue between comic Welsh woman and son, "Woss for supp-ar, Ma?" "Schloop, my boy, schloop." "Oh, bother schloop, I'm schlick of schloop, it's always schloop for supp-ar" ... She could make you absolutely hysterical when she wanted to.'

She had known Richard only a few months when they were married in February 1949 at Kensington register office. Burton liked to say she was 'posh Welsh, not poor Welsh like me'. Friends remember them singing folk songs together, playing the fool, usually happy, hoping to have children, which were a long time coming; sent a photograph of a friend's baby when they were away from London once, Burton wrote to say it had better be put behind bars when they returned because Sybil wanted to eat it. Years later, when Elizabeth Taylor was on the scene, Burton told a columnist that 'I shall never leave Sybil ... she thinks I'm a genius.' Sybil said that her husband was always 'wonderful ... about giving me confidence, making me feel people wanted to meet *me* equally'. When they married she had a minor part in a West End comedy, but her career was never intrusive, and it faded away after two or three years. They lived first in an apartment at the top of Daphne Rye's house, close to Emlyn Williams and his wife. When they moved to north London P.H. Burton lived only five minutes away. He had left Wales to become chief instructor at the BBC's staff training school. He, too, was glad to see his protégé settling down. The theatre meant hard work, and he thought Richard too inclined to play. Writing in his diary he noted with relief how 'miraculously' the future that he had dreaded was turning out.

About the time he married, Burton won and then lost a part at the St James's Theatre. A new play by Terence Rattigan was going into rehearsal. Called *Adventure Story*, it was about Alexander the Great, had Paul Scofield, still only a promising young actor, in the lead, and offered juicy roles in martial dress. Daphne Rye sent him along to the director, Peter Glenville. Burton was cast as Hephaestion, Alexander's aide and friend, but rehearsals had barely begun when he was told he was not right for the part and replaced. Glenville, later a film director who worked successfully with Burton, says it was simply that he was too short for the taller Scofield: 'Suddenly on came Paul and said, "You're my friend, my rock, on which I lean." He went to lean, and went down about two feet.' This is not entirely convincing. The difference was only a matter of inches. Burton may have been too strong an actor. The actor Noel Willman, who was also in the cast, says that height had nothing to do with it. 'Richard thought he wasn't that character. He stood there glowering in a wonderfully interesting way. The balance was wrong.' This time the result was more painful than when he failed to look innocent for Emlyn Williams. Hephaestion was a good part, Rattigan was a famous writer, and the play was not one of the subsidized productions out at Hammersmith but a commercial venture in the West End. To give himself something to do, Burton bought a quantity of green baize and carried it home. He spent hours cutting it up to fit the apartment floor and nailing it down. Richard Leech guessed that he was working with his hands to get over the disappointment. Writing in 1964, Burton placed the episode at the Lyric, which would have been less upsetting at the time; Glenville's reason for sacking him, said Burton, was that he needed someone wiser and more mature.

Behind the mask he was nervous. Frank Hauser, the theatre director, then working for the BBC, was to mount a radio production of *Henry V*. He wanted a new voice for the king, and Robert Hardy, a friend of his, suggested Burton. Hauser had to clear it with a superior, who asked to hear Burton. He read badly; Hauser thought he had been drinking. Fortunately his colleague agreed that nerves were to blame, and Burton got the part. Something similar happened when he was in the running for his next theatre play that spring. This was *The Lady's Not for Burning*, an extravagant verse comedy by a rising playwright,

Christopher Fry. The ubiquitous Daphne Rye persuaded Hugh Beaumont to put it on in the West End, with John Gielgud, the best-known actor on the British stage, and its most praised (and mimicked) speaker of verse, as both star and director.

The play came under the 'artistic merit' label, but it was scheduled for the West End, at the Globe, in May 1949. Set in medieval England, it was a brilliantly overwritten piece about a soldier of fortune who wants to die and a beautiful witch who wants to stay alive. Gielgud thought staging it 'a tricky business', and was uneasy. According to Fry he had already tried and rejected someone for the modest part of 'Richard, an orphaned clerk' when Burton was sent along with Daphne Rye's blessing. The author was watching from the wings with Pamela Brown, who played the witch, as Burton read for Gielgud. He was in 'a terrible state of nervous apprehension', scarlet-faced, legs twisted around the chair. Fry assumed it was because the *Adventure Story* incident (with which everyone seemed familiar – Hauser knew of it, too) had undermined his confidence. With him on the stage, reading for another part, was an actress of eighteen, Claire Bloom. 'I remember Pamela saying to me, "The girl's all right but not the boy." Thank goodness, John saw the state he was in, and told him to come back next morning.' This time he was chosen. At rehearsals he irritated Gielgud by yawning and looking at his watch when he thought it was time for a break. Leech continued to be amazed: 'Any other actor would have thought, I'd better behave or I'll be out on my arse. He didn't care if he *was* out on his arse.' Burton would later speak of Gielgud's 'profound' influence on his acting and remark that because of their 'vast differences' in voice, physique and temperament, no one had ever noticed. Gielgud said that when rehearsals began, 'I was immediately struck by Richard's instinctive feeling for the theatre.'

The story of how Burton attracted attention by scrubbing a floor has been told often by those who remember it. The odd thing is that it should be remembered at all. The scene was a romantic duologue between Gielgud and Pamela Brown, the centrepiece of the play. Burton had to scrub and interpolate a word or two. 'The first time we went through the scene,' said Gielgud, 'he felt immediately, without any direction, exactly where he should matter in the scene and where he should obliterate himself. He never changed it.' When the play came to London from the provinces, no one seems to have picked on that scene. Three or four critics gave Burton three or four words ('sturdy and forthright', 'an industrious apprentice'); Richard Findlater, ahead of his time, called him 'an outstanding newcomer to the West End'. It was other actors who noticed. Richard Leech says that when Burton was on his knees and scrubbing, 'you couldn't take your eyes off him. There was an inborn arrogance – "'tis I, and I'm not concerned with the effect I'm making". He just did it. But because he is who he is, it was totally compelling.' Alec Guinness noticed him in the play, and says that 'so did everyone in the profession, because of this marvellous head and shoulders'.

Guinness, in his middle thirties, was turning from a distinguished stage career to the cinema. He first met both the Richards, Burton and Leech, at Daphne Rye's, and they used to visit him and his wife at their house by the Thames in Hammersmith. 'They were great fun,' says Guinness, 'attractive creatures. I first knew about Dylan Thomas seriously when Richard Burton gave me a copy of *Deaths and Entrances*. He used to come and read poetry to me, which he did extremely well. He'd come to dinner or I don't know what. I had a collapsible dinghy on the Thames and he used to row in that. I was extremely struck by his quality of reading – his greatest achievement. And then once or twice I got Ernest Milton, who was an eccentric – I think he was the only English actor of genius, wayward and absurd, more often than not, but now and then illuminating something beyond anyone else. Past it, by then. He was vain, poor old thing. I said to the two Richards, "You're never going to see him play Macbeth or Lear, it's all gone, but at least I can get him to come and read." Which he did, and of course it was appalling. He'd done it for me and my wife, and it had been marvellous. But he was so struck by Richard's beauty that he lost all sense of proportion and was rather giggly.'

A formidable Burton begins to take shape. The voice is rich and pliable. The head (it is Guinness's image) has the imperiousness of a Roman emperor's bust. The wide-set eyes penetrate, perhaps intimidate. Some of this may have been learned; most of it is an accident of birth; all of it has been worked on. To Robert Hardy, who says he found himself cultivating a Welshness in himself, it was some quality that Hardy, in his romantic moments, liked to think derived from an ancestor, a shadowy figure on a horse, leading a squadron of cavalry. 'Some of you South Walians must have been princes in the past,' he would say to Burton as a joke, and Burton would smile and say, 'Oh yes, oh, indeed.' There was always a withdrawal, a mask, a distance kept. Guinness, intrigued by the eyes, noted 'an amused brightness about him, amused by life and people'. Leech remembers him turning down weekend invitations to Emlyn Williams's house in the country. Gregarious one moment, he would slip away, vanish from the scene. 'You don't want to get too involved with people,' he would say.

Does Burton, aged twenty-three, have to be anything more than a handsome actor with strong lungs and impudent ways? No doubt hindsight colours the picture. But there was some quality beyond the usual. *The Lady's Not for Burning* was a success and ran all that year. *The Last Days of Dolwyn* came out in April and was praised for its Celtic overtones. *Now Barabbas* followed in May and was praised for its realism. The *News of the World* called Burton 'that fine actor and star-to-be'. C.A. Lejeune in *The Observer* gave him the best review he had yet received for anything – 'an actor whose progress I shall watch with great curiosity. To my mind, he has all the qualities of a leading man that the British film industry badly needs at this juncture: youth, good looks, a photogenic face, obviously alert intelligence, and a trick of getting the maximum effect with the minimum of fuss.' Warner Bros released *Now Barabbas* in the USA, and the *New York Times* thought him worth mentioning. 'We cannot feel we have seen the last of Mr Burton,' said the item. 'The fact that he might almost be the double of Sir Laurence Olivier, as Sir Laurence looked fifteen-odd years ago, won't do him any harm at that.'

On a modest British scale, Burton was already in demand. BBC radio producers used him regularly in 1949. He read poems by Edward Thomas, took part in a broadcast version of *Dolwyn* and another of Peacock's novel *Nightmare Abbey*, and gave readings in half a dozen programmes for schools. By November, when he had an agent to act for him, the BBC contracts for ten and twenty pounds a time were no longer made out to Tennent's. People remember that his conversations came back to money. Leech shook his head when he heard him say, 'You can't be at the mercy of fate, you've got to invest so you don't ever need to work again.' What could be less likely? Someone else heard him talk seriously about wanting to be a millionaire. This was an implausible ambition; the British film industry, never more than a minor Hollywood, was shrinking fast. Still, there was far more money for a few weeks' filming by day than for his nightly appearance at the Globe. It was a lesson he learned early.

In 1949 Associated British Pathé hired him to play an Air Force lieutenant in *Woman with No Name*, a creaking 'psychological drama' set in wartime London. In the USA, where it had a tepid reception, it was released as *Her Panelled Door*. Phyllis Calvert, then a star of the British cinema, loses her memory in an air raid and falls in love with Burton before he flies away and is killed in combat, after which her memory returns and she spends the rest of the picture sorting out her relationship with a husband she had forgotten. They shared a few important scenes. In one, they sat on a sofa while Burton talked about himself and was supposed to show romantic interest with his eyes. It is all she remembers of his acting. The director, Ladislas Vajda, couldn't persuade him to look as if he was falling in love with her. 'Film work is to do with the eyes,' Calvert explained helpfully, but Burton's eyes remained unawakened. He could be what he was; when he tried to interfere with the signals he failed. Off the set she noticed what others noticed. He told her about a house he had just bought in north London, in Belsize Park; he and Sybil lived in part of it, and the rest was let as separate apartments, 'so we needn't ever be short of cash'. His working-class background was duly produced. Phyllis Calvert had humble origins, too, but 'I never admitted it, in those days – I didn't dare! I think he was one of the first actors to talk about it openly. One thing he used to say, I suppose to cover himself, "My uncle is a knight and my father is a night-watchman."* He didn't say that once, but over and over.'

Calvert, who co-produced the picture, thinks that Burton worked for ten days, and probably earned a hundred pounds a day. From early in his career he had the proper fear, well developed among Celts, that what Fate was handing out so freely it might take back again. Thus he was careful with his money. More films came along to improve his bank balance and do little for his reputation. After *Dolwyn* and *Barabbas* a rot set in. In *Waterfront*, a precarious melodrama made for the Rank Organization about dockland in the Depression, he was an out-of-work ship's engineer; the unit was on location in Liverpool in November 1949. Burton collected some warm reviews the following summer, but the picture itself was a poor vehicle. *Green Grow the Rushes*, made in 1950, was worse, an attempt by a film technicians' union to produce a picture and find work for its members as studios closed down. Burton's part as a romantic young smuggler in a corner of England that history has

---

* When Richard Jenkins was too old to go down the pit, they made him a night-watchman. The 'uncle' was a cousin of Jenkins Sr, a miners' agent and local figure who served as Member of Parliament for Neath and received a knighthood in 1931.

1 *Above* Richard Burton's parents, Richard and Edith Jenkins, on their wedding day.

2 *Below* Teacher and Pupil: Philip Burton, 'the magician', and the schoolboy Richard Jenkins who took his name.

3 *Above* Young actor and bemused father. They are on the 'Big Bridge' at Pontrhydyfen. Sister Hilda's house is in the row by Dic Bach's cap.

4 *Below* *The Last Days of Dolwyn*, 1949: with Emlyn Williams, writer and director, and actress Andrea Lea.

5 *Above* Prince Hal at Stratford, 1951: 'a shrewd Welsh boy shines out with greatness'.

6 *Left*   With brother Ifor and first wife Sybil at Pontrhydyfen in the early 1950s. The right-hand house at the foot of the hill is his birthplace.

7 *Below*   A new face in Hollywood: with Olivia de Havilland in *My Cousin Rachel*, the picture that was meant to launch Burton as the romantic hero of 1953.

8 *Opposite*   He has filmed *The Robe* in Hollywood. Soon he will be at the Old Vic in his first *Hamlet*. In between, Burton goes back to Wales, July 1953.

9 *Left* 'Moody, virile, baleful': Burton plays Hamlet in 1953 as the man of menace.

10 *Below* Eleven years later, Burton's American Hamlet, played in 'rehearsal clothes', probably made more money than any stage presentation of Shakespeare, before or since.

11 *Above* In Spain to film *Alexander the Great* in 1955 ('So Mighty it Staggers the Imagination!'), Burton talks to Harold Hobson, a leading London theatre critic, there with his wife and a friend.

12 *Right* With Claire Bloom in *Look Back in Anger*, 1959, as a mature Jimmy Porter.

13 *Overleaf* His last picture was *Alexander the Great*, his next will be *The Rains of Ranchipur*. Between dubious epics, he and Sybil leave London on the *Queen Mary* boat train, July 1955.

passed by was too artificial for him to make any impression on it. The
executive producer, who looks back at the enterprise as 'a disaster',
doubts if Burton was paid 'more than a couple of thousand'. But that
was a large sum by theatre standards.

Earlier in 1950 Burton was with the Company of Four at the Lyric,
Hammersmith, for what turned out to be a crucial role in another play
by Christopher Fry that opened there in January, *The Boy with a Cart*.
This was a one-act miracle play that Fry had written for a village church
jubilee twelve years earlier; now that he was famous, his old manuscripts
were in demand. The story was based on the legend of Cuthman, a
shepherd boy who wheels his ageing mother across England to a village
in Sussex, where he has been divinely commanded to build a church.
Burton, as Cuthman, was again directed by Gielgud. The part was long,
heavy with monologue. Fry says that Burton 'found the opening difficult, a sort of carefree running across the downs. 'I remember John
having a long go at him, trying to get him loosened up.' But his performance had 'tremendous simplicity and youth'. Wearing a striped shirt
with rolled-up sleeves, looking more boyish than ever, he trundled Mary
Jerrold about the stage in a wheelbarrow. The play itself received cour-
teous reviews; Burton was 'delightful'.

Once more he had a part that impressed a handful of insiders, not the
theatre-going public. But among the insiders was Anthony Quayle, then
planning the following year's Shakespeare season at Stratford, where he
was one of three directors. The season was part of the 1951 Festival of
Britain, a patriotic occasion meant to improve the nation's morale after
years of economic austerity. It was a good excuse to stage a cycle of
historical plays; a good excuse, too, as Quayle knew, to persuade successful actors to spend an exhausting summer for small salaries. One of
the problems was to find the right actor to begin as Prince Hal in *Henry
IV*, Parts 1 and 2, then to become the king in *Henry V*. Quayle browsed
in many theatres. The previous year, before he was looking, he saw *The
Lady's Not for Burning* and failed to notice Burton. Now, hearing the
gossip, he went to the Lyric 'and there it was, that was Hal, straight
bang off, no question about it. So I asked him to come and do it, and he
did.' Philip Burton, back in Wales briefly to produce a radio programme,
heard the news on his return, and wrote 'Wonderful' in his diary. He
still lived for the theatre and dreamt that one day his protégé would take
his true place as a classical actor. Despite indifferent films and the ragbag
of radio work, the future brightened up again.

In the autumn of 1950 Burton made his first stage appearance in America, when *The Lady's Not for Burning* was taken to New York. The Burtons, travelling with Richard Leech and his new wife, made the most of their four or five days in a Cunard liner, enjoying the cheap whisky, the thick steaks, the escape from a country where rationing was still oppressive. The play was warmly received. *Time* published a cover story on Fry; a photograph from the play was captioned, 'Pamela Brown, John Gielgud (right) and friend'; the friend was Burton, insufficiently known to the editors. Writing amiably to Fry he reported that audiences either stopped the show with belly laughter or sat in total silence. He sounded a little homesick for Britain. The play ran on, later moving outside New York.

It was still running when Burton had to leave the cast to prepare for the Stratford season. He sprang at the plays. In rehearsal, Quayle saw 'a confidence that the clock had struck, was striking. This was his hour.'

CHAPTER FIVE

Welshman at Large

THE Burtons stayed at The Old House in the village of Oxhill, ten miles out of Stratford, rented for the season by another Welsh actor, Hugh Griffith, and his wife. Griffith, who played the rebel Owen Glendower in the first part of *Henry IV*, was also responsible for seeing that anyone who had to speak or sing Welsh was up to the mark. The play's Celtic undertones helped bring Burton's character to the surface. Quayle and others remember him as aggressively Welsh that spring and summer. Brinley Jenkins and his wife Mair, school friends from Port Talbot, were with him in Stratford one evening. She thought he was swaggering and brawling too much in the little town and told him so. 'You should never let the Welsh down like that,' she said. He was taken aback. But he liked being Welsh in front of the English. 'They are afraid of us,' he said to Brinley Jenkins on another occasion.

Robert Hardy, a guest at Oxhill, was carried away by the atmosphere of romance, the clowning and the novelty. Osian Ellis, the harpist, was there with his wife. A joke, or perhaps not a joke, that the house had a ghost was perpetuated through the summer. Ellis hid in a cupboard and played his harp at night to make visitors think they were hearing phantom music; Charles Laughton, invited there by Griffith, is supposed to have paled. Dogs barked, the countryside shimmered, the future seemed certain. 'There were nightingales,' says Hardy. 'Too many nightingales.' When Hardy came to play the part of Scroop, Archbishop of York, in *Henry IV*, an aunt who went to see him at the Shakespeare Memorial Theatre said she agreed with the critics that he was very good, but why did he play it with a Welsh accent?

Anthony Quayle, rehearsing *Henry IV* for its opening in April, noticed the belligerence in Burton's approach to Prince Hal. It seemed to him a means to an end. 'When you have to produce some essence of yourself, some dynamic, you draw on whatever inspiration is around. I didn't care what the hell he drew on as long as he produced the answer, and he did, but what he drew on was largely his Welshness. It made him feel different and apart from people – fine, he was playing a man who *was* different and apart from people.' Quayle dismisses a suggestion that there was a dispute about how Burton should interpret the Prince. According to Burton years later, he was 'nearly fired from *Henry IV*, Part 1, because in rehearsals they didn't think that I was going to be very good as Prince Hal'. His intention, said Burton, was to 'be solitary, removed, cold and certainly not the thigh-slapping, stamping, roaring-with-laughter Prince Hal that we'd all been accustomed to'. Quayle says this is how he saw Prince Hal, too. His reservations were about something else.

Quayle talked to me in the sitting-room of his house in Kensington, recalling the Stratford season with a kind of angry candour. I was beginning to grasp that actors, especially famous actors, were not the easiest people to ask for interviews. By soliciting their views on Richard Burton, I was asking them to take part in someone else's performance. Loyalty to old colleagues in a close-knit profession was very likely another reason for tight lips and terse letters saying no. Envy was a possibility; so was apprehension, but these were harder to pin down. Whatever the reasons, several people who would have been helpful in understanding the early Burton were not available.

Claire Bloom, approached via her agent, said it was a long time ago and she preferred to keep her recollections to herself; the letter had no address. Sir John Gielgud, frequently interviewed for radio and magazines, where he tells genial anecdotes with stings in their tails, wrote that he did not wish to appear churlish, but he was reluctant to give his views about Burton. This surprised one or two people in the business who knew him and said he was the most helpful of men. But Sir John wrote that he was fond both of Burton and Elizabeth Taylor, and that any 'chat' about Burton's Hamlet in America – this was in 1964, with Gielgud directing – would be gossipy and not attractive. Burton was a controversial figure, said Gielgud, and he preferred not to commit himself. His happiest memories were of the early days, ancient history now. I replied that conversation about the early days would do very well, but the correspondence went no further. So it was encouraging to find an actor of Quayle's seniority, as it had been to find one of Guinness's, who was willing to talk.

Quayle had reservations about the way in which (he says) Burton could achieve effects at the expense of others, a mystery for those of us who don't understand stagecraft. He was friendly and painstaking, but I was disconcerted once or twice when he spat my name into dialogue that he was inventing to illustrate a point. 'He was very odd in his acting,' said Quayle. 'It is bad manners artistically to use a pause which somebody else has worked for. You work to create. An actor can increase the tempo or heighten the rhythm of the thing, "da-da, da-da, da-da, and you, Paul Ferris, you come to me and you ask me this, that and the other, da-da, da-da, da-da, da-da." ' Quayle paused for three seconds and added softly, ' "Well, bugger you." You see? You work for your pause, you drive it along, and then you stop. The audience says, "What is he thinking? He's led to a point and now he's left us on a cliff. The voice has taken him *up*." Now, if it's a duologue, and another actor cashes in and uses your pause, you think, "You bugger. I'm going to reshape the whole scene then. We're meant to be collaborating. You work for your own damned effects." But Richard would cash in on anybody else's.'

'What I don't understand is how the other actor is going to use the pause,' I said. 'He can't say anything if the dialogue isn't there.'

'I'm trying to think of a good example. A scene is written for me to say, "Da-da, da-da, da-da, da-da, and you, Paul Ferris, you come to me, da-da, da-da, da-da, you sit there, da-da, da-da, da-*dum*." You say, "Yes, well, what?" Pause. I say, "Well, to hell with you." Richard was very apt to move in, and instead of volleying the ball back, he'd have a long, long pause, take it all to himself, and *then* say, "Yes, well, what?" You're left with egg all over your face. Gone. There's no way that you can answer without looking a fool.'

Quayle said that none of this was to detract from Burton's theatrical qualities, 'which are enormous, just enormous'. But the technical tricks of thirty years earlier seemed to rankle. 'When a company is doing a play it is an ensemble, it is an orchestra, and the play is a piece of music, let's say, that Shakespeare has written. It has a shape, and it will build to a point where the king or whoever has to say, "Will you do this, will you do that?" They say, "No, we won't," and eventually he says, "Then *I* will decide, I tell you that that is what I demand!" Sensation. In other words, his voice is the climax, from which the Bishop of this and the

Lord of that say, "Well, I'm very sorry, very good, sir, we'll go away and think about it." The trigger line is where it's "dum-dum dum-dum dum-dum *dum*," and the king says "Shut up the lot of you, I'll tell you, I insist it is *that*." Silence. "Oh, very good, so sorry, forgive me, sir, I'll talk to my wife about it." Richard had a tremendous capacity, instead of coming like a swimmer over the wave, and breasting that wave and taking that climax – because it was terribly theatrically effective, he would deliberately go under it. When everything was leading to a climax, there'd be a long pause, and he'd say ...'

Quayle whispered, ' "Now listen, all of you, I have made up my mind, this is how I want it." Which is wonderful for him, but leaves *them* absolutely smothered with egg. They'd nowhere to go, nothing to do. He's undercut them before they open their mouths. It was gamesmanship of a very telling kind.

'I'm also talking about wonderfully magnetic and imaginative poetic qualities. An enormous appreciation of language, of poetry, but even in those days, a knowledge of power, a kind of 'fluence which he had. To you, to me, to the world, to everything – "Fuck you, I'll do it my way, and that's it."'

Quayle, who played Falstaff in the play as well as directing it, was already a distinguished classical actor, a dozen years older than Burton. 'He was the artistic director,' says Robert Hardy, 'but to us then he was the boss who drove about in a Bentley, and would have you to supper once in the season if you behaved well.' Having recognized 'Richard's beginning flame', and coveted it for Stratford, 'he may have been shocked when he came up against it, because Richard has a raw quality. Tony Quayle came to me from time to time – I was well-disciplined, and I never knowingly stole from other actors. Nowadays I know how to do it, and very few detectives would catch me at it. Also I take great delight in being part of an ensemble. Tony would come to me and say, "Your chum needs a kick up the arse," or words to that effect. Richard didn't fit into any of the categories of subordination. If there were other people playing, let them look out. Which is what the theatre is about. To be an actor of vast success you have to be self-centred. Anthony's judgment may be coloured by the fact that he happens to be the most generous of men and of performers.'

Quayle failed to make Burton alter his ways. 'I would say, "Don't do that, Richard, it's horrible, it puts everybody in a mess," but he wouldn't change it. It was no good saying, "Richard, could you do this, don't you see, it makes things frightfully difficult for everyone ..." [he mimicks Burton's soft rejoinder] "... Oh, does it? Too bad."' It was not that Quayle had any doubt about his quality. He saw 'an appearance, a voice and a magnetism that come once in twenty years to dominate and attract and fascinate an audience. Olivier had it when he was very young. It's a kind of animal quality. Maybe it's something to do with sexuality. I saw it in X [a young actor] the other day. X is a homosexual. It doesn't make the slightest difference. It's some peculiar quality which interests men and excites women, a latent power to disturb. You hardly need to open your mouth if you have it. Usually it comes with success – the success gives you the authority. You're not having to be friendly, not having to be anything. You can just *be*. "Here I am, and you come to me. I'm selling nothing." It's pride, a funny quality, and Burton had it before he had the success.'

Like others, Quayle noted the contribution that the parts made to the inexplicable whole. Cheekbones and length of nose, rough-textured skin (relic of the acne), eyes set in 'a sort of sculptor's head. He could be thinking about a horse-race or how to get out of an obligation, it didn't matter what. The face was significant and compelling, a magnificent mask. It made me laugh, some of the things that were said about his performance. Somebody wrote that "this young man brings on a cathedral in his eyes". Actually what Richard was thinking about was how soon he could get another pint of beer or who ... But that was a Godsent thing he had, that extraordinary face.'

Over the years Burton has speculated in public about the business of acting. Often he has been dismissive, like many actors on the subject. Now and then he takes it more seriously, and some of his observations agree with Quayle's. In 1964, while he was playing Hamlet in New York, he said on an American TV show, 'I'm supposed to be a "star", but when I go on stage with an actor who may not be recognized as a "star" – perhaps a superb performer such as George Rose ... [the grave digger in *Hamlet*] it's every man for himself. Nobody is going to protect me from George Rose, nobody is going to protect George Rose from me. In films, if I'm the star and he isn't, they might cut away from him and on to me to make me look good. But in the brutal equality of live theatre, it's George Rose and me, and God help me if I'm not up to George Rose.' A year or two later, discussing the way he isolated himself when acting, he suggested to Kenneth Tynan that on stage, 'I don't think anyone wants to help you particularly. Despite the agonies of a first night, and the nervousness and so on, you really have to look after yourself. I think that particular loneliness, solitude, the idea of carrying on your own private room, is not unique to actors, though all actors have it. I have it perhaps, or sometimes have it, a little more than most. When I go out there on the stage I'm battling the world, I have to be the best as far as I can.'

Is it the voice of the lonely man as well as the lonely actor? Whatever drove Burton as Prince Hal and in the handful of other classic roles he was to play, it came from deep in his nature; it was not something he put on, like armour and plumes. The critics, maligned often enough for short-sightedness, recognized the unusual when they saw it on 3 April 1951. The young Kenneth Tynan, not long down from university, and soon to emerge as a leading drama critic, observed that 'a shrewd Welsh boy shines out with greatness'. In the first interval, 'the local critics stood agape in the lobbies. Burton is a still, brimming pool, running disturbingly deep; at twenty-five he commands repose and can make silence garrulous. His Prince Hal is never a roaring boy; he sits, hunched or sprawled, with dark unwinking eyes.... "He brings his cathedral on with him," said one dazed member of the company.... In battle, Burton's voice cuts urgent and keen – always likeable, always inaccessible. If he can sustain and vary this performance through to the end of *Henry V*, we can safely send him along to swell the thin company of living actors who have shown us the mystery and the power of which heroes are capable.'

For the Burtons it was a gratifying summer. Sybil remembered 1951 as 'that wonderful year'. She and a Welsh actress friend, Rachel Roberts, later the wife of Rex Harrison, had small parts at Stratford. Sybil had found that she liked 'everything about the theatre, the casting calls, the rehearsals, the tea breaks, the backstage giggling and gossip – everything except the actual performing'. She came on stage in 'Lady-Something-or-Other' Shakespearian parts, nails varnished, wearing a wristwatch, hair tucked under her wimple; after Stratford she settled down to be an actor's wife.

Philip Burton was there, genial with pride but irritated when reporters, hurriedly boning up Richard's biography, described him as 'a miner's son'. He wrote in his diary of 'ecstasy' and 'bliss indeed', seeing a play one day, giving Burton 'notes' on his performance the next. His theatrical credo was the traditional one: if an actor aspired to be great, he must be tested against the great roles, most of all in Shakespeare's plays. He believed that his protégé had a natural grasp of the meanings within the poetry. Now, second-rate films forgotten, his hopes were renewed. In *Henry V* (from 31 July) there were reservations about Burton now that he was king – he lacked warmth or experience, or he shouted too much. But his only failure that season was in *The Tempest*, added to leaven the historical cycle, in which he was cast in too pretty a part as Ferdinand. His face stares uneasily out of publicity stills, a ruff around his throat like a bandage. 'We all had supper after the first night,' says Robert Hardy. 'He was so out of joint, so totally awful, that one said, my God, you know, *I loved the ruff*. That was all you could say.' Burton later dismissed himself in the part ('rather shortish as I am') for 'tottering about, with nothing to say of any real moment, bloodless, liverless, kidneyless, a useless member of the human race. I found myself incapable of playing such a role.'

His earnings were still modest. Nobody was paid much for acting at Stratford. Robert Hardy, in fair-sized 'feature' parts, received sixteen pounds a week; Burton's salary would have been around forty. His car was an old Standard. Hardy heard of a man at the theatre with a second-hand Lea Francis, and persuaded Burton to buy it. Potboiling work for the BBC continued. In July, while rehearsing for *Henry V*, he was narrator in a radio documentary about a new steelworks at Port Talbot ('Special fee for leading part and also in view of unusual nature of programme, 20 guineas'). The writers put Burton into the script as himself, and there were echoes of childhood tramps over Margam Moors, already covered by the steel plant. His voice at the microphone was thunderous, as if he was using flat prose about 'the steelworkers of Wales – I know them well' to test his lungs for 'Once more unto the breach, dear friends, once more.' The BBC producer in Cardiff, doing Philip Burton's old job, found him 'a nice, modest young man'. Burton was self-deprecating about events at Stratford. 'Before I play Shakespeare I go through the text with Phil,' he told the producer. 'I'm just a marionette.' Again there is that sense of backing away from the heart of whatever it was he did on the stage. Acting was only a craft, he wrote later, except for the occasional man or woman who could make it something odd and disturbing, once or twice in a lifetime. His reluctance to pry seems to be self-preservatory, almost superstitious; for someone who has given his opinions, drunk and sober, to reporters all over the world, on everything from sex and politics to literature and the Celts, his comparative silence on the serious side of acting confirms his view of it as a mystery, best left alone.

Towards the end of the Stratford season, in the autumn of 1951, Quayle spoke to Burton about the possibility of a new season that might include *Hamlet* and *Othello*. 'I said, "You've a marvellous gift. You'll learn so much – become a better actor." ' But Burton was non-committal. 'He said a most extraordinary thing. He said, "I'm frightened of all that, because I've got a knack. I don't know what it is, and if I ever started to know, I might lose it." ' Some of the mysterious *it*, as Quayle observed, was sex. He knew he was recognized as a sexual actor, although in spite of this, or because of it, he found the idea of kissing a woman on stage distasteful. He told Tynan in 1967, 'I can't play with girls,' perhaps implying that sex was to be taken more seriously than that. A quarter of a century after his Stratford season he said he had just discovered that it was women he acted for, not men – turning to them like a moth to a flame, 'old ones, young ones, fat ones, thin ones, short ones, dark ones, fair ones . . . it's an instinctive sexual thing, the male animal, the peacock in me.' Women could have told him that long before.

For the moment, in 1951, he had done with tights, doublets and the classics. In August the *Los Angeles Times*, reporting that Humphrey Bogart and Lauren Bacall had been to see *Henry IV* and had met Burton, said he was 'besieged' with offers from Hollywood. Allowing for columnist's licence it meant that after Stratford, talent scouts saw his potential as a romantic hero. His next engagement was in New York, to play the male lead alongside Dorothy McGuire in an Anouilh play, *Legend of Lovers* (*Point of Departure* in an earlier British production; *Eurydice* in France). The offer had been made and accepted early in the summer. After visits to Hartford and Washington, the play opened in New York on Boxing Day 1951, where its long-winded symbolism about love and death was not much liked. Burton himself made a good impression on stage. He was quoted as saying that 'after Shakespeare, everything seems curiously flat'.

His private life continued to impress those who shared it. Noel Willman acted with him in *Legend of Lovers* ('I played Death in it, and I *was*'), and found him convivial when they drank together. 'Between you and me,' says Willman, 'I had just taken my bachelor's degree in drinking in California, and I achieved my master's under Richard's supervision in New York. I don't drink any more, I may say. He enjoyed drinking tremendously, and he never seemed to be drunk. I remember we sat up one night drinking Scotch and talking interminably, because he was the most fascinating talker, he could *rivet* you. As far as I remember we stayed up all night and went to rehearsal next morning.' Willman has the patient look of a psychiatrist who is not going to be shocked by anything, not even by the deeds of a young, beautiful actor facing the ravages of pleasure. 'It seemed to me', he says, 'that Richard was beginning to live a kind of myth, invented partly by himself and partly by other people. He always loved to say that the Welsh had a great talent for decadence and corruption – and he liked that, he found that very agreeable. That was what life should be like for an artist. I don't know whether that was just youthful high spirits – it very often is. But Richard always thought he had the world by the tail, that he could cope with anything. Every one of his wickednesses – his drinking, his hell-raising – he felt he could stop them tomorrow if he chose. That's a terrible illusion, one of the worst. But that was something he had great pride in, being in absolute control.'

Willman, having known him in London since the *Adventure Story* incident, had seen Burton's flowering. He says that in 1951, after Stratford, there was no question of the future that was intended for Burton. 'It was not just what he had done. It was made quite clear to him that he was *the one*, he was the crown prince, he was the actor who would take the mantle of both Gielgud and Olivier.' I asked how uncommon it was for an actor to be acclaimed so quickly, almost overnight. Willman looked knowing and said it may have been sudden in terms of the critics, but 'the theatre knew'. The theatre had known for years.

Legend of Lovers soon died in New York. In 1977 Burton said it had been his only failure on stage 'out of a hundred' (what hundred, one might ask). By the beginning of February 1952 he was on his way back to Britain, writing to a former school friend before boarding a ship in New York. The letter is rough and jocular, as if Burton is reviving his old Port Talbot voice, one Welshman to another. He writes about rugby football and the Lea Francis, which was being looked after in Cwmavon by Ifor. But in the summer, he says, almost as an afterthought, he will be filming opposite Katharine Hepburn.

In the event it was not Katharine Hepburn but another fully fledged star, Olivia de Havilland, who was to partner him in his first Hollywood picture, which was made by Twentieth Century-Fox. He already had a film contract of some kind with Alexander Korda, who loaned him to Fox to make a limited number of pictures. In the early part of 1952 they were planning a movie set in nineteenth-century Cornwall based on a new novel by Daphne du Maurier, *My Cousin Rachel*. Fox had paid

$80,000 for it before publication. Darryl Zanuck, the rumbustious head of the studio, heard of Burton supposedly from George Cukor, who was meant to direct the film but in the end didn't. Cukor says that while casting *Rachel* he saw Burton in London in a play, whose title he has forgotten, and advised Zanuck to make him an offer. The story, like most stories about how stars arise and film contracts are agreed, is confused. The first reliable evidence appears some months before filming began on *Rachel*, when Zanuck wrote a studio memo dated 21 April 1952 to say that Burton would be 'wonderful' for a war film they were planning.

At that point Burton was still in London, marking time with 'Religious Interludes' and 'Senior English' for BBC school broadcasts. His one theatre appearance that spring was in *Montserrat*, a harrowing play by the American writer Lillian Hellman. He played a rebellious Spanish officer at the time of Simon Bolivar who is left alone with six hostages, and told that unless he betrays Bolivar they will be shot one by one. The play opened in Brighton, and went on 8 April to the Lyric, Hammersmith; critics spoke of his 'brooding manner' in a difficult part where his only room for dramatic manœuvre lay in a struggle with conscience, as the hostages in turn beseech him to save their lives and are taken out to die. After the final curtain on the opening night, insistent cheering, uncommon in London, broke out. Burton, replying on behalf of the company, said, 'We are overwhelmed.' From the gallery someone shouted, 'So are we.' But it was another of the Lyric plays with no commercial appeal. It ran for only a few weeks, and Burton was upset, or pretended to be. Noel Willman, who directed the play and had a part in it, heard him say rhetorically, 'One day, I tell you, they'll have to queue up to see me.' As far as Willman could judge, he enjoyed acting. 'I don't remember him ever walking through a part or being bored by it. He might be angry that the audience wasn't responsive. But he was always thinking of what to do.' He was difficult to direct, not because he was unfriendly or even unco-operative, but because 'his own thing was so idiosyncratic. He had to find it in his own way. His way of acting was particular, very much himself. I've directed quite a few stars, and it hasn't necessarily been so with them. His rhythms had to be *his* rhythms.'

When he spoke of queues, did he mean for cinema or theatre? Willman heard much talk of Hollywood and *My Cousin Rachel* during the run of *Montserrat*, which is almost certainly the play in which Cukor, or someone from Fox, saw him. Willman heard, too, Burton's old insistence on the need to be 'absolutely independent, so that I can do what I like'.

Rachel was the first serious step in that direction. The film industry in Britain was in a poor state of health; America beckoned; the deed was done. Burton was to emphasize how temporary was the move. Years later he was still implying that films were a mischief that had come upon him in the night. Talking of his early years in and out of Hollywood, which began in 1952, he told Darryl Zanuck's biographer, 'All I wanted to do was live, to pick up a new Jag and to act at the Old Vic.' At first in California he was an unknown quantity. He and Sybil arrived quietly and waited while the studio cleared up teething problems on the script. Nunnally Johnson, a veteran Hollywood writer, had been producing draft screenplays since March. A deliberate uncertainty in the novel (has Rachel poisoned her husband?) was incorporated in the film, causing anxiety. The original director, Cukor, walked out and was replaced by Henry Koster, who tried to have the story changed, without success. He had to direct the widowed de Havilland in her love scenes with Burton without knowing if she was a murderer. The script had some minor censorship problems. Burton was to shin up a wall to de Havilland on a balcony, where 'her eyes study him with a tender smile', and 'she kisses him with all her strength.' Then, 'as her ankle slips out from under her robe ... FADE OUT.' The Motion Picture Association of America, administering the Production Code, thought the ankle 'unmistakeably' suggested an illicit sexual affair, and it remained under the robe.

Photography began on 21 July. A second unit went to Britain to film exteriors; the actors did their work on sound stages in Los Angeles. Olivia de Havilland was in her middle thirties, playing what a biographer called 'one of the few interesting roles she would have in the next three decades'. Koster found Burton easy to work with. 'Once in a while' he lost his temper, but only with himself. In the balcony scene, the one with robe and ankle, he declined a stand-in for the long-shots of him climbing. Twice he slipped as he reached the balustrade. When it happened a third time, he 'went pale and ran with his head into the wall of the house, screaming something, I don't know what – it might have been Welsh'. The story of this strange British perfectionist banging his head against a wall, even if it was only a wood and plaster wall, spread quickly. Koster remembers little else about the filming, except that one day an actress, a young girl, appeared on the set, watching Burton 'with tears in her eyes'. Koster asked her what her business was. 'I just want to see him,' she said. As for Burton's acting in the film, he had a part not unsuited to brooding and melancholy, 'troubled' (as he said in one of

many narrative speeches) 'by strange and formless fears'. His performance impressed critics when the film was shown; even P.H. Burton found
a good word to say for it. In 1952 studio publicity had de Havilland
declaring that Burton was 'the greatest leading man in a decade', though
it was rumoured that they got on badly. Filming took nine weeks. He
earned, probably, $50,000 or $60,000, less Korda's share, if any, and was
immediately richer than any of his friends. It was 'incredible', he told
them, it was 'fantasia'.

Pleased with what they had seen of the incomplete *Rachel*, the studio
offered Burton a contract for ten pictures, and announced at the beginning of October that he had signed it. A million dollars was the rumoured
figure. But Burton appears to have resisted the temptation, although his
agent came over from London and half committed him to the deal.
Richard Leech later heard funny stories from Burton about how the
moguls of Fox, 'very genial, very Hollywood', together with lawyers and
accountants, tried to convince him, in 1952 or 1953, that it was too late
to back out. From geniality they moved to threats. At this, says Leech,
reporting the story as he heard it, 'He did his usual thing, he went
berserk. He said, "I haven't signed an effing contract, and as far as films
are concerned, I much prefer *acting*. I did all right in London, and as for
suing me, I've got thirty pounds in the post office," and walked out.'

He made no move to leave Los Angeles, but it was understood that
the following year he would return to London and play Hamlet. His
next film part was being written as work on *Rachel* was finishing in late
summer, 1952. *The Desert Rats* was to be a war picture set in North
Africa, about the second siege of Tobruk ten years earlier. James
Mason's Rommel is at the gates; Richard Burton's Captain MacRoberts
has to stop him. Zanuck had redesigned the script at story conferences,
turning MacRoberts from an older man into 'a tough young English
officer who has been in combat for a year or two. A young fellow like
Richard Burton, for instance.' Filming began in the desert near Palm
Springs in the middle of November and they were back in Los Angeles
to finish the studio work by Christmas. Robert Wise, the director, says
Burton was an agreeable fellow to work with, 'able to get a feeling, a
motivation. He was highly professional. He never held us up for a
minute.' This time Burton's fee was $75,000. His acting was efficient
enough, as those who see the picture in its old age on television may
judge. Burton spits out sentences that sound like extracts from a military
manual ('Only a line officer knows that any decision he makes in battle

may involve somebody being killed or wounded'); Stratford was far away.

The Desert Rats disposed of, it was time for Burton's third and last film before he returned to play Hamlet at the Old Vic. This was *The Robe*, a picture much derided since, but in its day, and in the intentions of Twentieth Century-Fox, a 'Hollywood epic', with all that that implied. Lloyd C. Douglas's documentary novel about early Christians, and the Roman officer Marcellus who becomes a convert, had been bought by an independent producer, Frank Ross, ten years earlier. In theory everyone wanted to film it; in practice studios feared the cost. Fox eventually agreed to make it in 1952. Ross said supernatural powers had been at work: 'Ten years ago ... people did not need *The Robe* as much as they need it today. Someone was guiding us.' Divine intervention did not stop Fox worrying about the budget. According to Henry Koster, Marcellus was to be played by Tyrone Power; but the director's budget for the film was sixteen million dollars, an unheard-of sum, and when the director was replaced by Koster, who said he could do it for six, Power had to be replaced too. Among those considered for the role was Olivier; Burton was determined to have the part for himself, or so P.H. Burton remembers. It would be 'a sign of ultimate success' if he, rather than his senior, were selected. Whether Olivier was interested is another matter. The columnist Louella Parsons quoted Burton ('who has a great sense of humour') as saying that 'I'm really called the Poor Man's Olivier.' Then and always, Olivier was a yardstick for Burton.

By the end of September 1952, and before work on *The Desert Rats* had begun, Burton was cast in *The Robe*. This was made to attract a great deal of publicity while it was in production, in the early months of 1953. There were overtones of godliness. Clergymen, nuns and church groups visited the set. The film was shot on Fox's extensive 'back lot' in the middle of Los Angeles (later sold for development and planted with glittering towers); feature writers were brought in to see and write about the crucifixion, on a studio Golgotha of piled-up earth, with a painted backdrop of Jerusalem. A new process called CinemaScope had been pressed into service, just in time for filming, and this generated more publicity.* Fox encouraged writers to pay attention to Burton, and for

---

* CinemaScope was part of Hollywood's anxious response to falling cinema attendances. A wide-angle lens compressed the image on to film; the projector used a compensating lens to expand it again for a large screen. Only one camera lens was available at the start of filming; a private detective guarded it. Publicity implied that the product was three-dimensional. But it was just big.

the first time he came under the scrutiny of experienced American journalists. Hedda Hopper, in a column written before *The Robe* was under way, said Burton's career was already 'the most exciting success story since Gregory Peck's contracts of ten years back'. Louella Parsons wrote that he was 'one of the most delightful and unaffected actors ever to come to our town'.

Blurred details of a private life emerged. The Burtons lived in Beverly Hills, to the north-west of the city, renting or borrowing houses from other British actors – among them Stewart Granger and Jean Simmons, then married to one another, and the James Masons. Sybil did her own housework. Burton slept in his pyjamas. He could sing five hundred Welsh songs without stopping. He was careful with his money. He drove a Jaguar car. One of his great-grandparents was a Jew. Until he was ten he could speak only Welsh. He was a brilliant raconteur. Once upon a time his grandfather William (he had no grandfather William) won twenty-six shillings on a horse called Black Sambo. He sped down the steep hill in his wheelchair.... Aged thirteen, Richard played the organ so well that a dying man recovered. Poverty in his childhood was so terrible that 'our entire family lived for eight months on the equivalent of one dollar!' Sometimes the reporters knew they were having their legs pulled, sometimes not. Sometimes they were not having their legs pulled, but it was not easy to tell. The distant mentor was given his due. Mr Burton had told him that the essence of technique was to obtain the biggest possible effect with the least possible effort. 'I was fourteen, chubby and short, spoke only Welsh and had pox marks [*sic*] on my face. Mr Burton took me and made something from nothing.'

The articles multiplied, fed on the studio publicists as well as on Burton, doubled back on themselves, cannibalized other articles. Did he really tell *Look* magazine, 'This is damned gratifying to a man who came up from the lowest depths of the working class'? Did he really tell the *Hollywood Citizen-News*, 'Half the satisfaction of being an actor is getting away from your own disgusting self'? (He denied it and blamed the public-relations men.) The *New York Herald Tribune* saw him on the set of *The Robe*, declaiming speeches from *Hamlet* between takes, 'his green eyes flashing and his curly head bobbing up and down in iambic pentameter'. His determination not to be seduced by the cinema was reported time and again. When the PR men did corner him, he smiled and looked happy. The *Christian Science Monitor* printed a photograph of him in sandals and Roman skirt, teeth flashing, arm in

arm with the lady from Ohio whose idea in 1940 had led Lloyd Douglas
to write the book. But the surest source of publicity was Burton in his
role as odd-man-out. *Look* reported, with an echo of the balcony scene
in *Rachel*, that when he failed to do a scene in *The Robe* to his satisfaction, 'he battered his head against a wall, and, recovering, hurled a
sword across the set'. Richard G. Hubler, writing a perceptive article in
the *Saturday Evening Post* that carried warnings for the future, noted an
'inward uncertainty' and a 'wry defensive humour which may make
Burton miss by miles being a matinée icon. He has neither the patience
with the public nor the calculated personality which a top-drawer
motion-picture star must have.' No doubt behind the 'natural' Burton
was a sharper awareness of himself than reporters suspected. Talking, in
1966, to a Welsh TV interviewer, Burton said he thought it was the
English who were 'romantics and sentimental', not the Welsh. The
Welsh were colder and more calculating. 'Somewhere or other along the
line,' he said, 'calculation does enter my tiny Welsh head.' In Hollywood
in 1953 he could play a simpler part, the brave and cheerful underdog
who meant to preserve his identity. Hubler, taking Burton's word for it,
described him as 'a firm follower of the fiery Welsh leftist, Aneurin
Bevan'. He had 'invaded the social purlieus of the movies like a shaggy
Welsh griffin, invariably wearing a leek-green tweed coat and green
unpressed corduroys. His procedure was to devour the *hors d'œuvres*,
lay down a basis of beer and go on from there – meanwhile reciting,
singing and wooing, Welsh-style, any unwary lady within reach.'

Seen from close range, in a letter to a friend, the Burtons didn't let
Hollywood encroach. They went out infrequently at night and were
intermittently homesick, Sybil in particular. Emlyn Williams, in America
for his stage readings as Charles Dickens, came to stay, and they emerged
from the quiet life for a round of parties. Williams was with them for a
week, acting, tongue in cheek, the part of the sly Welsh lodger; it made
them more homesick than ever. *The Robe* seemed never-ending. Burton,
knowing it would be an indifferent epic, was both angry and amused at
the surrounding air of pseudo-reverence. The cardinals and priests who
came to watch were watched in turn by Burton with a cold, nonconform-
ist's eye. When press photographers were on the set, he was asked not
to smoke in case it spoiled the illusions of the women's clubs, and refused.
His temper was precarious, his nerves on edge; several times during
filming he exploded with rage. He clung to the notion that acting in a
film should be a sort of holiday. The frayed nerves he blamed on over-

work and dislike of Los Angeles, the mad city where all assumed that if he resisted lucrative contracts, it was only to raise the price. Film people made him uneasy, their flattery persistent and somehow rapacious, with undertones of fear. Yet the newcomer who finds the film world meretricious while continuing to work for it is himself part of the tradition, one of Hollywood's stock characters. Burton, pleased at having turned down a long-term film contract, was now contemplating a further, shorter agreement with Fox, after his next season in the London theatre, to make two or three films at £50,000 each. The Old Vic was looming up already, exciting and alarming him. He would wake in a sweat, thinking of *Hamlet*, then smoke cigarettes and walk about until his confidence returned. Photography on *The Robe* finished at the end of April, though Burton was not released for another four weeks. He and Sybil planned to move to the other side of Los Angeles, to a bungalow by the Pacific at Santa Monica, ten miles away, for a month of swimming and sunbathing. *My Cousin Rachel* seemed to have turned out satisfactorily; Sybil liked him in it and so did Philip Burton. But he hadn't seen it, or *The Desert Rats*. Soon he would be home. A year in Hollywood was over.

CHAPTER SIX

Moving Away

By returning to London for a season at the Old Vic, 1953-4, Burton disposed of fears that his admirers had entertained about the actor and the fleshpots. It is true that having talked about the need for money before he had any worth speaking of, he could now be heard grumbling that the government took it all away in tax. Money weighed with him; whether it weighed more than with others was hard to say, but instead of suffering in silence he was quick with figures to show how the taxman was bleeding him. Earnings from his three American pictures of £82,000, less tax of £76,000, leaving a profit of £6,000, was one of his public calculations. At the high rates of personal tax then in force, the calculation was roughly correct; though it said nothing about expenses claimed and other possible benefits. The figure of £6,000 or thereabouts seems to have been written on his heart. In a television interview more than twenty years later he said that 'when I was a baby, about twenty-three or twenty-four [he was twenty-seven], I remember earning in one year, I remember the figure exactly, £68,000, which in those days of course was considerably more than it is now. And I paid £61,000 in tax. I thought, there's something wrong there, isn't there?' Burton's dismay at seeing a fortune melt away is not surprising.* His earnings were enormous, and he was a novice at the business of legally avoiding tax. The lesson sank in.

* In 1981 terms, and taking the earlier figures, he was earning roughly £400,000 (£82,000 × 5) and retaining £30,000 (£6,000 × 5). With the lower rates of tax in 1981, a screen actor who remains in Britain and pays the full tax on earnings of £400,000 would be left with £165,000.

For the time being he was safely home with Shakespeare, a salary and the London critics. His film career was doing well enough. He had received an Academy Award nomination for his part in *Rachel*, and both this film and *The Desert Rats* had preceded him to London, where they were judged to be modest achievements, nothing to be ashamed of. British newspapers had begun to pay attention to him as a celebrity. Reports of his return to South Wales in June to stay with Cissie in Port Talbot depicted him as a magical figure come back to a world that had more or less stood still: his sisters bringing up families, his brothers at work as miner, fitter, bricklayer, sergeant-major, police sergeant and clerk.

Rehearsals for *Hamlet* began in July at the Old Vic in the Waterloo Road. The play was to open briefly in Scotland, at the Edinburgh Festival, the following month, then settle in London as part of a long Shakespeare season from September. Burton told a reporter that the stage was 'more nerve-racking' than films, which were 'rather dull at times'; he was 'a little nervous' about his Hamlet. Philip Burton hovered over the preparations, an unofficial presence, ready with an encyclo-paedic knowledge of the text. Master and pupil had talked about it for years, off and on; as the master put it, 'my only chance of ever playing Hamlet was through Richard'. The director, Michael Bentall, 'didn't try to direct him. Whenever there was a soliloquy he'd say, "OK, Richard, that's yours, now let's get on with the scene." '

The reviews were good, with reservations. He was inclined to be aggressive rather than thoughtful. The by now familiar phrases were pressed into use: 'moody, virile and baleful'; 'a sturdy creature of blood and thunder'; 'dash, attack and verve'. Burton recalled that 'at the end of the first act I used to be dead tired'. One reviewer said he looked and sounded like the Olivier of fifteen years earlier, his passions running away with him, his voice 'close to hysteria'. If, as Philip Burton and others assert, Hamlet is 'the most naked of all parts', unactable except in terms of 'the Hamlet that is in you', a wrathful if changeable person-ality was to be glimpsed behind the costume; perhaps it was some version of the man of menace as seen by Robert Hardy, who was in the play as Laertes, though Hardy was not keen on his friend's interpretation. The Jenkinses came from Wales to see it, and Cissie was in pleasurable tears when he stepped on to the stage. Trevor George from Port Talbot and his wife were in London on their honeymoon. They met one of the Jenkins brothers in a pub in the Waterloo Road before the play, 'wearing his tuxedo and bow tie – his Afan Glee Singers outfit'. They all went round to the dressing-room afterwards, where Burton introduced them to Claire Bloom, his Ophelia.

The play was the most popular part of a popular season. Winston Churchill saw it, and according to Burton, who improved the story over the years, sat in the stalls mumbling the text, to Burton's alarm ('God! – here in front of me is this, this religion, this flag, this *insignia*') before going to Burton's dressing-room in the interval and saying, 'My Lord Hamlet, may I use your lavatory?' All Robert Hardy remembers is Churchill shaking hands with the cast on stage, and telling Burton he was a virile Hamlet. Among the many colleagues who saw it was Gielgud. The story of his visit, well attested, has Gielgud, who secretly disliked the performance, waiting for Burton to change out of his costume so they could go to supper. A stream of visitors caused delay. Gielgud, a noted dropper of bricks, said, 'Shall I go ahead or wait until you're better? – I mean ready.' Gielgud's biographer says that following this, Burton was seen to be imitating Gielgud's Hamlet, 'but failing to hold the audience because there was no emotional backing to the façade'. Since he gave more than a hundred performances, it can be assumed that he made experiments. In fact he told Tynan that 'I played it as if I would like to be John Gielgud' (1967). He also said he was 'inadequate ... the Tommy Steele of the Old Vic' (1963) and that 'I played him as a raving maniac' (1964). Burton's way of speaking verse was far removed from Gielgud's 'poetic' diction, which Burton mocked good-humouredly to his face, mimicking his vowels, 'In a dreeeam of passion'. That was when Burton was playing Hamlet for the second and last time, ten years later in America, with Gielgud directing. His problem, he was heard to say at rehearsal then, was that he spoke the verse too flatly. But he was not much interested in refinement, in delicate touches. 'John, dear,' he was also heard to say, when Gielgud wanted an 'I' given special emphasis, 'you are in love with pronouns but I am not.'

His other career was being advanced by the money that Fox had spent to promote CinemaScope and *The Robe*. The film appeared in 1953, when the Old Vic season was under way. Reviews were mixed on both sides of the Atlantic; Burton's uninspired performance, speaking uninspired lines, was more kindly received than seems justified now. Because of *Hamlet* he was unable to attend the New York première. Hedda Hopper, writing her column about the Hollywood showing a few days later (it 'held our most sophisticated audience speechless and soundless, as though they were on their knees in a cathedral'), quoted Darryl Zanuck as saying that they could not have done the picture without Jean Simmons, who played a Roman lady in love with Burton. The article did not mention Burton; this may have been an early hint that his popularity with the studio had declined. On film he lacked the presence that he had in the flesh; he was merely a good-looking actor with a rich, theatrical voice and eyes that were deadened by the screen.

His sub-career in radio had not been abandoned, and he found time, between *Hamlet* and the other plays in the programme, to earn himself more guineas at Broadcasting House. He was in several productions before the end of the year, including an appearance as a 'guest star' in *The Frankie Howerd Show*. Presumably he saw nothing incongruous in a Hamlet, or a Marcellus for that matter, setting himself up as a joke adversary for a comedian in a sketch. Perhaps he liked an excuse to play the fool in a way he never found possible, or was never asked to attempt, in 'serious' acting. As an actor he was unrelaxed and unamused; childhood friends in Port Talbot can still be heard to say, with a trace of puzzlement, that 'all his films are a bit serious', that he is 'not funny in them, not like he was then'. Perhaps it was an indiscriminate streak in his nature, and thirty guineas was thirty guineas. The show was recorded at the Camden Theatre before an audience:

Frankie: What did you think of my rendition, Mr Burton?

Richard: I can almost hear Shakespeare clapping his hands.

Frankie: (*pleased*) You can?

Richard: Over his ears.

Frankie: Ha, ha. Will you excuse me while I clout him? ...

Early in December he was approached by Douglas Cleverdon of the BBC to take the lead in Dylan Thomas's 'play for voices', *Under Milk Wood*. Burton had not begun his long march to inaccessibility, and could be found by addressing a letter to him at his house-turned-into-apartments in Belsize Park. Cleverdon was the patient radio producer who had waited three years for Thomas to write his play. No sooner was it completed the previous October than Thomas went to New York and died there. As it happens, Richard Burton had spoken to the poet shortly before he left on his last journey. Thomas was visiting Philip Burton in London to discuss an idea for a play to be called *Two Streets*. Desperate to raise money, as usual, he telephoned Richard from Philip's apartment, needing £200 'for the education of my children', and offering in exchange the rights in the unwritten work. Burton refused – 'I told him I simply did not have the money, although I suppose I could have raised it by selling things' (1971). For the first broadcast of *Under Milk Wood* in January 1954 Cleverdon used Burton in the role that Thomas had written for himself, the 'First Voice'. Sybil was in it, too, as Miss Price the Dressmaker, and so was Philip Burton.

During the Old Vic season, Burton worked longer and harder at the theatre than ever before. It ran for thirty-seven weeks, until the early summer of 1954, and was followed by engagements in the north of England and then Elsinore, in Denmark. The Old Vic had decided to present all thirty-six plays of Shakespeare's First Folio over the next five years. This season had six of them, beginning with *Hamlet*, and Burton was in five – the others were *Twelfth Night*, *King John*, *Coriolanus* and *The Tempest*. Before the Old Vic season he had been a professional actor for five years, 1948-53. In that time he had only a dozen parts in the theatre, still regarded, at least in Britain, as the actor's basic training ground, where a live audience judges him, and he is in sole charge of his performance; there is no film editor to interfere and make him seem better, or worse, than he really is. (Gielgud, born 1904, played nearly forty stage parts in his first three years as an actor, when there were fewer alternatives to the theatre.) Eight films and the radio work, most of the latter calling for 'reading' rather than 'acting', complemented Burton's stage experience.

His only disappointing role that season was as Toby Belch in *Twelfth Night*, in which he was thought to be too sober and withdrawn. It was a 'character' part, and the character under the old-man paint and feathers was still Burton. When Richard Leech saw it, 'I said "Well, it's lovely, it's enchanting and you're so sweet, but what about the old man bit?" He said, "You've got to think of the fans, haven't you?" He could have been much better, if you think it's better to give a character performance, but he quite deliberately didn't. It was just Richard, our lovely lad, pretending to be Toby Belch.' Otherwise he was bombarded with praise. In *King John* he was the Bastard, 'fiery', 'bold', 'rising in power and magnetism'. Critics clapped him on the back for having renounced Hollywood for the Old Vic at fifty pounds a week. *The Times* drew a comparison with Olivier's 'silent momentousness' in the part of Hotspur. 'Even when silent among the brawling barons [Burton] rivets attention....' Philip Burton, disciple of stillness, says with satisfaction that the director, George Devine, had to rearrange some scenes because Burton, sitting to one side of the stage and doing nothing, attracted attention away from the action. Ten years later the 'silent momentous-ness' had become one of Burton's funny stories, about a director who annoyed him at rehearsals by poking him with his pipe and criticizing. Burton said he retaliated on the first night by yawning, scratching and speaking his lines in a monotone; the critics thought it was brilliant.

In *Coriolanus*, in the name part, he attracted glowing reviews and con-fident predictions. His Roman traitor, aloof and fascist, brought him 'a sturdy stride nearer the greatness that so surely lies ahead of him'. It put him 'in the first rank, and restores a real star personality to the Waterloo Road'. Philip Burton says that 'he was the definitive Coriolanus, and Olivier agreed with me', but that when the part was first suggested it took several days to convince Burton that 'you don't have to commit murder to play a murderer'. According to Philip Burton, he had no sympathy with Coriolanus, the tyrant, seeing himself as 'the socialist product of a socialist family'. This was soon after he left Los Angeles; perhaps a year of American capitalism had sharpened his working-class propensities.

The last play to come into the programme was *The Tempest*, in which he was a muted Caliban: 'A fine end to this actor's astonishing display of vigorous versatility in five major roles.' His false nose fell off on the first night. Near the end of the season, in May, Burton was briefly ill and told to rest. But soon after he and the company finished *Hamlet* in Elsinore, he was meeting Darryl Zanuck in Paris to discuss the date of his next film, *The Prince of Players*.

The pattern was repeated: from a successful season in Britain, the Burtons went back to California. The new film, an anti-climax after *The Robe*, was an account of the nineteenth-century American actor Edwin Booth taking Shakespeare to cities and mining camps. Moss Hart, the impresario, had written the script from a novel. Comments, probably by Zanuck, scribbled on an early draft, say it won't be a '*regular* movie' but '*special* material'. Philip Burton, in Hollywood that summer, sat up until three o'clock one morning reading the script, and thought it dread-ful. The story was a vehicle for the cast, led by Burton, to perform scenes from Shakespeare. A little *Hamlet* was seen from backstage. A bit of *Romeo and Juliet* was set in 'a house of pleasure'; Zanuck ruled that no girls should be visible. Sitting around on the sets, Philip Burton was struck by the splendour of Richard's dressing-room and the boredom of film making. Now nearly fifty, he had decided to take his chance and live in America, and a New York film producer had put him in charge of a script department. P.H. Burton realized he was meant to be a lure for Richard; he had been sent to California to interest him in a war film about a German sea raider. Nothing came of it. Philip read bad scripts that agents sent to Richard, dined at Hollywood tables – the Cukors', the Masons', the Bogarts' – and returned to New York.

The undistinguished film was completed. Burton said his fee was $150,000, say £53,000; another fortune for the taxman. Philip Dunne, who directed it without enthusiasm, says it had the distinction of being the first flop in CinemaScope, 'a picture about a dead actor that nobody ever heard of, too heavily larded with Shakespeare'. This was not apparent in 1954. Producers and agents were pursuing Burton with projects that seemed a good idea to someone at the time. Ideas for 'great shows' and 'terrific pictures' thickened now that he was a celebrity. Little of this gaseous industry leaves behind any trace in the careers of actors. A few documents that happen to survive in a library catch Burton for a moment in New York, returning to Europe after making *The Prince of Players*, being solicited one Friday afternoon in November to sing a baritone part in a musical, *Shangri-la*. An agent wangles a quick interview, hands over a script, and follows it up with a letter to Burton in London. He tells an associate there to get the red carpet out, that Burton is 'a helluva nice guy' and 'hot as a pistol', that he 'won't sell a ticket, but we should be able to get him reasonably'. On a list of candidates for the part, Michael Redgrave is first, Burton second, Robert Donat third; runners-up include George Sanders, Trevor Howard and James Mason. Olivier has already said no. The agent has high hopes of Burton. He keeps referring to him as 'Dick', which is what strangers call him; those who are friends, or who wish to sound as if they are, say 'Richard', 'Richie' or 'Rich'.

Burton went on to make two more pictures in his latest cycle of film work. *Alexander the Great* was another epic. Robert Rossen, its writer, producer and director, signed him in New York on the same November visit, and it was filmed in Spain between February and July 1955. The money came from United Artists; Burton's commitment to Fox was not exclusive. His fee is unlikely to have been less than $150,000. Before *Alexander* he was back in Britain for a month or two, spending Christmas in Wales and doing more work for the BBC.

After *Alexander* he was back in California, playing an Indian doctor in *The Rains of Ranchipur*, a CinemaScope version of a Hollywood old faithful, *The Rains Came*. 'More sex', someone has written inside the cover of a draft script. His leading lady was Lana Turner. Filming began late because she was ill, and was done in a rush so that the picture would catch the Christmas trade; photography ended early in October.

Burton was now almost thirty and ready for more Old Vic. His second bout of film making outside Britain had hardly improved his standing. *The Prince of Players* gave him an excuse to play Shakespeare on the screen, but he could do it better in a theatre; in any case the object of being in pictures was to make money, and a 'picture about a dead actor' was of no help in building up a commercial reputation. *Alexander* had the right ingredients, with battle scenes and a conqueror's role, but the result was turgid. When he looked stern he was striking; when he smiled he looked unnatural; when he spoke he was rhetorical, rarely at ease. It was not enough to be a good-looking chap in armour with a loud voice, speaking purple prose, declaring that 'There is not world enough, and not time enough, for these men to escape my vengeance.' There was something cold and awkward about him on the screen. A few years later a magazine wrote that 'the cinema, far from enlarging Burton's talent, has been a crippling influence. . . . The earlier promise of *My Cousin Rachel* flattened out into a frozen-faced taciturnity.' Films like *The Robe* and *Alexander* seemed to inhibit him. Very likely his contempt for the material was a factor. 'Peopled With a Cast of Thousands!' roared the publicity for *Alexander*. 'In Preparation For Over A Decade! So Mighty It Staggers The Imagination!' The following year he said, 'None of my films has done me any good. I know all "epics" are awful, but I thought *Alexander the Great* might be the first good one. I was wrong. They cut it about – played down to the audience. I say if the audience doesn't understand, let 'em stay ignorant.' Elsewhere, and at a safe distance in time, he was quoted as saying that *The Robe* was 'rubbish . . . tastelessly sentimental and badly acted by me'. *The Rains of Ranchipur* ('At last! In all its breathtaking fury and torrential force!') was 'beyond human belief'.

Few screen actors, however eminent, expect to go from peak to peak in their careers. Gregory Peck once said that when he was new to Hollywood he met James Stewart, who 'asked me how many movies I had made. I told him two, one good, one bad. "Well," he said, "I've made sixty-two and you're already ahead of the game. All you need here is two good movies out of five to keep the old bicycle wheels turning." ' Burton's bicycle wheels were not turning very fast, but he was entitled to feel that the theatre made a difference; it was his excuse and his reward. Like Laurence Olivier he could, perhaps, touch fire without being burnt. Olivier, after early unhappy experiences in Hollywood, became a leading actor in the London theatre before being tempted back in 1938 to play Heathcliff in Sam Goldwyn's *Wuthering Heights*. Until then, he said later, 'I was snobbish about films.' Although he was too theatrical ever to be one of the cinema's 'natural' stars like James Stewart, Olivier had continued to enhance both his careers without sacrificing plays to films.

Returning to Britain in November 1955, Burton went into rehearsal at the Old Vic for another season of Shakespeare. By Christmas he was appearing in *Henry V*, too busy to go back to Wales. The notices surpassed anything that had been written about him, even as Coriolanus or at Stratford. There were more touches of chauvinism, hints that here was a patriotic Briton come back in triumph to act in this patriotic play. His Henry V at Stratford was cited only to say how much he had grown in stature in three and a half years. In some of the speeches he ranted. Otherwise he was 'equally at home in love and war'. He was 'a cunning warrior, stocky and astute, unafraid of harshness or of curling the royal lip'. He had 'a steely strength which becomes the martial ring and hard brilliance of the patriotic verse'.

Whether or not he knew it then, he was coming to the end of his work in the London theatre. *Othello* went into the programme in February 1956. Burton and John Neville took turns to be Othello and Iago, hero and villain. In the name part, Burton was commended for his sincerity and criticized for making the verse sound like prose. As Iago he found his stature again. Kenneth Tynan, writing as though he had a presentiment of Burton's coming flight, provided a summing-up: 'We may now define this actor's powers. The open expression of emotion is clearly alien to him: he is a pure anti-romantic, ingrowing rather than outgoing. Should a part call for emotional contact with another player, a contemptuous curl of the lip betrays him ... Mr. Burton "keeps yet his heart attending on himself", which is why his Iago is so fine and why, five years ago, we all admired his playing of that other classic hypocrite, Prince Hal. Within this actor there is always something reserved, a secret upon which trespassers will be prosecuted, a rooted solitude which his Welsh blood tinges with mystery. Inside these limits, he is a master. Beyond them, he has much to learn.'

But it was not in Burton's nature to try. He was not a disciplined actor. He seemed to take pleasure in indifference; perhaps to take refuge in it. Behind the indifference there were traces of something else, if Burton's word can be accepted – not always a safe assumption, because what looks like bursts of frankness can be denied later and passed off as leg-pulling or black humour. But one has to assume that all the clues are buried somewhere. A journalist asked him in 1969 why he didn't return to the theatre. He said, 'I think I'm afraid. It's been quite a time. And one is so vulnerable. Waiting for those wretched notices the next morning. With the cinema, by the time the reviews come out you're two films ahead anyway.' Better not to risk being vulnerable. Others might have a vocation, he had a trade. Peter O'Toole, Albert Finney, Paul Scofield and Marlon Brando were 'actors from the womb, whereas I became an actor by accident. I've never really taken it as seriously as they have' (1977). He was to float away into a theatrical limbo, never able to stop talking about the stage, never letting it be seen to get the better of him. 'Look at my contemporaries – Olivier, Gielgud, Scofield, Richardson. They love acting. Me, I'm different. Much of the time it's just tedium for me' (1969).

Sometimes he would admit that he liked 'the acting, the job itself', or be heard to say that if only things had been different, he might have stayed in the theatre. When Tynan asked him in 1966, ten years after the valedictory review of *Othello*, whether he would have joined a National Theatre 'on a long-term basis' had one existed at the start of his career, Burton replied, 'Oh, good God, yes, of course I would. Yes, if they gave me enough money to keep me alive. After all, the fundamental basis of being an actor is ... simply to make money. And therefore if anybody had asked me then, or indeed even now, to play in a theatre which offered me a suitable arrangement of roles, I would unquestionably do it.' If this set of cryptic statements meant anything it was presumably that he liked the theatre but he liked the money more. In the same interview he said that he had no self-criticism, that if people wanted to pay to see him in plays or films it was their responsibility, not his. He went on working because 'I rather like being famous, I rather like being given the best seat in the plane, the best seat in the restaurant, the best food in that particular restaurant.' Acting was put in its place. Burton was beholden to no man. Money was freedom.

From the Old Vic he went to Jamaica in summer 1956 to make a film called *Sea Wife* for a British production company using Fox finance. This was to be no more successful than the previous year's efforts. *Variety* summarized it as 'another nun-shipwrecked-at-sea yarn ... with Joan Collins as the nun plus three men on a dinghy in the Indian ocean'. Miss Collins, when she came to write 'an honest, perhaps overly indiscreet account of my life', gave a glimpse of Burton taking things easy during the filming, at first in his suite 'with his pretty Welsh wife, Sybil, drinking tea and playing Scrabble', later climbing aboard an offshore diving raft and telling her that women always succumbed to him 'even if they were not receptive at the outset'. She listened to a 'lengthy saga of lust and intrigue on sets and in dressing-rooms and elegant boudoirs'. Despite a salty kiss and much persuasion ('My dear, what the eye does not see the heart does not grieve for') she took up with a junior member of the camera crew instead. A final exchange of pleasantries is recorded, one day 'lying side by side on our stomachs in the warm, and waiting for the crew to set up:

' "Richard, I do believe you would screw a snake if you had the chance," I laughed unbelievingly.

' "Only if it was wearing a skirt, Darling," he countered smoothly. "It would have to be a female snake." '

From now on he would see more of the sun and less of London. In 1956 he was planning to take up residence in Switzerland. While he was still at the Old Vic, Ifor, by now his personal manager, was heard to say that Richard would have to go abroad because of tax. Towards the end of 1956 a reporter spent an evening with him in South Wales, drinking beer at pubs in Port Talbot and Pontrhydyfen, ending up at Ifor's house for 'eggs and bacon and peas and potatoes and tea'. He endeared himself to the visitor by his unpretentious manner, but even in the process of harmonizing with his background he was distancing himself from it: 'This part of the world is vulgar but honest. I couldn't settle down here – the life's too starved. But I was born here and I like to come back.'

By early in 1957 the story that he was to pack up and move to a house near Lake Geneva was common knowledge; it was said to be for three years. A television producer wrote to say how sorry she was, and asked to be told if he returned, when 'I will have the entire whisky resources of the BBC mobilized and waiting for you.' Like Dylan Thomas, whose convivial ways he admired, Burton found ready audiences of fellow drinkers for his anecdotes and monologues. Glib (he said so himself) and charming (as few failed to notice), he could be the best of company, though inclined towards melancholy; he blamed his Celtic blood. In March he was in Libya, making a war film for Columbia and a European consortium, talking cheerfully to reporters about his career. The film was *Bitter Victory*, a confused melodrama about two commandos in the desert who love the same woman. A reporter who went to Tripoli told Burton that people were calling him 'a tax dodger, placing an unfair burden on the people who are left behind'. This patriotic argument, which only very upright citizens are entitled to advance without being suspected of hypocrisy, doesn't seem to have troubled him. When he received a letter addressed to 'Richard Burton, Welsh Actor, Tax-free Switzerland', he thought it a good joke and told people about it. In Tripoli he said he had been thinking of the move for 'a couple of years', adding that money was not the whole story. The theatre was produced as another reason for leaving Britain, making a virtue out of what looked like a necessity. 'My real interest in life is the theatre,' he said, 'and I think I've shot my bolt in London as far as classical roles are concerned. I've played all the parts I think I can play, and one or two that I should have given a miss. But there is nothing left until I'm older and can play parts like Lear.'

Thus Burton turned his back on the classical stage with the air of a man who knew better than his admirers: as no doubt he did know better in the end, recognizing his appetites and fears as more real than the attempt to make him play some role in other people's estimation as heir to the leadership of the English-speaking theatre. Philip Burton met him and Sybil on the French Riviera in April and did his best to welcome the 'big move', if only because Richard seemed so happy to have made it. Burton was driving a Cadillac. As though helping to mark off another section of his life, Sybil was pregnant at last. They were so anxious for a child that they had been taking steps to adopt one. The following month Burton's real father died in hospital near his home. He was eighty-one, and for years had featured in his son's Welsh fantasia as the hard-drinking ex-miner who rarely saw Richard's films because there were too many pubs between house and cinema. Dillwyn Dummer was in the village a few years earlier when Daddy Ni went for a ride in Burton's new Jaguar. When asked what he thought of it, he peered short-sightedly from the back seat and said, 'It's not a car, mun, it's a bloody boat.'

Burton was to stay close to his family in sentiment, paying expenses for his brothers and sisters to visit him, buying them houses and presents, and eventually sending them regular cheques; the remittances still arrive twice a year, summer and Christmas. But the centre of his life had shifted. In Switzerland, Burton would live in seclusion at Céligny, outside Geneva, and call the villa Le Pays de Galles, French for Wales. He would come back to Britain, often at first, then less and less. He would turn into that equivocal figure, bound to arouse curiosity and envy, the rich exile.

CHAPTER SEVEN

Marking Time

ALTHOUGH the cinema had made Burton wealthy, he was not in great demand for films; or if he was, he failed to respond. Several years passed without his career making much progress. He caricatured it in an interview with the *New York Times* in 1970: 'Actors go through cycles, remarkable, weird cycles. There was one period from 1956 to 1961 or so when I couldn't do *anything* right. My voice went foul, my luck was bad, I chose badly. I thought I had lost what I had, and I nearly retired right then and there.'

No doubt he was exaggerating; at the time he said it, he was in a mood to talk about escaping from work. But in 1957 his career in the cinema certainly looked mediocre. Whether it was he or the studios or both who were disenchanted, the result was that after *Bitter Victory*, where filming finished in May, it was eighteen months before he began his next feature film. For much of that time he worked in the theatre in the United States, appearing in a romantic fantasy by Jean Anouilh, *Time Remembered*. He was also seen in one or two television plays there, notably as Heathcliff in a version of *Wuthering Heights*. He left Switzerland to go to America in September; Sybil had just given birth to her child, Kate, and followed him later.

The play, which opened in Washington and New England before making its way to New York in November, had Helen Hayes in the lead, and was well received, running until well into the following year. The cast also included Susan Strasberg, then aged nineteen, whose father, Lee Strasberg, founded the Actors' Studio and taught the 'Method' of realistic acting. In the play Burton was a prince and she fell in love with him; roughly the same thing happened off the stage. Like Joan Collins, she wrote the story of her life when she was older, devoting eighteen pages to *Time Remembered* and a passionate affair with Burton. The account of a callow girl in love with a famous man is given baldly. Burton flattered and alarmed her, making no secret of the relationship, she wrote, relying on his 'charisma and charm', which 'set him above the ordinary man, allowed him his own rules of life, including acceptance of our affair. You could not judge someone like Richard.' Sybil remains on the edge of the stories, apparently no obstacle. The lovers even rented an apartment in a friend's name for occasional use. At Christmas she was delighted to be given a white mink scarf and muff, 'until I saw the full-length mink he had bought Sybil'. Celebrities wander in and out of the narrative: Olivier (in New York for *The Entertainer*, John Osborne's play), Henry Fonda, Peter Ustinov. When relatives arrived from Wales to see the play, she was introduced as his 'pocket princess' and told to speak to them in Welsh. 'I gazed into his green eyes and recited the words he had taught me. "Who do you love?" he asked. "Ti," I said. "Rwyn dy garu di." "Faint?" he queried. "Mwy na neb arall yn y byd," I replied.' She was telling him that she loved him more than anybody else in the world. Burton lost no opportunity to bring Welsh into a conversation. Appearing on *The Ted and Jinx Show* on NBC Television he was asked to contribute to a 'Guidelines Book', and obliged with 'Cofiwch o hyd dy fam', 'Always remember your mother'. Having Sunday brunch with the Strasbergs, he told them about grandfather and the wheelchair. They visited Philip Burton and she found her companion 'more comfortable, less theatrical' in his presence. Drink loomed up; it was years before Burton became one of the best publicized drinkers of his time, but he told the girl, possibly for effect, that he had given it up, or was about to, because if he didn't he would die, and if he died he would not see her again; this came in a letter which included references to dust, worms and the grave. Talking to her in a sombre mood, he spoke of his childhood, his dreams and his family. He said, 'Christ, what if I bore the piss out of everyone? Without the alcohol, when I'm stone-cold sober, I feel I belong in a university town somewhere, teaching literature or drama to grubby little boys.' Or so Strasberg remembers. If he meant it, it is a bleak insight into another Burton. Presently the play came to an end and so did the affair. The girl grieved. The Burtons went back to Le Pays de Galles.

Many of Burton's acquaintances are unwilling to say what they know or believe about his sexual escapades. Emlyn Williams, thinking in particular of Elizabeth Taylor, who came later, says, 'He never discussed that sort of thing with me. He knew how fond I was of Sybil.' An American actor who saw a lot of him in New York says that 'he always told me about the ladies and what he got up to. It was almost invariably people he was acting with. This is all old stuff now. It was not that he was a great sort of Casanova, he had to know that everybody loved him. That's a very common thing with star actors. The need to be loved is very strong. It is what they put their energy into, making audiences love them, and he carried it into his life to an astonishing extent. I think very often the affairs were not lust, only the seeking reassurance that he was loved. But that's all speculation. I found some of the stories fairly horrid, but he always said, "It's all right, I'd never leave Sybil, you know. I'd never let her know that I've done this." He really was absolutely convinced that he could never leave Sybil, never divorce her. He always said that he said to the ladies, "I won't, I warn you now".'

The same actor is not certain how much Sybil knew. 'She wasn't the sort of wife who clings,' he adds. It is an area where everyone treads carefully. Sybil was patient, forgiving, perhaps preferring not to know more than she had to about ills she couldn't remedy. 'She hated it,' says Robert Hardy. 'Her attitude to life was that marriage should be perfect. And there was nothing insipid about her. She was certainly not the little woman waiting with a boring smile when Lothario came home.' At the time of *The Robe* in 1953 Richard Hubler wrote that Sybil had 'a good deal of spirit', adding that her formula for dealing with her husband's flirtations was to tell him, 'She's a nice girl, don't do anything to hurt her,' in the first week, and 'Richard, don't do anything to hurt us' in the second. 'Only once', wrote the reporter, 'has a further admonition been necessary. At a New Year's Eve collation Burton was dancing at the witching hour of twelve with a lovely English actress. On the hour he bussed her soundly. Sibyl observed it, darted through the crowd and rocked his head with a resounding slap. Burton turned slightly sour on the festivities thereafter, but by morning they had reconciled.' Hubler prefaced the story by saying that Burton was 'unreservedly devoted' to Sybil. This is where most of the stories begin and end. Burton was a paradoxical man with a strong sexual appetite who loved his wife and cared about his marriage.

Returning to Europe after *Time Remembered*, he had a new film in prospect, a screen version of John Osborne's play about youth and disillusion, *Look Back in Anger*, first seen in London in 1956. Osborne and Tony Richardson, who was to direct it, interested a Canadian producer, Harry Saltzman, who later made the James Bond films. On the strength of the play's reputation and Burton, Saltzman raised something over £200,000, most of it from Warner Bros, to make a low-budget English picture. Burton was not Saltzman's first or even his second choice. His fee of $125,000 (£45,000) to play Jimmy Porter, the original angry young man, was by far the largest in the budget. Burton was back in Britain to make the film in autumn 1958, working at the Elstree studios where he had filmed *Woman of No Name*.

Susan Strasberg, at the Brussels World Fair to do a play, went to see him there. She was still in love with him, and had been sending letters to his 'private post office in Geneva'. A car was sent to meet her at London Airport, but when she arrived at the studios Burton said that Claire Bloom – playing Jimmy Porter's wife's best friend, who becomes his mistress – was on her way to his dressing-room to discuss their next scene. Would she mind stepping into the bathroom? The young Miss Strasberg was slow to grasp the point. 'It was so unexpected that I could not comprehend what he was asking. "But I don't have to go to the bathroom ... oh, I see, you're afraid Claire will call Sybil if she sees me here. Claire is one of your oldest friends. Why should she care?" ' She waited miserably, trying to see through the keyhole, while they talked. Eventually he took her for a drink in a pub and on to her hotel in London, the Savoy, where he said he wouldn't come in because 'someone might see us'. The melancholy scene ends with her on Waterloo Bridge in the autumn mist, contemplating suicide, before she comes to her senses and catches the next plane back to Brussels.

Look Back in Anger was released the following year and brought renewed respect for Burton as a film actor, although he was too mature for the tormented youth. Saltzman concluded that it had been 'a monumental miscalculation' to give the part to Burton, who was 'too old anyway' and 'looked as if he could handle himself so capably that he'd lay anyone he hated out flat'. As usual Burton's strength lay in his voice and his presence. There were touches of Shakespearian rhetoric about the way he made some of the speeches ring out. The performance leaned towards theatre. Burton said it was a change not to be 'dressed eternally in togas or whatever. It was fascinating to find a man who came presumably from my sort of class, who actually could talk the way that I would like to talk.' Commercially the film was a failure. Saltzman showed it out of politeness to Jack Warner, whose company had put up the money. After a few minutes Warner asked sarcastically what language they were speaking. 'English,' replied the producer. 'This is America,' said Warner, and walked out. While Burton was in Britain making the film he did one last radio play for the BBC, taking part in two versions of *Brad* (*Treason*), in Welsh and English, by the nationalist writer Saunders Lewis.

The following year, 1959, was spent largely in America, making two more films for Warner Bros. As far as journalists and publicists were concerned he was no longer interesting. The novelty of his earlier appearances on the Los Angeles scene had worn off, and his films had failed to make him a major star. Perhaps he didn't want to be one, or only half wanted it. Talking to a reporter on the *Los Angeles Times* he spoke of the prospect facing 'the actor who limits himself to appearing only before cameras': that he may grow 'soft' and 'afraid to appear in a stage piece that might not become a smash hit'. He gave details of the low tax levels in Switzerland. 'One big picture is worth ten small ones,' he said. 'The actor who is fortunate enough to get two or possibly three big subjects a year benefits from their long runs. He's never absent long from public view.' *The Bramble Bush* seemed unlikely to help with a career that was hanging fire. The complicated plot involved sexual scandal and euthanasia in a small town, with Burton as a doctor who has an affair with the wife of a dying man, before dispatching him (for charitable reasons) with a lethal injection. A new director, Daniel Petrie, made a serviceable job of it, though the Legion of Decency forced him to truncate the case for mercy killing and make nonsense of the ending.

Petrie, until then a television director, had worked with Burton on *Wuthering Heights*. As an actor he found him friendly and accommodating. 'He would respond to practically anything. "Where do you want me to go?" – he'd do it. He had that kind of ease. OK, you want to play this scene all seated – he'd play it seated. You want him to roam around the room, he'd do that. He was very easy to direct. Odd that I had almost the same situation with Laurence Olivier on *The Betsy* [in 1978] – within whatever structure you lay out for him, he can still operate at the height of his powers. Unlike working sometimes with American actors, who are very conscious of what the staging might be.' Burton made no bones about his attitude to film making: he liked or needed the money. The subject came up as regularly as in London five and ten years earlier. Petrie heard him recall 'a conversation he had had with ——, a famous actor he admired tremendously. Here was ——, aged forty something, highly successful, and he had a Rolls Royce and a house, and that's it. And Burton said, "I decided that I was not going to do that. I was going to go for the money." Because *The Bramble Bush* was not exactly a great venture in terms of the script. It was a poor man's *Peyton Place*, though it did well at the box office.'

For all Burton's competence on the set, Petrie was struck by the difference between Burton in the flesh and Burton on film. 'I used to say about him that pound for pound he's the best actor in the English-speaking world, in terms of equipment – his voice, his body, his looks. But something happens to him on film. A coldness seems to assert itself. He doesn't have the compassion or warmth that some of the great film actors have had. Off the screen he is one of the best of raconteurs. He is articulate, vivacious – delightful company. Some of that warmth and wit translated to the screen would be rewarding. But he doesn't use himself in his roles, and perhaps that's the reason that in any of his films, I haven't seen the kind of thing you'd see in his dressing-room.' Petrie, who grew to like Burton during the filming between March and May, noticed that every day on the set his first drink of the evening arrived precisely at five o'clock. They would shoot for a further hour but 'when the sweep-second hand of the clock came up to five, he would put his hand out like that, and his dresser would have his drink, *choonk*, right there. An hour of polite drinking wouldn't affect him at all. But that was the routine.'

The second of the year's films was larger but no better. Edna Ferber's novel *Ice Palace*, an Alaskan saga, had been bought by Warner for $350,000. Despite unkind opinions within the studio – one memo called it 'a rambling, plotless social tract with cutout characters that never come alive' – it went ahead as an expensive production, calling for location filming in Alaska and elaborate sets in Los Angeles complete with snow, crevasses and a bear. The director, Vincent Sherman, says the script was so poor, 'I told Jack Warner that I would do it if he could get a cast – thinking he couldn't.' Sherman's experience of Burton was not unlike Petrie's. The unit left Los Angeles on 1 August and filming began two days later at Petersburg. They filmed long hours in bad weather, and Burton was unfailingly co-operative. 'He is such a facile actor', says Sherman, 'that I'm sure sometimes he doesn't dig deeply enough, and God knows, *Ice Palace* didn't require any great depth of digging. The character, Zeb Kennedy, was very simple. But Richard was most pleasant to work with. The women were crazy about him. The crew loved him too. He was a very democratic type of guy. He had what is always I think attractive in a man, you felt he had a working-class background, he wasn't afraid of having dirt under his fingernails, which gave him a certain reality. There wasn't anything affected. In some ways he reminded me of Clark Gable, with whom I once did a Western – the genuine professional, always on the set on time, never gave you a moment's trouble as long as you explained to him what you wanted.'

Burton was paid $125,000 for eight weeks' work; according to Sherman he guessed the film would take longer and was eventually paid as much again in 'overage'. Sherman suspected that one reason Burton harped on his finances was that he was 'sending money back to the various people he supported'. Jim Backus, the character actor (and the cartoon voice of Mr Magoo), who had a part in the film, spent long hours in Alaska drinking and talking with Burton, and heard much about Wales and the family. 'Here we are,' Burton said to him one night, or day, 'sitting on top of the world, having a drink at three o'clock in the morning with the sun out and the dogs barking, making this piece of shit. If they want to pay us, let them. But they must be out of their minds.' In the films he is at his best in the more extravagant scenes, standing up for oppressed workers at the cannery near the start, in action in the snow and ice at the end. As the rising tycoon in between he is not very believable. Nor does he age successfully over the picture's half-a-lifetime.

Various projects were linked with Burton. The entertainment industry is all hope, bravado and speculation. Reports said he would make a film in Rome and another in Africa, or sing in a new musical on Broadway with Julie Andrews. What he showed no sign of doing was return to the London theatre, at least not yet. He was still available for modest enterprises. Aled Vaughan, then a BBC radio producer, visited him at Le Pays de Galles at the end of 1959. Burton asked him to bring laver bread, a Welsh seaweed that is made into pats and fried; originally a survival food for starving villagers, it has achieved the status of a delicacy. Vaughan bought supplies at Swansea market and took two empty film cans of the stuff, arousing the suspicions of the customs at Geneva. Over the next two or three days there was much drinking, but Vaughan recorded Burton talking off the cuff for the radio profile he was preparing.

After an especially heavy night, they sat in a milk bar in Geneva before going into a local studio to record another item, a Christmas talk by Burton. He was writing and rewriting the script on scraps of paper almost until it was time to record.

Another visitor at about the same time was Richard Findlater, who had been among the first critics to notice Burton in the theatre. He found him contented though still muttering about the Inland Revenue. Sybil had just given birth to a second daughter, Jessica. The Cadillac was parked outside. Ifor was installed in a garden chalet. Burton said lightly that he had 'been in a lot of rubbish' in films. Findlater thought he was 'smouldering with ambition to tackle some of the great classic roles – notably Richard II and Lear – and to find the right way for our time of delivering Shakespearian verse'. But he had no plans to return. His technique for talking about his film career was to disarm criticism by making it himself. When he said the films were awful but he liked the money, he endeared himself to many by admitting that he had done what they would probably have done, too, given the chance. Another writer from London, Roderick Mann, who went to Switzerland six months after Findlater, was told that 'if you're going to make rubbish, be the best rubbish in it. I keep telling Larry Olivier that.' There was more on these impertinent lines, chiding Olivier for 'playing a minor role in an epic like *Spartacus*, which he's just done. Larry had a dressing-room half the size of Tony Curtis's on that film. And he got about half Curtis's money. Well, that's ridiculous. You've got to swank in Hollywood. When I go there I demand two Cadillacs – one for my family – and the best dressing-room at the studio. Of course I'm not worth it, but it impresses them.'

The Broadway musical, unlike the films in Rome and Africa, became a reality in the shape of *Camelot*, one of the dominant shows of the 1960s. The writers, Alan Jay Lerner and Fritz Loewe, drew on the novels of T.H.White about King Arthur and the Round Table. The Arthurian legend set to music suited Burton better than anything he had done on the stage since Shakespeare. Moss Hart, who had written *Prince of Players*, and who was to direct *Camelot* in autumn 1960, first suggested him as King Arthur. Burton's singing voice was adequate and he liked the idea of using it on a stage. The fee, $4,000 a week with a share of the profits, was not to be sneezed at. Rehearsals were to begin in September.

Earlier in the year Burton kept the old bicycle wheels turning with some work for television. He was in at least one American production, and in the spring went to London to tape a short John Osborne play, *A Subject of Scandal and Concern*, with Tony Richardson as director. This was a piece of documentary drama based on the case of a nineteenth-century schoolteacher, George Jacob Holyoake, who ruins himself and his family by clinging to radical and atheistical principles. Burton did it at short notice for the BBC,* who booked him in to a suite at the Savoy Hotel for a fortnight and gave him a fee of £1,000. The BBC negotiators were unable to resist pointing out to him that this was the largest fee they had ever paid for an engagement of that length – it ran for less than an hour; this delighted Burton, who was soon telling reporters in America about it, adding that the least he had ever been paid for a television show in that country was roughly nine times as much. The production itself has vanished more or less without trace, in the way of television drama, though archive copies exist. In the part of Holyoake, who manages to be meek and stubborn at the same time, a stammering little man behind rimless spectacles, Burton extinguished his fieriness and gave an inkling of what he could do with 'character' parts if he chose. However, he did not choose. *A Subject of Scandal and Concern* was a lucky accident, a worthwhile play by a writer he admired, with a director he had worked with in *Look Back in Anger*, which turned up while he was still accessible.

More in keeping with his need to be visible and rich was a series of television documentaries about Churchill, *The Valiant Years*, in which his voice was heard – on ABC in America and the BBC in Britain – reading extracts from Churchill's war memoirs. The recordings for twenty-six episodes overlapped the early days of *Camelot*. According to Burton, Churchill asked personally that he should take the part: 'He'd seen me play Hamlet and he told them, "Get that boy from the Old Vic." There's been a million boys in the Old Vic but he roared, "That boy!"' According to the producer, Jack Le Vien, who had bought the television rights to Churchill's memoirs, Burton's name came up in the normal way as a candidate for the part. The fee was large, probably $100,000 or more. Burton's delivery, brooding and restrained, was well liked. Rather than attempt a Churchill imitation he settled for a voice that was socially approximate – 'I based my voice slightly on a Peter Sellers imitation I once heard of an upper-class Englishman, dropping aitches and changing

---

* Osborne's play was originally intended for the independent television network, but the company made difficulties because it was supposedly 'controversial'. Osborne and Richardson then took it away and offered it to the BBC.

RS into WS.' There is a touch of uneasiness about his reported comments on the part. He was 'worried' at the thought of the series being shown in Britain – 'They know me as a Welshman. I didn't know how they'd take me as an Englishman.' When the American reporter asked 'if his was naturally the accent of the British upper classes', Burton roared, 'Good Lord, no. I'm the son of a Welsh miner.' Years later a fear that he, the Welsh leveller, might be seen deferring to Winston Churchill, the English patrician, would be painfully evident. It was not in Burton's nature to kneel to a Sir Winston Churchill, any more than to a Sir Laurence Olivier.

The centre of his working life for the next year was *Camelot*, or 'Costalot' as the jokers called it. The show was a slow starter and had teething troubles. Moss Hart was ill before the opening in Toronto in October; a change of style in the play as it stood, from comedy in the first act to sterner stuff in the second, emerged as a major flaw, and led to much rewriting, and Philip Burton was called in to help reshape the production before it went to New York in December. In his autobiographical *The Street Where I Live*, Lerner wrote that 'God knows what would have happened had it not been for Richard Burton', who 'radiated a faith and geniality which infected the company'. Burton, back on a big stage, seems to have been in his element, resplendent and heroic, a king again. It was the style that suited him best. He could be heard denying it – 'The unfortunate thing is that everybody wants me to play a prince or a king. . . . I'm always wearing a nightdress or a short skirt or something odd. I don't want to do them, I don't like them, I hate getting made up for them, I hate my hair being curled in the mornings, I hate tights, I hate boots, I hate everything. I'd like to be in a lounge suit, I'd like to be a sort of Welsh Rex Harrison and do nothing except lounge against a bar with a gin and It in my hand' (1963. The interviewer said, 'Your voice is against you. It has the ringing heroic note.' Burton said amid laughter, 'Yes, my father had that too, very difficult. He said "Good morning" and we all fainted'). But kings appealed to Burton, as he admitted from time to time. He told Kenneth Tynan in 1967, 'I am the son of a Welsh miner and one would expect me to be at my happiest playing peasants, people of the earth. But in actual fact I'm much happier playing princes and kings. Now whether this is a kind of sublimation of what I would like to be, or something like that, I don't know, but certainly I'm never really very comfortable playing people from the working class.'

King Arthur was not Shakespeare, but his silver-painted armour suited Burton, and his songs were sad as well as amusing. Lerner had to rewrite some sections where he 'stands silently, lost in his own thoughts, while the action swirls around him', so as to 'bring him articulately into the scene in order to keep it alive'; otherwise, as usual, his presence outside the action was too strong. Offstage his 'devotion to the bottle' struck Lerner, who added that he never saw 'any sign of intoxication. He was not always *compos mentis*, but at no time did it impair his memory.... From time to time his voice was a little croaky, but only in the wings.' Lerner concluded that Burton was 'a driven man, but a remarkable fellow and a remarkable actor'. According to Burton years afterwards, he once, for a bet, drank a bottle of vodka during a matinée of *Camelot*, and another during the evening performance, without ill effect. But the Welsh like stories about prowess in drink even more than about prowess in sex.

With two shows to attract attention – *Camelot*, which turned the corner when excerpts were included in Ed Sullivan's television show, and *The Valiant Years* – Burton was enlarging his reputation in America. Reporters were at the door of his dressing-room, having salt put on their tails. His father was half Jewish. He played Henry V when he was twenty-one. He never went to bed the night before a first night, to give himself energy. Did somebody pay for him to go to Oxford? 'Yes, darling, 'twas on a scholarship.' Did he walk in the same bowlegged way even when he was playing a king? 'Darling, whenever I walk onstage, I *am* king.' As for acting, 'Darling, I dislike actors who analyse to the nth degree. They're self-indulgent – entertaining themselves. An actor's first duty is to be heard, then seen, then to act.' Never mind what it meant, it made good copy.

Camelot prospered through the spring of 1961. His engagement had months to run. There was talk of taking it to London. Then one day the moguls of Twentieth Century-Fox, in serious trouble with a film called *Cleopatra*, asked him would he go to Rome and be Mark Antony, if they bought him out of his contract. Burton said yes. Scandal, farce and change were on the way.

CHAPTER EIGHT

Cleopatra and Friend

THE making of *Cleopatra* was as absurd as anything that ever happened in the film business. It was Hollywood at its most endearing – extravagant, foolish, hell-bent, and in the end a sort of victory against odds. There was a film and it made money. What more could a reasonable man expect? Burton, who arrived on the scene long after the story began, seems to have had some hopes of an artistic success, speaking well-written lines in a psychological drama in which the vast settings, the battles and processions, were mere backcloth to a serious study of Antony as he ruins himself for the charms of Cleopatra. No doubt Burton also saw the advantages of being in a film that was already creating its own publicity. In the event *Cleopatra* made him the world's best publicized actor, but in a way that suggested some joke among the gods, who wanted to show him, or Hollywood, or us, what happens when mortals let things get out of hand.

The film was conceived in 1958, three years before Burton became involved. Rehashing a subject that had been used before, it was to be a 'tits and sander', a potboiler with a lascivious heroine in exotic settings, made for a modest amount, below a million dollars. Over the next year it became a more ambitious venture. But Fox was in a muddle. The studio was falling on hard times. Darryl Zanuck had left to be an independent producer.

The president, Spyros Skouras, had little flair for film making, and sat uneasily at the controls; Groucho Marx once said that 'Mr Skouras faces the future with courage, determination and terror.' There were vague yearnings for a picture that would make everything come right. Under the wing of Walter Wanger, a senior producer at the studio, the budget grew larger. Elizabeth Taylor, newly married to the actor Eddie Fisher after the noisy scandal of his divorce from the actress Debbie Reynolds, was talked of as Cleopatra; so were Brigitte Bardot, Marilyn Monroe and many more. Olivier might be Caesar; Burton might be Antony, except that Skouras, disenchanted by Burton's earlier films for Fox, thought he lacked box office appeal.

By the middle of 1960 large sums had been spent on scripts, sets, travel and all the other things that eat up money in pictures. Caesar was to be Peter Finch; Antony, Stephen Boyd. Taylor, after blowing hot and cold, had asked for a million dollars to play Cleopatra, bold even by her standards, and wept when told she couldn't have it. Her eventual contract was for three-quarters of a million dollars, but so packed with special conditions and sub-clauses that when Wanger read it he decided that if filming ran over schedule she stood to make 'two or three million dollars'.* Another of her conditions was that the picture should be made in Europe, for reasons connected with tax and a Swiss company, MCL Films, through which she sold her services. Fox stumbled ahead with a plan to make the film, Egypt and all, at Pinewood film studios outside London. No expense was spared. Palm trees were brought from Hollywood and fresh palm fronds were flown in from Nice and Egypt. The summer weather was cold and rainy in the months before photography was to start. When the director, Rouben Mamoulian, first saw the bogus city of Alexandria in the English landscape he is said to have been physically sick. Thirty miles away, Taylor and Fisher took up residence at the Dorchester Hotel, and the disaster gathered speed. The star was not in good health. Illness, like celebrity, was always part of her story, and part of her appeal as well, the violet-eyed pleasure queen made to suffer. A cold in October became a fever; an infected tooth was involved. At Pinewood, weather permitting, they filmed scenes that didn't require Cleopatra. One day it was so foggy that the gloom swallowed up five hundred extras. Before the end of 1960 the farcical production, which had cost between two and three million dollars already, was suspended.

Early in 1961 Fox rubbed the slate clean and tried to start again. Mamoulian resigned in disgust and was replaced at enormous expense

---

* Her *Cleopatra* earnings by the end of 1963 were put at just under two million dollars in fees, more than half of this in overtime, plus above a quarter of a million in expenses.

by the stern, cerebral Joseph Mankiewicz, who was to write a new script ('psychiatrically rooted', noted Wanger) as well as direct the picture. Mankiewicz saw Antony as the conqueror ruined by love; he wanted Burton, now appearing in *Camelot*, for the part, and eventually he and Wanger were able to persuade Skouras to see if he was available. But in March, before the new ideas bore fruit, Taylor was ill again, this time with influenza that turned to pneumonia. She needed a tracheotomy and nearly died. In her own account, 'It was my subconscious which let me become so seriously ill.' Taylor makes it plain that she married Fisher out of her grief for an earlier husband, Mike Todd, the impresario she was in love with, who died in a plane crash in 1958. Thus, unhappy in her life with Fisher, 'I just let the disease take me', because 'my dream world which was Mike was much more satisfactory and much more real. As I've said, I was not a very healthy girl. Poor Eddie.'

The Queen's doctor was in attendance; the Queen's portable lavatory, used in distant parts of the Commonwealth, was rushed to the London Clinic, according to Wanger. The illness was real but the images of the stricken star, dying and then born again, were part of a powerful fantasy that press and public were happy to conspire in. She was never out of the headlines; her mail had to be stored in laundry baskets. Convalescing in the spring, she won an Academy Award for *Butterfield 8*, a film she had made the previous year. Taylor on form is a better actress than some people give her credit for. In this case she was frank enough to say that her Oscar was a reward for not having died: 'The reason was, I am afraid, that I had come within a breath of dying of pneumonia only a few months before.' As the star come back to life, her fame was multiplied. Hyperbole set in. Anyone who came within her reach could hardly fail to be influenced by the kind of special prize she now represented. At the same time, as the illness had hinted, she was a vulnerable woman, not happy in her marriage. A new strong man, more on the pattern of Todd than Fisher, might work wonders, or wreak havoc.

Negotiations for Burton took some time. His Hollywood agent then was Hugh French, a stylish Englishman. French is dead; his son Robin, a partner in the business, suggests that Burton was keen to play Antony. 'It was not a breeze to get him the part, and having got him the part, my father said to me, "Now the fun will start".' The resistance came from Skouras. Mankiewicz finally got his way in mid-May 1961, after which it was only a question of how much it would cost to buy Burton out of his contract. The answer was $50,000, a modest sum, considering that it had cost three million dollars to buy Mankiewicz out of his existing commitments, half of which went to the director himself.

Belatedly the studio had agreed to make the film in Italy, and photography began at the Cinecittà studios on 25 September. Burton was told to hurry there and stand by; Mankiewicz's biographer reports him as saying, 'I've got to don my breastplate once more to play opposite Miss Tits.' In Rome he found himself with little to do for the rest of the year. Taylor and Rex Harrison, the final choice as Caesar, dominated the first part of the screenplay, which Mankiewicz was having to write as he went along. Burton, guaranteed a quarter of a million dollars for three months' work, earned much of it for doing nothing, then moved on to overtime; by the end of the picture he seems to have received a total of half a million dollars. Sybil was in Rome with him; so was Ifor. His air of detachment was as marked as it had been when he first went to Hollywood. He was a singular fellow to have around, cast in his own peculiar mould. 'Doc' Merman, the production manager in Rome, noted a lack of vanity where his wardrobe was concerned. He found Burton 'defiant' rather than 'arrogant' in his dealings with the world. Rex Harrison, who knew how to make his demands felt on a film set, was surprised to hear Burton complain that his Roman officer's boots hurt, because, it turned out, he was wearing Stephen Boyd's leftovers, not having thought to insist on a pair of his own. Burton's entourage was small and barely worth the name. He lacked airs and graces. In the right mood he was a flashy wit and raconteur, but in some mysterious way, and in spite of his eye for women and taste for drink, he had a look of stability. Wanger found him wordly, well-read, the 'rugged male' who 'combines the best qualities of the physical man and the thinking man. At thirty-six he is a solid citizen, independently wealthy, thanks to wise investments.' He also saw him as 'the ideal lover', quick to put women in their place, yet without illusions about himself. A remark about the Welsh, first picked up by reporters in Los Angeles eight or nine years earlier, caught Wanger's fancy when he heard it in Rome: we are a strange people, said Burton, and we gave the world the verb 'to welsh'.

Like Wales, the theatre continued to be a point of reference for Burton. Movies passed: the stage endured. In December 1961 he was writing enthusiastically to Christopher Fry about Fry's new play, *Curtmantle*.

He was supposed to be in a Sartre play, *Le Diable et Le Bon Dieu*, in London the following May, *Cleopatra* permitting. Perhaps he could do them both. But he didn't want to visit Britain until he went there to work because that would complicate his business affairs. He remained detached, a man on holiday in Rome.

In the background – or the foreground as far as the publicists were concerned – Elizabeth Taylor proceeded in her imperious way to make the first half of the film. Secretaries and assistants hovered about her. She, Fisher, her three children from two previous marriages, servants, dogs and cats shared a villa in parkland near the studio. When she was late on the set, she always had excuses. Her real excuse was that she was Elizabeth Taylor. She had the film industry in her blood; she was genuinely beautiful, a breathtaking woman whose looks and moods were part of her professional equipment, their use perfected over the years. Things constantly happened to and around her. Fans, photographers and policemen kept one another in a continual state of agitation whenever she appeared on the streets. Dancing a rumba with Mankiewicz at a party, she stepped on a match, which ignited and set fire to the ostrich-feather fringe on her dress; musicians leaped to her aid. When the script called for her to be massaged by handmaidens, the set was closed and stories of nakedness were put about with much nudging. There was never any getting away from her body. Just before Christmas she was having trouble with veins in her leg, and there was gloomy talk of what would happen if a blood clot developed.

No rumours about her and Burton seem to have circulated until several weeks of 1962 had passed. They played their first scene together on 22 January; 'electricity' between them was duly reported. The usual story is that this marked the start of their affair. Doc Merman, who was not there at the time, heard that the real date was a month earlier, at Christmas. It may have been even earlier than that, when Burton was still in *Camelot* and they were both in America; some members of Burton's family say they know this to be true because he told them. Wanger wrote that Taylor had known Burton 'as a friend' for years, then 'met him again when she was tired and confused after her near-brush with death in London and after the boredom of her convalescence in California'. In Elizabeth Taylor's written account, on 22 January Burton was incapacitated with 'trembling fits' from a hangover, his face bore red blotches, he fluffed a line, and 'my heart just went out to him'.

So began the public affair, stared at to begin with by the film crew, the cast, the extras, each circle ringed by another, peering hard to see who was doing what to whom, the press, the Jenkinses, the Welsh, the Europeans, the Americans, the human race. As Brenda Maddox wrote, it was 'the most public adultery in the history of the world'. The Associated Press bureau in Rome thought it the biggest story they had ever handled from the city apart from the death of a Pope. It took weeks for the rumours to take root in newspapers. Among those with a close view of the affair was Fox's assistant publicity manager, Jack Brodsky, who was in Rome to keep an eye on things. The studio's Italian publicity chief asked him if he knew there was 'much rushing back and forth between villas', but Brodsky told her not to be silly, that to invent a sexual liaison between stars was very old hat. 'And then', says Brodsky, 'it became apparent she was telling the truth.' Private letters exchanged by Brodsky and his chief in New York, Nathan Weiss, were later published as *The Cleopatra Papers* after both had taken the precaution of resigning. On 15 February Brodsky was writing that Burton's affair with Taylor was plain fact and not rumour. 'It started about three weeks ago and is now the hottest thing ever. It seems that Fisher found out about it and started squawking, so Taylor said, quote, I love him and I want to marry him, unquote. Mank[iewicz], Wanger, not to mention Fisher, died. Burton has told Taylor he wants her, too, but Wanger believes Burton will never leave his wife. . . .'

Sybil flew to New York, where she talked to Philip Burton. As a result he sent a cable reproving Burton, who telephoned angrily from Rome. 'I was indiscreet,' says Philip Burton. They were estranged for two years. The affair proceeded. According to the Brodsky letters, when Sybil left for America, Burton tried to extricate himself. A day or two later Taylor was in hospital with 'food poisoning', and there was talk of a suicide attempt. Anything seemed possible. A detailed denial about 'Elizabeth and myself' was issued in Burton's name by his press agent without Fox approval. This gave reporters the chance they had been waiting for, since it enabled them to direct readers' attention to what was being alleged. Burton's denial that he had made the denial stoked up the story, and so did the press agent's insistence that Burton had approved the original denial.

Did constant publicity help to influence the affair, or did it merely provide glimpses of what would have happened anyway? Brodsky reported a conversation at the beginning of April. Burton said, 'Jack, love, I've had affairs before. How did I know the woman was so fucking famous? She knocks Khruschev off the front page.' Brodsky said, 'Rich, it's none of my business, but you can't very well deny everything in print and then go out on the Via Veneto till three in the morning.' To which Burton replied, 'I just got fed up with everyone telling us to be discreet. I said to Liz, "Fuck it, let's go out to fucking Alfredo's and have some fucking fettucini."' John Heyman, then acting for Burton in London, later film producer and friend, says that for obvious reasons, none of Burton's previous associations had 'garnered so quickly the imagination of the yellow press of the world. In a way they were locked up together. There was nothing they could do about it.' Still, publicity apart, Elizabeth Taylor, who had her thirtieth birthday on 27 February, was a determined woman who presumably knew what she wanted. She once wrote in another connection that 'I will get away with murder if I can.' In Rome she made the most of circumstances. 'It's an insane asylum here,' wrote Brodsky on 2 April. 'Taylor told Burton she'd live in a cold-water flat to be with him. He said he wanted to go back to the Old Vic and she said she'd give up acting just to be out front.' Brodsky, wondering if 'R.B.' could outmanœuvre 'E.T.', concluded, 'I'd bet on her.'

It was widely supposed that Taylor took the affair to lengths that Burton had never intended. Ungallant motives were attributed to her. Sheilah Graham, a Hollywood columnist who went to Rome, later quoted 'an eyewitness on the set' who 'believes the swiftness of [Taylor's] assault on Richard was to punish a recalcitrant admirer'. Friends assumed that no one was a match for Sybil. 'I don't believe Richard would have left Sybil in a million years', says John Heyman, 'if it had not been absolutely impossible for him to extricate himself from the situation he was in.' Burton was frequently quoted as saying there was no question of a divorce. Even as events turned out, it was almost two years before his marriage wore away. In spring 1962 the Jenkins family, always fond of Sybil, couldn't believe that their prodigal but much loved brother was 'serious'. Twenty years later his sister Cecilia says that 'we all rue the day when he met Elizabeth'. Ifor had no time for her at first. She took pains to be nice to him in Rome, and make him an ally, 'and of course', says Hilda, 'he had to accept her in the end – we all did'. Emlyn Williams arrived, suave, old enough to be his father, to do his bit. Burton told him, in Welsh, that he meant to marry Elizabeth. When he met Taylor, Williams said something to the effect of 'Why not have a lovely affair?' ('Not surprisingly,' says Williams, 'she didn't warm to my suggestion. She walked out.') Williams turned to Burton and remarked, not realising

Taylor was within earshot, that 'she walks like a chorus girl'. What Burton said is not recorded. It was 1964 before Emlyn Williams met her again; she was married to Burton by this time and he was in *Hamlet* on Broadway. 'In Rome you met Mr Hyde,' Williams assured her, all smiles. 'This is Dr Jekyll.' 'I think I preferred Mr Hyde,' she said.

Events can hardly have taken Burton by surprise, whatever he said about not realizing the extent of Taylor's fame. If *Cleopatra* had appealed to him as a vehicle, part of its attraction was that it enabled him to play opposite a wonderfully famous film star. Wanger noted that the 'canny Welshman' was suddenly a household name: 'The romance has changed his life.' Hugh French the agent was there, looking pleased. By May Burton was telling Sheilah Graham that his price per picture had doubled. David Lewin, a London journalist who had known him since they were both making their way after the war, had dinner with him in Rome. Burton told him he had found Elizabeth's contract for *Cleopatra*. 'He couldn't stop talking about how much she was making,' says Lewin. Yet Burton was not the unblemished artist, sneakily corrupted. He had made no secret of his liking for money. He told Sheilah Graham that a 'famous actor' in London had sent him a telegram to say, 'You must decide what you want to be – a household word or a good actor.' Burton allegedly replied, 'Why not both?' Brodsky, who was at the interview, wrote that in speaking the friend's message Burton imitated Olivier's voice, without saying who it was. The telegram anecdote has followed Burton around, denied by him on at least one occasion, on the grounds that Olivier 'wouldn't be so vulgar'.* If Burton invented it on the spur of the moment for the benefit of Graham and Brodsky, it may indicate what he felt below the surface of the interview: that there was, as there had always been, a choice to be made between 'actor' and 'household word'.

The making of the film, which continued to spawn technical problems, became entwined with the love affair. Fox went through a period of fearing that either the company or *Cleopatra* or both would suffer because of the scandalous connotations. At the New York and Los

---

* In a radio interview by Philip Oakes in 1963. Oakes had spoken of 'a wire chiding you that either you became an actor or a star', and mentioned *Time* magazine, in which the anecdote was said to have appeared. *Burton:* '*Time* – oh well, you know what time is. Time out of mind and time like an ever-rolling stream must bear its sons away. Time, time, time, it's like the quotation from some idiotic writer who doesn't quite know what he's doing. No, obviously he never sent me a telegram of any such kind, he wouldn't dream of doing it. After all, he's a man who would understand, isn't he?'

Angeles offices, wrote Wanger, 'They refer to it as a "cancer" and say it will destroy us all.' It turned out to have been excellent publicity, but at the time, says Brodsky, the studio's anxiety was not hypocritical. Ingrid Bergman had been damaged in the United States a decade earlier because she left her husband for the Italian director Roberto Rossellini. 'There was a real fear that the churches might say, "Don't go and see *Cleopatra*."' The Vatican City's weekly newspaper made an oblique attack by means of a reader's letter. Taylor's uneasiness echoes in her cry years later that she couldn't help loving him, that 'I never felt dirty because it never was dirty.' They were spied on by journalists and servants. One employee was found to have a camera hidden in her hair. On board an Italian publisher's yacht for Sunday lunch, Taylor kept insisting that someone was taking photographs. Burton told her not to be paranoid, but she insisted she could hear a whirring sound. Newsreel and still cameras were then found behind a curtain.

Talking about it to a friend years later, Burton said he had been 'enormously emotionally disturbed because of the various heartbreaks that were going on around.... It was in a sense a kind of nightmare, lighted occasionally by a flash of happiness.... We often refer back to those days. It's rather like a war, you only remember the humorous things – one rarely remembers the agonies of war, or its boredom, even – being separated from Elizabeth, which I was for days at a time, she was living on the Via Appia Piatello and I was living on the Via Appia Antica, and though we were only about a mile away from each other, we couldn't get to each other without running through a gauntlet of a thousand *paparazzi*. And I'm perfectly convinced that the phone was tapped.' As filming dragged on, Brodsky noted that Burton, 'usually the great guy', was 'nervous, irritable, drinking'. In a scene where he was on horseback in a crowd, he lost his temper with Mankiewicz because they had to shoot it several times. 'Can't you bastards get the thing right once?' he shouted. 'Don't you know what bloody torture it is riding through this crowd?' Mankiewicz, still writing as well as directing, was widely assumed to be inserting lines in the script that reflected what was going on outside the picture. Wanger wrote that it was 'hard to tell whether Liz and Burton were reading lines or living the parts'. In a scene where Cleopatra finds that Antony has temporarily abandoned her, she had to slash his clothes and bed with a dagger. The same day, newspapers were quoting Burton as saying that he would never leave his wife. 'She really went wild,' wrote Wanger with satisfaction, 'lashing out in such frenzy that she banged her hand.' The doctor, still a busy man, had to come running.

It was July before filming ended, with scenes in Egypt. Mankiewicz, worn out by his labours, was seen being carried across the desert outside Alexandria on a stretcher, scribbling on a pad. 'How's it going?' called a colleague. 'I'm writing the last page,' said Mankiewicz. Soon after this a boardroom upheaval at Fox removed Skouras as president and replaced him with Zanuck, who had remained a major shareholder. Zanuck took the final editing away from Mankiewicz, who has maintained ever since that the real picture was thus destroyed. He says that Burton's part is the one that suffered most, largely because Zanuck 'didn't understand the character of Mark Antony *at all*, and would not accept the fact that a woman like Cleopatra dominated a great general like Antony. It had never occurred to him. He'd never read it in the schools of Wahoo, Nebraska, and wrote me a letter that "if any woman ever treated me the way you have Cleopatra treat Mark Antony, I'd cut her genitals off".' As a result, says Mankiewicz, 'He destroyed an extremely good performance by Richard Burton. And a well-written one, too, that no one has ever seen. Literally, no one has ever seen.' Three and a half hours of film were lost to posterity. In the version that comes round from time to time on television, Burton can be heard speaking heroic lines in his prince's voice, which as usual overpowers the more colloquial dialogue. It is the rhetorical passages that succeed, as in 'The ultimate desertion: I from myself' when he is dying by his own hand. The tone of the film and Burton's performance are uneven, but everyone can safely blame Zanuck. Burton has described the part as 'a sort of Roman Jimmy Porter ... brilliantly written – how they cut it is another matter'. Taylor has said that 'they cut the film so all you see is him drunk and shouting all the time, and you never know what in his character led up to it. He just looks like a drunken sot on campus.' In the vaults at Twentieth Century-Fox the cans of dead film await the millennium.

When their part in the film was over, Burton and Taylor were able to escape the worst of the publicity. According to Rex Harrison they stayed with him at his villa in Portofino for several weeks. According to Taylor she wrote him a letter to say they must part, and they did, in the summer or early autumn of 1962. Both went to Switzerland, he to his family at the villa outside Geneva, she to a house she owned at Gstaad, sixty or seventy miles away; her marriage to Fisher had been effectively over since she told him the stories were true, after which 'Eddie and I never did live together again.'

Burton and Taylor were in touch again soon. A relative heard about their meetings. 'Elizabeth had a home in Gstaad and his home was in Céligny. He was going up there quite a lot, because when we went out to Switzerland in 1976, he took us up to Gstaad – he had parted from Elizabeth then. He said, "Imagine the runs I used to do up here from Céligny" – Sybil was there then – "and going back in the early hours of the morning".' In a television interview with David Frost in 1972 Burton spoke first of the meeting that is supposed to have ended a three-month separation – for lunch in a hotel on Lake Geneva – then referred to 'meetings', in the plural, that 'weren't strictly what you'd call Byronic, they were by no means romantic, it was a a desperate rush for lunch and a desperate rush to, er, to, er, get home, and anyway I'd rather not talk about that period if you don't mind, it was, er, far too personal and far too – tormented.' His private life quietly tore itself apart. He had two small daughters. Acquaintances all say that he wanted to keep family and marriage intact, but Taylor had him under a spell: he wanted her, too. A thread of violence was to run through their relationship, at least in public. Sheilah Graham noticed that 'while Richard sometimes called Elizabeth "Fatty" he has always called his first wife by the affectionate diminutive of "Syb".' He spoke of Elizabeth's charms but slipped easily into a knockabout invective that she returned with interest. It was part of their display, like birds at courtship. 'I'm pretty fond of that Jewish girl,' he said on a film set, adding, as she came near, 'Look at her. She walks and looks just like a French tart' (1963, before they were married). 'Does the burnt-out Welshman know his lines?' she asked (1964, after they were married). They were in love but they were also actors, unable to escape the fact that people expected them to act the part of turbulent lovers. This was a long way from life with Sybil. 'I think', says a friend, 'that Sybil was so deeply damaged, not only because she loved him and would have died for him – which is not the rarest thing in the world – but because she had tried so hard. What defeated her was to be so dependent on his love, on his being finally there, whatever had gone on in the dark and in the distance, on the fact that he would finally come back to her, and that he didn't. She did try and cut her wrists – I saw the scars. How genuine an attempt, I have no means of knowing. But she did it.'

In the aftermath of *Cleopatra*, Sybil continued to be quoted as saying there would be no divorce, by reporters who may have been making it up or copying from the next man. One reliable remark, to Elaine Dundy in 1965, was that her 'lowest point' came when she found she could no longer relax by reading: 'There I was in a Swiss village after the filming of *Cleopatra*, and I looked down at the page and *I couldn't read it*. Then I knew I was really in trouble. It was awful. I couldn't go anywhere – couldn't go to England or anything because the bloody press was watching, actually watching through the windows!' But the bloody press was only conspiring with the bloody film stars. Burton and Taylor both thrived on publicity, even if the present kind was not to their taste. It could not be turned on and off like a tap to suit anyone's convenience.

During and immediately after *Cleopatra*, other, smaller projects floated in and out of Burton's life, leftovers from the pre-Taylor days. Any chance that he might have appeared in the plays by Sartre and Fry had been ruled out when filming over-ran. In the spring, in Rome, he had accepted a part in a television play by Terence Rattigan. In September he was cabling the producer from Switzerland to say that doctors forbade him to work before the end of the year. In October John Heyman, acting on his behalf in London, was haggling with the BBC over the fee for a few minutes of poetry reading in a radio programme, *London Lights*, that Burton had agreed to record. Offered 100 guineas, Heyman asked for £200, citing Burton's 'fantastic' earnings in films and on American television. After long bargaining 150 guineas was agreed, a small fraction of what he earned for a morning's work on *Cleopatra*. Heyman says that the only reason Burton agreed to take part in the programme was to do with 'the single most important factor in his life, the constant re-establishment of roots.... The BBC for Richard was much more important than Twentieth Century-Fox, MGM and Warner Brothers put together.' If the past and his origins were important to Burton, he was in need of them then.

The verse reading was recorded in Paris near the end of October. The press said Burton was there, together with Taylor, to re-record dialogue for *Cleopatra* in a dubbing studio. In November it was announced that the two were to make another film together, thus confirming that their relationship continued. Both were said to be in Paris again, discussing the contract. Reporters, lucky or imaginative, described conversations with Sybil in Geneva, in which she said that she and Richard understood one another perfectly. Writing from Switzerland to a BBC producer earlier in the month, Burton had sent greetings from his wife. By the end of the year the family were all back in London for Christmas, and Burton and Taylor were filming the first scenes for their new picture at Elstree studios, *The VIPs*.

Burton liked to make out that after *Cleopatra* he had trouble finding his next part: 'As a result of "Le Scandale" with Elizabeth Taylor, I couldn't get a job at all for months. . . . Finally a kind gentleman offered me something, the first part I'd had in about eight months. I accepted, of course' (1965). The 'kind gentleman' was Anatole de Grunwald, the producer of Burton's earliest British films, who was now working for MGM. *The VIPs* was a project he had been nurturing for years, the story of a rich man whose wife is about to leave him for a lover, the action squeezed into a day or two and a single location. At first it was to be a hotel; then they decided on London Airport, where passengers, among them the wife, are delayed by fog. Terence Rattigan had written the final script by 1962. The wife could be Ingrid Bergman; the husband, William Holden or Laurence Olivier. With the *Cleopatra* affair still fresh, MGM decided they could do no better than hire the protagonists. De Grunwald travelled between New York, Paris, Rome, Geneva and London to negotiate with the players, their lawyers and their agents. In three weeks he made seventeen trips between London and Paris; in one afternoon, twenty-seven transatlantic phone calls. 'I am usually exhausted at the end of a production,' he said. 'This time I was exhausted before we even started.' Burton's agreement, signed on 16 November, provided his services for ten weeks at a fee of half a million dollars: his price had doubled, as everyone said it would. Taylor, who said she went into the film as 'just an excuse to be together', was paid a million dollars.

Filming began a few days before Christmas, with MGM anxious to rush through the production and take advantage of the Burton–Taylor publicity, which was certain to flare up again when *Cleopatra* was released in 1963. As well as the familiar worries about having to censor words that still passed for 'strong language' ('whore', 'bitch', 'goddam') and about whether there might be any 'undue revealing of breasts', the studio was afraid that the screenplay would be seen as implying that the hero condoned his wife's infidelity. De Grunwald was told to beware. The more the film hoped to excite sexual curiosity, the more careful it had to be not to give hostages to the prudes. MGM's publicists longed to exploit the real-life situation, but were afraid to make too much of it. As one of them remarked, 'Burton is, after all, still a married man.' This exquisite dilemma extended to the matter of the title. *Very Important*

Persons or *The VIPs* was the working title, but *International Affair* was tried out by market researchers, who reported a favourable response. In the end MGM trod carefully and went back to *The VIPs*. As such it was a commercial success, probably making Burton an extra half a million dollars in percentages for a dullish performance in a dullish picture, kept alive by the supporting cast of fogbound passengers, among them Orson Welles, Margaret Rutherford, Richard Wattis and Maggie Smith.

Filming took longer than MGM had hoped. Burton was away for a week at Pinewood, shooting additional scenes for *Cleopatra*. He was unable to work for a while following an incident at Paddington Station, when he returned to London late one Saturday evening after watching an international rugby match in Wales. A gang of youths was said to have attacked him for no apparent reason, and left him badly cut around the eye (in 1978 he called it 'a street fight', in the course of which 'they fractured my spine').

Burton, newly famous, struck an uneasy figure. He was quoted later as saying that when he was in Rome, 'I always carried a knife with me.' Now, in London, where the press took comparatively little interest in his behaviour, he managed to avoid attracting much attention. A friend says, 'It was the time of major melodramas. Would Sybil take too many sleeping pills tomorrow? Would Elizabeth take too many sleeping pills the day after tomorrow? If they went out on the street in Italy or Spain or France or wherever, they had a thousand people around them in three minutes. The only place where they felt remotely untampered with was London, and there they could only spend ninety-one days a year, or an average of ninety-one days over five years, or whatever it was, before their lawyers got incensed. And taxes and that sort of thing don't ever really seep through to Richard' – an unrealistic view to take of Burton the canny businessman.

Time reported that he was 'maddened with guilt', repeating over and over that 'my name is writ in water', Keats's epitaph. Hyperbole was still the order of the day. At first he continued to see his wife. 'It was neither one thing nor the other,' wrote Taylor. 'He couldn't leave his family. We were all there.' Taylor was installed at the Dorchester with entourage and little dogs. Burton was there too, although at other times, and perhaps at this time also, he had been known to slip away from the hotel to find a quieter refuge at a house in Hampstead that Ifor and his wife kept ready. At the Dorchester they occupied separate roof-garden suites, the Terrace and the Harlequin. 'Eight floors below,' says Heyman, 'reality and the world continued.' Burton told a reporter in 1971 that 'apart from the fact it was quite absurd, it meant it cost us double the money to live'. He told Romany Bain, a journalist he had known for years, 'In those days things were less permissive, so that there was all that fuss about separate rooms in hotels.' Appearances had to be maintained.

MGM were worried at anything that might upset Taylor. A report circulated within the company that Burton had left the hotel to walk with his wife and children in Hyde Park; word went out to keep the news, true or false, from reaching Taylor. Old friends watched from the sidelines. Robert Hardy and his wife had Sybil to dinner at their house in Chelsea. Driving her back to Hampstead, Hardy unwisely chose the route through Hyde Park, past the Dorchester. Sybil was distraught. On another occasion Burton and Taylor visited the Hardys. She was anxious to be accepted for herself. As they left she seized Hardy's arm and spoke a line from a script, or perhaps her heart, 'Don't hate me.' John Heyman says that when he had finished work on *The VIPs*, Burton was still telling his wife, 'I'll be home on Monday.' According to Burton (1972) Taylor told him, 'We don't have to get married. I can be a friend, a sort of mistress if you like.' But, said Burton, 'My Welsh Presbyterian puritanical background took over, and a clean break was made.'

In April 1963 Sheilah Graham was reporting a legal separation, with a financial settlement of one and a half million dollars. 'Clean break' was another euphemism. Sybil continued to hope for a reconciliation. David Lewin interviewed her in New York in June, where she had taken the children and moved into an apartment. She said that any question of divorce was 'in the future', insisted that she knew of no financial settlement and wrote off 'the past two years' (which pointed to troubles well before *Cleopatra*). Rome was a blank: she had made it so. 'We had good times there, Rich and I - and with Elizabeth. The rest I forget.' And, 'I live in the present. I am happy.' Burton was left to enjoy life with the woman he loved, 'pulchritudinous beyond one's imagination', while lawyers worked to resolve the financial affairs. Ahead lay a decade and more of interviews in which actor and actress might have been conducting a seminar on their affections. Burton would talk of love at the drop of a hat. 'I loved before. I loved Sybil but in a different way.... I would say my love for Sybil was much more a love of a man for his daughter.... Before Elizabeth I had no idea what total love was.... I was shocked.' He was not an empty-headed man rattling off pleasantries for the press. He must have felt some need to state and restate, to speak when he could have been silent, to spin out an explanation of a life, like a patient on a couch.

A new element had entered Burton's affairs. Previously he had stood apart from the unreality of the film makers' world. Now, though he would continue to smile at it, to be his own man, he was seen to have lost something of his detachment. Few thought of 'Burton' any more. It was 'Burton-and-Taylor', or even 'Taylor-and-Burton', she being the more famous of the two. A magazine article about Taylor, based on a visit to the set of *The VIPs*, gave a taste of the stuff that lay in wait for him. A close-up of Taylor with a sad expression was called for. Burton 'walked slowly towards her intoning a poem in a melodious, melancholy voice. When he reached the word "beauty" he repeated it with languorous, hypnotic effect: "Beauty ... beauty ... beauty...." And an expression of exquisite sadness obediently crossed Elizabeth Taylor's beautiful face.' For whatever reasons, Burton went along with this sort of thing for years to come. On the practical side, romance in print was publicity; it was, in the end, money. The Burtons' private affections could no more stay private than his flashing eye or her heaving bosom. They were cast as Great Lovers and that was that. Many would benefit. As Darryl Zanuck, a practical man, put it from Fox's point of view, 'I think the Taylor–Burton association is quite constructive.'

CHAPTER NINE

Pictures of Success

BURTON has often hinted that he should not be taken at his face value. An actor, yes, but what after all is *acting*? As he approached middle age – five or ten years ahead of this point in the narrative – his tongue grew sharper when he spoke of the profession. 'I am totally alienated from the craft that I employ so superficially and successfully' (1970). 'It seems to me the most ludicrous, undignified job in the world to sit down and learn tedious lines written by some tedious man' (1972). 'Acting is somehow shameful for a man to do. It isn't natural to put on make-up and wear costumes on stage and say someone else's lines. So you drink to overcome the shame' (1975. Later he said he must have been drunk when he said it). Most of his close friends were writers, not actors, he told an interviewer in 1974, offering a clue to one of his identities. The same interviewer asked him if he meant to write the story of his life. 'If I do,' he said, 'it won't be a theatrical biography. [That] will be very much on the side, it is only part of my life, it is only one-tenth, it is like an iceberg, that is the only bit that shows.' She asked what the other nine-tenths consisted of. Burton said, 'You will have to wait until the book is written, It is hidden under water.' So now we know, or rather don't know. To be nourished by a sense of a hidden life, inviolate and secret from the world, is common enough. What is he keeping hidden? Conceivably the man behind the mask is no more than a would-be writer who seeks reassurance and identity in Wales, his past and the Jenkinses. John Heyman talks of the 'constant re-estab-lishment of roots'. 'I would like to write about my father, my mother and my ancestors,' Burton told an interviewer at Pontrhydyfen in 1977.

Because of shared hardship, the valley Welsh have sometimes thought of themselves as a race apart, better than most and especially the English. In 1965 there was talk of a film that Burton and Taylor were to produce from a script by the Welsh writer Gwyn Thomas, another valley man, about the Great Train Robbery of 1963, when a mail train bound for London was waylaid. Burton said the idea was 'completely dominating my mind', adding that 'what really interests me is the social phenomenon: why should men as intelligent as that ever become criminals? What makes them do it? What I want is to explore the social problem.' He saw the chief robber, his part, as 'a Socialist, a left-winger, a bit of a misfit'; he also saw him as Welsh ('We'll probably call him Williams, or something really original like that'), which the real chief robber was not. But the film was never made; the clue, if it was a clue, disappeared.

Whatever may be hidden under water, Burton remains what he has always been, a working actor, no more entitled than the rest of us to shake off the suspicion that 'how we live measures our own nature'. In 1963, after *Cleopatra*, he managed without excuses. He put his life in order and embarked on a fruitful period. His stature as an actor was glimpsed in the cinema. He even went back to Shakespeare on the stage and played Hamlet. Much of this was in train by 1963. The first of the successful ventures was a film about royal England in the twelfth century, *Becket*. Olivier had played Archbishop Becket on Broadway in 1961, in the Jean Anouilh play on which the screen version was based. When the film was announced early in 1962 it was Olivier's name that was mentioned, before Burton accepted the part later that year; once again their names appeared together, as if joined by an invisible thread. Hal Wallis, the American producer, obtained backing from Paramount, signing Burton either during or immediately after *Cleopatra* at his 'old' fee of a quarter of a million dollars. The director was Peter Glenville, who had dismissed Burton when he was a young actor rehearsing *Adventure Story* on the London stage. They worked together without incident. Burton played Becket, the 'meddlesome priest' whose emotional friendship with Henry II turns to a conflict of wills, Church against State. Peter O'Toole, in demand for films after *Lawrence of Arabia*, was cast as the king, a showier part. Burton claimed to have been given the choice of roles, and says he chose Becket on Elizabeth Taylor's advice: 'She said the king was the kind of part I was always playing, and she was right.' Wallis and Glenville both say there was no question of Burton playing Henry, who had to be a younger man against Becket's comparative maturity; perhaps it was Burton hoping for another royal part. Filming, all in England, lasted from May to September 1963. The cast included Gielgud. Burton wrote in 1964 that 'I was, for about only the fourth time in my somewhat uncertain film career, really trying to be a good film actor.' Already Elizabeth Taylor had taught him that 'my very penetrating voice need not be pitched louder than a telephone conversation'. Also, he said, she had persuaded him that film making was 'as exciting and as serious as playing Shakespeare on the stage'.

Burton, easily bored, seemed bored no longer. Talk of a new *Hamlet* in New York had begun in the spring, before *The VIPs* was finished. Alexander Cohen, the Broadway producer, had lunch with John Heyman, and discussed what Burton might do in the theatre. Heyman 'asked if I'd ever seen Burton's Hamlet', and telephoned later to say that Burton would like to do it in 1964. Until he met the actor in London in June, during the filming of *Becket*, Cohen thought it was too good to be true. Perhaps Burton saw a return to Shakespeare as an omen for his future. Taylor wrote that for years, 'Richard had felt completely empty, used up as a serious stage actor.... Then came the offer of *Hamlet*. Richard very sweetly gives me all the credit for his accepting that.' But was it offered, or, as in Cohen's account, did the proposal come from Burton's side? In Burton's version it is different again, the result of a casual conversation with Gielgud on a cold summer's day in the north of England where they were doing location work on *Becket*. 'On an impulse,' Burton said he would do *Hamlet* again if Gielgud would direct it. 'I don't know why I said it. I hadn't the slightest desire to do it again. I'd probably had a few drinks.' Witnesses to how things start, like witnesses to accidents, seldom agree. Burton may not have wished to seem over-keen. Fate sweeping him into the part made a better story.

Cleopatra, released in America in June, had its European première at the end of July. The crowds were more impressed than the critics. A week later *The VIPs* was out. Work on *Becket* ended soon after, and Burton moved on to his third film of the year. As preparations for the Broadway *Hamlet* went ahead, with Gielgud as director, he got ready for *The Night of the Iguana*, Tennessee Williams's melancholy comedy about a party of American tourists, all women, in Mexico in the shaky hands of a fallen clergyman. John Huston was to be the director for MGM. Burton, the clergyman, was guaranteed his 'new' earnings figure

of half a million dollars, this time for twelve weeks' work. Paid weekly
– the Hollywood custom that continued long after actors ceased to be
on a salary – this came to twelve cheques of $41,667 each. A large income
was more important than ever to Burton, following the financial settlement on Sybil and his daughters that had been reported in April; he
needed to accumulate capital again. It is said that in making the settlement he gave away most of his fortune. In 1966 he told a reporter that
when his marriage broke up, he gave half a million pounds (or very nearly
one and a half million dollars) to his 'first family' and to charities.
'Perhaps money had become too important,' he said. 'Perhaps it was a
sort of corruption. Whatever it was I wanted to start again from scratch.
So I got rid of it. Every penny.' He had always been generous to his
brothers and sisters as well as to good causes. To leave himself with
nothing sounds like some parable of a rich man's conversion. John
Heyman says it is the truth – 'a totally conscious decision to give Sybil
and the children everything he had. He was earning by that time two
million dollars a year, and in the foreseeable future would continue to
do so. Still, almost everything that he had earned and built in the
marriage with Sybil was made over to her. He did start from scratch
again.' While he was giving away his money, Burton and Taylor were
putting their financial affairs on a new footing. They shared a skilful
lawyer in New York, Aaron Frosch, who made the necessary dispositions
in 1963 or 1964. Henceforth most of her money went into trusts. It is
likely that as part of the new tax structure Burton moved his legal
domicile to Switzerland.* Glenville thinks it took place about this time.

The Night of the Iguana was filmed in black and white in Mexico
between September and November 1963. Taylor was there with secretary, cook, chauffeur and children, and was never far from Burton's side.
For most of the time the unit was at Puerto Vallarta, then a little port on
the Pacific coast, and on a wild peninsula nearby. Heat, insects and the
claustrophobia of an isolated location helped give accounts of the goings-
on a febrile air. Huston's biographer says that 130 journalists were there
from time to time. Ava Gardner, the female lead, was good value in her

---

* 'Domicile' is a step beyond 'residence', which Burton probably obtained in Switzerland in 1957.
An expert in these matters describes domicile as 'a medieval, in some ways Biblical, concept, of
great significance in tax : the place to which you intend to return. It may be accompanied by the
purchase of a burial plot, by evidencing in wills and like procedures that it is the place where you
intend to die. Once the British Revenue accept that you have acquired the domicile of another
country, there is considerable tax relief on investment income. The long-term emigrant rapidly gets
shot of UK domicile. It doesn't affect passport or nationality.'

own right. As usual it is difficult to be sure whether events at movie locations provide insights into people or merely into the peculiarities of the movie business. Burton was quoted on familiar subjects, on love, Elizabeth, his childhood and the theatre. A secretary on Huston's staff kept a diary that later found its way into print. Burton was seen swimming in his underpants, to Taylor's dismay; reciting poetry; lapsing from hilarity into gloom. Irritated when she kept rearranging his hair after the hairdresser had finished with it, he poured a bottle of beer over his head. He was the wit, story teller and hard drinker. It was here he made her weep with his remark that 'the only thing in life is language, not love'. When she was out of earshot he told his audience it was ridiculous to marry and be tied to a contract, adding, 'I'm not going to marry Liz. Of course I haven't told her that yet.' Later that night he didn't know where he was. In general he and Taylor seemed happy. Meanwhile Huston, making the most of the private tensions that flourished there, drew exceptional performances from his cast. Burton's clergyman is a wry, defeated piece of flesh with glimmerings of the spirit; a comic creation that may have been his best achievement in fifteen years of film making.

In late November, while they were still filming, Burton wrote to Alexander Cohen, refusing to visit New York to help with the final *Hamlet* auditions, as Gielgud wanted him to do. He feared embarrassment and bad publicity if he appeared there; time enough to take his chance with what he feared would be an unsympathetic press when the play opened on Broadway the following spring. Cohen had to deal with Burton in Mexico and Gielgud in Australia, where he was on tour. Rehearsals were to be in Toronto, again to avoid the powerful curiosity of New York's press and public; Gielgud cabled his reluctant agreement. Burton and Taylor found Puerto Vallarta a useful refuge; they bought a house and were there over Christmas 1963.

Burton's marriage was finally dissolved in December, when his wife's lawyers obtained a divorce in Mexico. According to Sheilah Graham he had continued to protest to his wife that he did not want a divorce; it was not until he was filming at Puerto Vallarta that he drove the last nail in the coffin, writing to her that divorce would be best for all concerned. Sybil, finally cast adrift, began a career in New York as an impresario of offbeat plays, and founded a fashionable discotheque called Arthur. It was the time of the Beatles and British pop culture, and the former Mrs Burton did well out of Anglophilia. She cut herself off from Europe and her past. Aged thirty-six, she married an American rock-and-roll musician, aged twenty-four, and had another daughter.

Taylor's marriage lasted into 1964 because of unseemly wrangles with her husband about money. Burton called on Fisher to do 'the gentlemanly thing'. Fisher said, 'He deserves an Oscar for sheer gall. He should stick to his Shakespearian roles.' By the time they were divorced it was March, and Burton was appearing in *Hamlet* in Canada. He made his return to the classical theatre, after eight years away, in an eccentric production that was acted on a bare stage in 'rehearsal clothes', in Burton's case black sweater and trousers. Gielgud's intention was to strip the play of 'extraneous trappings'. Rehearsals in Toronto began on 30 January, shut away from the public gaze. Two of Burton's fellow actors, William Redfield (Guildenstern) and Richard L. Sterne (A Gentleman), kept their eyes open and wrote books about the four weeks of rehearsals. The Burton they saw was hard-working, unpretentious, ready to listen to what Gielgud had to say though less ready to act on it, the 'Flying Welshman' (Redfield's phrase) meeting the part head-on. Sterne used a tape recorder hidden in a briefcase and was able to reproduce exchanges between director and star. Gielgud thought he shouted too much. Burton, who seems to have agreed with him, resisted actions and stage business that he found undignified. In the gravediggers' scene Gielgud had him vault over a table to represent jumping into the grave with Laertes. Burton was not happy with it. 'John, you don't think we could fight outside the grave? There's such a danger of this being comic.'

Gielgud: 'No. Hamlet is competing with Laertes. It's in the text and the lines require it. Try it again.'

Burton: 'No, John! ... What if I came in from above and jumped off the platform?'

Gielgud: 'That might work.'

On another occasion Gielgud recalled an effective piece of business when Alec Guinness was playing Hamlet:

Gielgud: 'When he said to Ophelia in the play scene, "That's a fair thought to lie between a maid's legs," he reached right up her skirts in front of the whole court.'

Burton: 'Well, John, that's good for Alec, but I'm liable to get a sexy reputation.'

Gielgud: 'I could add a programme note.'

The two friends from different generations regarded each other tolerantly, worlds apart: Gielgud the golden voice of English verse, Burton its earthier, more masculine exponent, liable to break up the rhythms into prose. Here they were in the fourth week:

Gielgud: 'Richard, you said "In a dreeeam of passion". You rather imitated my habit of dragging out a word.'

Burton: 'Well, I'm working with you, aren't I? [Affectionately] "In a dreeeeam of passion".'

Gielgud: ' "Plucks off my beard, and blows it in my face, tweaks me by the nose, and gives me ...".'

Burton: 'Yes, love. I was doing that at half past two this morning and I buggered it up again.'

Gielgud: 'Nobody will notice except me.'

Redfield caught similar echoes, as when Burton told him, 'The play is a series of theatrical effects. If you try to figure them out pedantically, you're lost.' What interested Redfield was the future of so good a stage actor as Burton, his career deeply involved with the cinema. Redfield looked at the temptations for a successful actor, examining what had happened to Olivier, who had resisted them, and Marlon Brando, who had not. A few years later Burton had a chance to comment on both the books, when a magazine asked him to review Sterne's. He found it unexceptional, but in passing mentioned Redfield's. This he belittled, saying that the anecdotes it contained were 'mostly apocryphal and sometimes outright lies invented I am proud to say for the most part by me'. But Redfield knew this already. 'He does them to a turn,' he wrote, 'as a good chef does a soufflé.' They were 'legends', some of which, 'perhaps', were true. Redfield did try to get to the bottom of one anecdote, about Olivier and *Coriolanus*, which he thought might have been a true story, except that the dates didn't fit. It was about the stage business as Coriolanus dies – Olivier fell backwards from a platform, Burton slithered down a flight of steps. After hearing the anecdote, Redfield went back to Burton and pressed him about what happened when, without success. The point is hardly worth pursuing. But the way Burton reacted to the book is odd. Was he impatient with the way Redfield tried to look behind his anecdotes? Did he resent speculation about his future as an actor? For a decade and more after the American *Hamlet* he was to repeat time and again in interviews that he would return to Shakespeare on the stage, this year, next year, some time, 'soon'. He talked but did nothing.

Hamlet opened in Toronto in the last week of February 1964 to full houses and unfriendly reviews, but Burton's acting fared better than

Gielgud's concept of a 'rehearsal'. Four days before the opening Philip Burton had a phone call from Toronto; Elizabeth spoke to him, and then Richard. It was their first conversation since the events in Rome two years earlier. Before he would go to Canada he insisted on talking to Sybil, with whom he had remained on close terms in New York, to see if she objected. He arrived three days after the opening, had an unembarrassed reunion with Richard, saw the matinée (it was a Saturday), went back to the royal suite at the hotel to meet Elizabeth, and saw the play again in the evening. He thought the production was unfortunate, Richard as magical as ever. On Monday he had to be back in New York to swear an oath of allegiance before a judge: at fifty-nine, he was taking American citizenship. He now ran an acting school in New York, renamed the American Musical and Dramatic Academy later that year. Burton and Taylor raised money for it with a poetry reading in June.

Two weeks after *Hamlet* opened, Burton, aged thirty-eight, and Taylor, aged thirty-two, were married in a hotel suite in Montreal by an English minister, a Unitarian. Presents from the cast included pots, pans, an onion chopper, two rolling pins and a mousetrap. From Toronto the play went to Boston for a short run, well received; at Logan Airport, where the cast arrived in a chartered plane, adolescent fans trapped them all for an hour, shouting insults and flattery. Among the cries heard were 'Kiss me, Dick' and 'Liz is a ba-a-d girl.' Outside the hotel fans manhandled them, tearing hairs from Mrs Burton's head and ripping her husband's shirt. Burton made a joke of his celebrity in a film released the following year, *What's New, Pussycat?* He had no billing in the film, which starred Peter O'Toole and Peter Sellers, and his appearance lasted only a few seconds. O'Toole, looking for someone in a crowded bar, brushes against Burton. Burton says, 'Haven't you seen me somewhere before?' O'Toole says, 'Give my regards to what's-her-name', and moves on.

By now they were famous simply for being themselves. In New York, *Hamlet* was in the shadow of their love affair. Crowds swarmed around the theatre, the Lunt–Fontanne, every night, marshalled by squads of police. Taylor put her finger on it when she said to her husband in the hearing of a *New York Times* reporter, 'You're the one they're coming to see. You're the Frank Sinatra of Shakespeare.' Burton replied, 'Get a hold of yourself, love.' He sounded fed up, complaining that marriage ought to have lessened the public's interest by ending 'the somewhat illicit quality of our relationship', instead of which it had made things worse. It was 'nasty' to be pawed by crowds, an interference with freedom; he had even stopped his wife attending the theatre, 'but the crowds got bigger'.

The crowds were inside the theatre as well as outside it. The thunder of money was heard at an early stage. When the play closed in August 1964 Burton had given 136 performances (and missed two because of a throat infection), filling a theatre of nearly fifteen hundred seats at unusually high prices, with gross takings over the eighteen weeks estimated at one and a quarter million dollars. *Variety* said respectfully that it was 'the highest grossing and almost certainly the most profitable presentation of the Shakespeare classic in US, if not world, stage annals'. Burton's share was thought to be fifteen per cent of the gross. He also had a share of the takings from a film that was made of a performance on stage. This was a fuzzy reproduction in black and white, shown over a period of two days at nearly a thousand cinemas in the United States. Archive copies can still be seen; the play seems to happen at a distance, with dusk falling; Burton's voice is raw and enraged, and when he comes to '*dreeeam* of passion' he shouts it like an order.

Behind the publicity, the crowds and the undercurrent of curiosity, Burton and the rest of the cast had played Shakespeare as well as they could. The play received warm reviews. 'Electrical', 'bold', 'virile' and 'unprecedented' were among the words used about Burton. Walter Kerr in the *New York Herald Tribune* thought him 'one of the most magnificently equipped actors living', although he suggested that 'his passion is always a *way* of doing passion, not passion proper, passion unpremeditated'. This has an echo of notices Burton was receiving in London ten years earlier. He told Tynan in 1967 that 'I played it absolutely as myself.' But whatever the merits of his Broadway Hamlet, it was harder to see him as an actor now that he was a celebrity.

CHAPTER TEN

Married Couple

BURTON the married man said once that he liked washing dishes with scourers and detergents as long as he was left alone to do it. He was tidier around the house than Taylor, who always assumed that someone would pick things up when she dropped them. 'Wherever we go,' he told an acquaintance, 'I insist on having a separate bathroom, if it's possible. Hers looks as if it's been hit by an atom bomb – pants, brassieres . . . Elizabeth calls me "Craig's wife" sometimes – a man killed his wife because she was so houseproud. But gradually Elizabeth has become more tidy than she was, and I've become less.'

The picture of their marriage that emerged was a mixture of the domestic and the sexual. Burton didn't talk to reporters about his personal life with his first wife – it would have seemed incongruous if he had – but he did it as a matter of course with Taylor. 'She brings me repose, especially at night,' he told David Lewin in 1971. 'Since being with her I have never wanted another woman and I have never *had* another woman. When I married her it wasn't marriage to a big star, or someone who had been married three or four times before, that was my worry. What I was concerned about was whether I could stay faithful, because I had been a great womanizer – knocking off everyone there had been in sight.'

All through the 1960s it seemed a successful marriage. They treated their quarrels, sometimes reported, as a joke. Taylor called them 'delightful screaming matches'. She also said that he made her 'feel an intellectual equal of his, which of course I'm not'. Sexually, at least seen from the outside, they were a match for one another. She was still the beauty queen, he was still turning women's heads. A youngish woman in Beverly Hills remembered him (1979) 'at some charity do in Los Angeles ten years ago, with all the upper-class ladies of thirty-five and forty fawning on him and getting hot. Me, too. You wanted him to take you away somewhere and do things.'

Burton's views on women were made known. 'Total nudity' was not to his taste, 'unless it happens to be a personal contact'. Taylor's 'sort of trouser dresses, which are terribly tight to the body', he found 'very erotic and provocative'. Cleanliness, dark hair and good bosoms met with his approval. On the debit side were raddled thighs and hairs that stuck through stockings. Feminists were not high on his list. 'Most of the fem-libs I've met are diabolically unattractive,' he said in 1974. 'They all seem to me to be lesbians. Something funny about them.... And when you have these arrogant, militant, idiotic, maniacal, stupid, ugly, ferocious, repulsive women trying to be as powerful as men, which they can't be, then I tend to vomit.' Years before that he was saying, 'I am an arrogant Welsh bastard. I'll be dependent on no woman.'

As father to his children he provided security, homes in two continents, trust funds, armed guards and affection. It was a complicated family. By Sybil he had the two daughters, Kate and Jessica, aged six and four respectively when he married Taylor. Jessica was a chronic invalid, kept in the background, and absent from most reports about the children. Taylor had three children from previous marriages. Her first marriage, to Conrad Hilton Jr, heir to the hotels empire, was brief and childless. From her second, to Michael Wilding, the British actor who fell on hard times and became an agent, she had two sons, Michael and Christopher, aged eleven and nine when she married Burton. She had a third child, Liza, by her third husband, Mike Todd, who was killed the following year. Liza was six when her mother took Burton as her fifth husband (the fourth was Eddie Fisher, but they had no children). She spoke sometimes of wanting to have Burton's children, but all three of her babies had been born by Caeserian section, and she had been warned not to have more. Instead, she completed the adoption of a German child, Maria (not her real name), begun when she was married to Fisher. Taylor said that the child was suffering from abscesses, malnutrition and a damaged hip, later corrected by surgery.

When the children were younger they were discreetly but closely protected when there seemed any danger from abductors. Romany Bain saw 'everyone at panic stations' in Mexico when one of the girls was half an hour late arriving. On another occasion Burton talked to her about his 'insensate jealousy' if a man looked at the two older girls in a restaurant – by this time they were both fifteen years old, Liza 'dark and rather Satanic-looking', Kate 'tall and blonde'. But there is not much to be said. His private life with his children remained private.

After the New York *Hamlet* Burton and his new wife were in Mexico, on holiday for the first time since they were married, and then, by the late summer of 1964, they were off to California to make another film together. This was *The Sandpiper*, a further exercise in exploitation. *Becket* and *Iguana* might never have been. According to the man who wrote *The Sandpiper*, Dalton Trumbo, it began life differently, as 'a nice, taut little drama about a poor young woman living on the beach with a four-year-old illegitimate kid who becomes involved with a minister'. The idea had come from a producer, Martin Ransohoff. Whatever the original intention, it became an excuse for more of the Great Lovers. Ransohoff made a package of Burtons and script for MGM, and fees of one million and half a million dollars respectively were approved, together with the usual large expenses allowance, running to thousands of dollars a week.* Burton and Taylor had been advised that for tax reasons they should not film for more than four weeks in the US. To accommodate them, only the exteriors were shot in California, at Big Sur, after which everyone moved to Paris, where the beach house, larger and more glamorous than Trumbo had envisaged, was conjured up in a studio.

   The Sandpiper made money, as no film with the Burtons hand-in-hand and lip-to-lip could fail to do at the time. It looked what it was, a vehicle for two characters to commit adultery in. Afterwards there was a move to disown it and blame the other fellow. Trumbo remarked ungallantly that Taylor 'checked in at 145 pounds and never looked hungry in her life'; his biographer accused Burton of ad-libbing, 'often changing the content of scenes'. The director, Vincente Minnelli, wrote that he found the premise of the story 'ludicrous and dated', but 'let the Burtons' enthusiasm colour my judgment'. The Burtons spoke scathingly of the project. Taylor wrote that because of *Cleopatra*'s troubles, and her difficulty in obtaining health insurance, 'I didn't think I could get a

---

* Compare other fees that MGM was contemplating at the time: $750,000 for Paul Newman, $400,000 for Sophia Loren.

job. So I grabbed *Sandpiper*.' She claimed to have talked Burton into accepting the part. Burton said that 'we knew this one would be bad before we started', that 'the dialogue was so awful, you'd die a little each day from sheer embarrassment', that 'we used to break out in cold sweats when saying our lines. Before the notice came out in the *New Yorker* I had a telegram from the critic saying, "Have just seen a run through of *The Sandpiper*. Run and hide."'

At the end of filming, on 8 December, Taylor received a piece of jewellery from the producer, a tribute her employers often felt impelled to pay her. 'I mean, I love presents,' she wrote. 'There is certainly nothing blasé about me in that area.' This time it was a gold brooch with precious stones, bought at Cartier for $4,250. When the studio in Los Angeles heard of it, there were long discussions about who should pay and whether it was to be a charge on the publicity budget. Burton was caught up in the lavish ways of film stardom. The gifts he gave his wife were only one side of it, the best publicized. He now shared a personal entourage. Sterne counted a bodyguard, a chauffeur, a dresser and two secretaries. The Burtons lived on a fine old scale. While a picture was being made, $70,000 or $80,000 could easily be swallowed up in hotel bills and plane tickets for them and their party. Sometimes a film company, groaning under its breath, had to meet some of the living expenses on top of the expense allowances.

Burton himself seemed largely unchanged. If he was less accessible to old friends, that was only because it was necessary to have mail and telephone calls filtered out by henchmen. His sister Hilda was dismayed to see a secretary ripping up unopened letters. 'They're only rubbish,' he assured her. Philip Burton said once that he would as soon 'put a letter in a bottle and throw it in the sea' as post it in hope of a reply. But when reached at last, Burton was his amiable self. Nor did he show signs of being deflected from what he saw as his new aim, over and above the other aim of making money: there was more talk of Shakespeare, this time *Coriolanus*. Alexander Cohen would produce it in New York for a run of sixteen weeks in a year's time, October 1965. His *Christmas Story*, the reminiscence of a Welsh childhood, appeared as a short book in America and as a feature article in *The Observer* in London. As for films, he was now under contract to make a version of Le Carré's novel *The Spy Who Came in from the Cold*, playing the shabby British double agent. Photography began early in 1965 and continued until May in Ireland, England and Bavaria. Again Taylor was a spectator. In Dublin the party, which included her three children and the fourth adopted child, together with nanny and tutor, filled suites on at least two floors of the Gresham Hotel. Barry Norman, a friendly reporter, shook his head at their 'almost total isolation'.

Journalists made their customary visits to sets and locations, allowed to talk to Burton, and occasionally Taylor, for an hour or two at a time in the interests of publicity for the film. This is standard practice; but the pair were bigger news than most, and Burton was an unfailing source of copy. A writer for the *New York Herald Tribune* had returned from the *Sandpiper* set with a report of Burton declaring, 'Life with Elizabeth is like waking up and finding a wonderful new toy on your pillow every morning. You never stop marvelling or being surprised. I worship her.' At other times, as the writer pointed out, he said things like, 'Where's that fat Jewish wife of mine?' Some of it sounds like mockery of his listeners or even of himself. The *Herald Tribune* heard him in Dublin arguing with a make-up man, at the end of a day's filming on *Spy*, about a faked head wound. ' "Let's leave it on for the night," Burton insisted. "It takes too long to take off. I'll wear it into a pub with pride. The Welshman saunters in with a bloody big bruise like this, but very cool, very debonair. I'd like to see anybody pick a fight with me tonight." ' To another reporter he described how, during an earlier scene in the film, 'I had to knock back a large whisky. It was the last shot of the day and I decided to use the real hard stuff. We did forty-seven takes. Imagine it, love, forty-seven whiskies.' It might have been Dylan Thomas saying 'eighteen straight whiskies, I think that's the record'.

Burton's price rose again for *Spy*. His agents successfully asked Paramount for three-quarters of a million dollars. Burton attributed it to *Hamlet*, not to his private life. In retrospect it turned out to have been a good choice of film, given the difficulties of estimating the finished product from a script. Ideas were always in the air – for him to play Napoleon or James Bond or Simon Bolivar. He was on the receiving end of other people's enthusiasms. Ransohoff, producer of *Sandpiper*, wanted him for an adventure story, *Ice Station Zebra*. MGM wanted him for *Goodbye Mr Chips* in a version by Terence Rattigan; after failing with an offer of three-quarters of a million dollars in October 1965, the studio was soon offering him a million. Negotiations petered out some time the following year, perhaps because Taylor wanted a part and none was available. Unwisely, the Burtons kept looking for films in which both could appear. Burton has said that 'frequently we did films that we didn't really want to do but simply to be in the same place as the other person. So the careers both became affected by it' (1978).

They worked together to good effect in the film that came on the heels of *Spy*, a black and white adaptation of Edward Albee's play about an unhappy marriage, *Who's Afraid of Virginia Woolf?* This over-rode fears of gimmickry, was taken seriously by the critics and made money. It was the one picture of real quality that they made together. The deal was arranged in 1964. Ernest Lehman, who was to write the script for Warner Bros, had recently finished adapting *The Sound of Music*. An intense and painstaking man, he was also the producer, and in this capacity thought of Taylor to play Martha, the soured wife. She was too young for the part – Martha was fifty-two in the stage version – but he decided that this was not crucial and talked to Hugh French not long after *Hamlet* closed. Taylor and Burton read the unadapted text of Albee's play on a train journey across America, and Burton advised her to accept the part. In Burton's account he said, 'I think you're too young. I don't think you're enough of a harridan. Maybe you don't have the power. But you've got to play it to stop everybody else [*sic*] from playing it. I don't want any other actress to do it. It's too good a part.'

For another fee of a million dollars, to which Jack Warner agreed with reluctance, she accepted in principle when she read the draft screenplay while filming *The Sandpiper* in California. She then began a campaign to have Burton play the equally important role of George, the bloody but unbowed husband. The Burtons and Lehman were in one of the bungalows in the grounds of the Beverly Hills Hotel in Los Angeles. Champagne was being drunk. Lehman was suggesting candidates for George. In his account Taylor pointed to Burton and said, 'There's your leading man. My husband.' Burton said, 'Now wait a minute, love.' Taylor said, 'Shut up, darling.' No decision was taken then. At first Lehman was not enthusiastic. Burton would be expensive, he might be too powerful for the part, and the studio would be accused of looking for sensation. But the idea grew on him. So did his conviction that Burton was itching to have the part but was too proud to be seen to want it, especially since he knew that the producer had reservations. In October Lehman changed his mind and persuaded Jack Warner to offer Burton three-quarters of a million dollars. Afterwards Burton said that he had intended to write 'a splendid book' while his wife was making the film, but 'Elizabeth started in on me, and those great eyelashes started to wiggle. Eventually I thought, well, if I play it a certain way, and am totally unlike Albee's lean and haunted man – if I could play him as a sort of decaying, seedy, gone-to-fat, almost obese intellectual – it might work.' Burton was also heard to say during the making of the film that 'virtually everything I've done in movies in the last three or four years has been Elizabeth's choice'.

The director, not appointed until the end of 1964, was Mike Nichols, at that time known only in the theatre, where he had been directing successful comedies. He and Burton had been friendly since they met during *Camelot* and discovered a mutual taste in jokes. When Burton was in *Hamlet*, Nichols sent him a moose's head with a note that read 'O! for a moose of fire', a pun on 'O! for a Muse of fire.' When Nichols's next play opened on Broadway, the Burtons sent him a life-size moose made of flowers. And so on. Nichols seems to have liked the Burtons, respected their talents and been at ease with them. This was not an easy thing to be, as several film directors were to find in the coming years. The Burtons in their heyday could be figures of menace. Nichols wasn't afraid of them, or their aides and sycophants. No doubt the effect that film stars have on their colleagues is as much a result of what the colleagues expect as of anything the stars themselves do. Sandy Dennis, the wife in the other married couple in *Virginia Woolf*, and relatively unknown in pictures at the time, was asked about the Burtons a year later. 'They were just people you work with and then you go home and forget them,' she said. Elizabeth was 'very sweet' and 'Richard gave us a lot of expensive books. There was no big star treatment. I can understand how when you get famous and make lots of money, how you'd ask for things like air-conditioned cars, things I'd be too embarrassed to ask for. But *they* don't have to ask. People just give them things. On the set, Elizabeth didn't really get anything more than anybody else. Richard had a big dressing-room and she had one two feet bigger in lavender. Big deal.'

But film-making generates enormous tension, especially when expensive celebrities are involved. Apart from their 'compensation' (her million to be spread over three years, his three-quarters over one), Taylor was guaranteed $70,000 for those useful 'miscellaneous expenses'. She and Burton were to have first-class travel and living expenses, including all hotels, when working more than twenty-five miles from the Warner studios at Burbank, Los Angeles. The man to do Taylor's make-up was specified. So were her hairdresser and the man who was making her wig or wigs ($5,000, fringe benefits and $200 for every day he was called in), and Irene Sharaff, who designed her wardrobe. Burton's only stipulation was his make-up man. Work began on 6 July 1965 with three weeks of rehearsals without cameras at Burbank, an unusual start to a film, insisted on by Nichols. 'Principal photography' began there on 26 July and lasted a month, when the unit flew across America to Massachusetts to do location work at Smith College, returning to Los Angeles to film on into the winter, by which time they were far behind schedule.

Throughout, the Burtons were watched and monitored. Their comfort and safety were prime considerations. Before the unit moved to Smith College, in the small town of Northampton, assistants tried to anticipate problems. The chartered plane from California would taxi to an isolated part of the airfield, away from press and public. A company Cadillac would stand by night and day. Taylor was advised that New England weather in late August and September could be warm in the day, cooler in the evenings – it was cold and rainy most of the time, one reason why filming over-ran. Photographs of the house selected for them to live in were sent for their approval, together with details of the property: screened patio, thirty-foot living-room with organ, large master bed-room with large bath, the whole tastefully appointed and secluded in 150 acres with fine views. Off-duty policemen were hired and given instructions. 'When on the set stay at a short distance from them, keeping them always in view.' When they were at home, it might be that the Burtons would 'make a sudden departure' on foot or by car. If so, one patrolman of the two guarding the house would follow; had they left by car, he was to radio his base so that two more men could hurry to their destination. Guards were told on no account to speak to the Burtons 'unless they initiate the conversation, and then make it brief. Do not ask them any questions.' The film company kept a close watch on Taylor's timekeeping and the state of her health. Reports noted each lapse from punctuality, even if it was only a matter of three or four minutes. Any event with the slightest medical implication was reported at once: she had caught her heel and stumbled, she was thrown against the side of a car by Burton in the course of a scene, bruising the back of her head (this was night filming, at 2 am), she was unable to work for 'personal health reasons' – allowed for in the contract at the rate of two days per month, with any additional days to be offset against her stipulated period of employment.

The film had more literary pretensions than most 'commercial' pictures. *Virginia Woolf* was an important victory for sexual freedom – or a sad day for sexual traditionlists – in the cinema. Its language, which Burton and Taylor use against one another like blunt instruments, was studded with words and phrases still unacceptable in the American cinema of the mid-1960s. Early thinking at Warners was that the text would have to be laundered, unless it was decided not to conform to the industry's Production Code, which would mean 'art house' distribution and less chance of commercial success. A meeting with Jack Warner produced a list of words that would have to go, among them thirteen goddams, twelve variations on Christ and Jesus including a Jesus H. Christ, three bastards, seven buggers, four screws and screwings, four sons-of-bitches and SOBs, two scrotums and a right ball, together with such phrases as 'must have made it in the sack' and 'on the living-room rug'. Lehman and Nichols eventually decided that the film demanded the language, and most of Albee's dialogue was restored, without disaster.

One of the few writers allowed to spend time on the set, Roy Newquist, caught glimpses of Burton. On the sound stage at Burbank one afternoon he walked into a shaft of sunlight that was coming through the roof, stopped, and recited a passage from *Hamlet* about 'this brave o'erhanging firmament'. Puzzled, George Segal, who played the other husband, asked him why. 'Because no actor should resist a spot like that,' said Burton. 'Straight from God, you know. Even Jack Warner couldn't supply it.' Burton was observed telling the tale about Wales, about going to Oxford ('an Exhibition in English, which I won'), about the critic who had remarked that in his 'wretched part' in *Druid's Rest* he showed 'remarkable ability'. But for that, said Burton, getting into his stride, 'I would have become a preacher, a poet, a playwright, a scholar, a lawyer or something. I would never have become this strange thing, an actor, sitting in a remote corner of the universe called Northampton, drinking a vodka and tonic and waiting to learn the next line. He's got a bloody lot to answer for, that man.'

Is it imagination, or is there more than usual in these vignettes of the Flying Welshman about writers and writing? One wet Sunday afternoon in Massachusetts Burton read aloud the review he had written for the *New York Herald Tribune* of FitzGibbon's biography of Dylan Thomas. Change was creeping over Burton, the penumbra of a new dissatisfaction. Earlier in the year, while filming *Spy*, he talked to a reporter in London about his desire to write more, and said he had been offered $100,000 for a book. Perhaps he had; perhaps he meant to write it. To another reporter he talked of retiring in three years, when he would be forty-two. In November, still at work on *Virginia Woolf*, he spoke to the *New York Times* about his ambition to play Lear. The tentative date for *Coriolanus* had come and gone.

The cameras finished with *Virginia Woolf* on 13 December; it had over-run by thirty-five days. At their contractual rate for 'overage', $100,000 a week for her, $75,000 for him, they were entitled between them to further payments of more than a million dollars. The Burtons waived these; Warners reimbursed them for 'certain expenses' instead. Taylor was reported to have been given a modest present of ear-rings. She was also said to have sent word to Jack Warner that she wanted a matching brooch at $80,000. He replied, 'I'm paying her a million dollars and ten per cent of the gross. Let her buy her own brooch.' The circus moved on.

Burton had seemed anxious at times not to be identified with the part. 'My only concern is that my quality is not exactly this, an American college professor going to seed,' he grumbled. After looking at the rushes one day he remarked, 'I was fascinated by that fellow up there. He's not me, that moon-faced chap beaten down by a woman.' But why should anyone think he was anything but an actor playing a part? He protested too much. Ten years earlier Susan Strasberg heard him say that he feared his place was in 'a university town somewhere, teaching literature or drama to grubby little boys'. Perhaps what he really feared was shades of Port Talbot, 'Poor Albert', and the grimmer career, a teacher's, say, that he had escaped – as he might feel on a bad day – by the skin of his teeth.

When the film was released the following year he went to see it, without pleasure. 'I wanted to kill myself because I thought I was so indifferent,' he said. 'Not bad, indifferent.' It was not the general view. The film was a genuine article, with both Burton and Taylor absorbed into the sour fabric of the story. But Burton was never one to sound pleased with his performance. There was always discontent, hidden under water.

CHAPTER ELEVEN

Paradise Lost

BURTON had his fortieth birthday while *Virginia Woolf* was being made. Wealthy, famous and respected, he remained an odd man out among his peers. Modest and almost homely from some angles, he cultivated or let journalists cultivate the style of a simple fellow who ate cod and chips from a newspaper in the back of his Rolls-Royce, had pork sausages sent by air freight from London to wherever he was, and could never find a suit when he wanted one. Stories like that only emphasize the wealth, as in accounts of millionaires who have to borrow a coin to buy a newspaper because they never carry money. Was he really the Briton in exile who is tired of international living, longing to come back? He told a reporter in 1965, 'I get terrible bouts of homesickness, like most provincials who remember seeing London for the first time.' He told another in the same year, 'I want to go back to England and pay taxes like everyone else.' He also said, 'I wake up in the middle of the night with my gums aching for a walk through London. And those dusty brown squares . . . [but] I wouldn't much like the thought of paying these exorbitant taxes' (1968). He spoke as the mood took him.

In February 1966 the Burtons returned to Britain to appear on the stage. The occasion was a week of Marlowe's *Dr Faustus* at Oxford. It was not to be a long visit. The producer was Professor Nevill Coghill, Burton's admirer since the wartime *Measure for Measure*, who was soon to retire. This production by the Oxford University Dramatic Society, with Burton as Faustus and Taylor as the conjured-up Helen of Troy, both appearing free of charge, helped round off Coghill's career. Tickets were expensive, with profits going to the Oxford Playhouse. While he was in Oxford, Burton kept open house for undergraduates at the Randolph Hotel every evening. Police and photographers were in evidence, but there was no Burton mania; there never was in Britain. Burton told reporters, 'I've been wanting to play Faustus for more than twenty years. I know the part but not as well as I thought. A lot of Marlowe's lines started coming out as Burton lines.' Of his summer at Oxford in 1944 he said, 'I was going to come back after the war, but instead I became what for lack of a better word is known as a star.' A reporter asked him if he thought the part of Faustus appropriate in his case. Burton's reply was cryptic. He said, 'Everybody is offered a choice: one easy, one difficult. Most men, regardless of their craft, profession or background, are faced at one time or another with an obvious, easy one and a difficult, more rewarding one.'

The play received some indifferent notices, Marlowe for having written poor melodrama, Coghill for a tedious production, Burton for 'walking through the part', Taylor – with no lines to speak – for 'looking impossibly pretty in a filmy nightie, on a carpet of smoke ... like a cunning soft-sell for lingerie'. Once again it was difficult to disentangle the performers from their reputation. There was no point in blaming the reviewers (Coghill was heard muttering that they were upset because tickets were short and 'no critic could bring wife or mistress'). 'Richard' and 'Elizabeth' were characters from a serial story in the newspapers; like a jury that is supposed to forget all it has read and heard before the case comes to court, a reviewer might find an unprejudiced mind easy to promise but hard to achieve. The reception of *Faustus* at Oxford, a place of strong associations for Burton, may have helped unnerve him when he thought of making a serious return to the stage. It was three years after this that a journalist asked why he didn't do another play, and he answered, 'I think I'm afraid.' The same interview raised the ghost of Faustus, a parallel that some critics had sought to draw with his own life. 'What can I say?' he replied. 'I could go to Scunthorpe to act in rep for nothing. Admirable, maybe, but an exercise. What would be the point? As Elizabeth said, would people say she'd sold out if she deserted films for the theatre?'

The Burtons moved on to Rome to spend the summer of 1966 making a lavish film of Shakespeare's *Taming of the Shrew*, of which they were co-producers, followed by a more modest film of *Dr Faustus* with the same supporting cast of Oxford amateurs. By keeping a low profile at their rented villa and working long hours at the film studios, the Burtons gave the Roman press no excuse to hound them. No location work was involved, Burton remarking that 'I believe acting to be an indoor art. I've never felt comfortable in the open air, and the vagaries of climate, aeroplanes passing overhead in the middle of a soliloquy, are not the most attractive ways . . . of entertaining oneself. So when I do have some smattering of power over any film that I'm in, I try to insist that everything is indoors.' *Shrew* was directed by Franco Zeffirelli. The Burtons had a bitterly negotiated financial arrangement with Columbia that seems to have included little money 'up front' but gave them a large percentage of profits, if any. Burton said the picture was being made 'in a commercial way, that is, it is a great mudpie-in-the-face romp'. As Petruchio and Katharina, the tamer and the tamed, the Burtons overflowed with energy. Disliked by many reviewers when it was released the following year, the film found large audiences and according to John Heyman added several million dollars to the Burton fortunes; one result was the scheme to provide the Jenkins family with regular remittances. The *Faustus* film was less fortunate. Burton and Coghill were joint directors, with the best technical assistance. Burton, directing for the first time, said he found he needed seven heads and would not try it again. For whatever reasons, the result was a curiosity, lurid and awkwardly 'poetic'. Certain profits from the film were to go to the Oxford Playhouse, but *Faustus* failed to generate them. (Four years later, in 1970, profits from another Burton film, *Villain*, were similarly earmarked, again without success.) The Playhouse had been hoping for something in the region of £100,000. Anguished discussions went on for years. Elizabeth Sweeting, the Playhouse's manager then, says that 'I have never encountered anything so complex in my whole life.' But Burton and Taylor were 'marvellous people' to deal with, and in the end, the Playhouse benefited by roughly the amount it had been expecting.

Neither of the attempts to turn a classic play into a film, *Shrew* or *Faustus*, led to anything. Separately or together, the Burtons returned to more conventional work. Burton told Tynan in the course of a long television interview, recorded late in 1966, that by marrying Elizabeth he had become a far more important actor, 'though it's not very easy for me to say that'. This is the interview, published later in *Acting in the Sixties*, that has been cited more than once because it shows Burton taking serious questions seriously. When, confessing that he was 'a frightened man' at the thought of facing a live audience again, he said it was fear that made it necessary for him to try, he sounded as if he was telling the truth. The interview, recorded soon after *Dr Faustus* was filmed, contains one curious passage. Near the end Tynan asks whether 'the thing that drew you to the stage was rhetoric?' 'Oh yes,' replies Burton, 'unquestionably, and I think – we have a word in Welsh called – misused I believe by you lot – called *hwyl*, and nobody can ever translate it, but it's a kind of longing for something, a kind of idiotic, marvellous, ridiculous longing.' *Hwyl*, though, means 'fervour', in particular the excited oratory of the preacher in his pulpit. It was the word that made sense in the context. But having used it, Burton pinned to it a different but even more potent idea in the Welsh consciousness. 'A kind of longing' is not *hwyl* but *hiraeth*, a word used especially for the homesickness of the exile. Burton was a natural Welsh speaker; it is an odd mistake to have made, as though some different train of thought has broken into the sentence.

His Welshness was always present at one level or another. His film contracts contained a clause to say he did not have to 'render his services' on St David's Day, but if necessary would work an additional day later on. From time to time Elizabeth Taylor was taken down to Wales, and the circus moved briefly to Pontrhydyfen, the big cars racing up the derelict valley, home to the family. Hilda, in the house beside the Big Bridge, remembers Richard and Elizabeth arriving with the chauffeur, who was expected, and a hairdresser and two secretaries, who were not. There were other visits when Burton went alone, running the bath at six in the morning, scribbling in his notebook in the living-room with a view of washing on the line, before Hilda and her carpenter husband were up.

February 1967 found the Burtons working together in West Africa on an MGM film of Graham Greene's novel of farce and terrorism, *The Comedians*, with Peter Glenville as director. Greene had worked on the screenplay; according to Glenville, the author's name was enough to make Burton accept the part – of Brown, the seedy hotel-keeper – the minute it was offered. Taylor, Brown's mistress, was there because MGM wanted a famous actress, against Glenville's better judgment. Having resisted the idea of Sophia Loren, he gave in when Taylor let it be known that she was anxious to join her husband in the film, and was willing to take half her normal fee.

Alec Guinness, the bogus Major Jones, had a leading part, and worked happily with Burton, though he raised an eyebrow, as did others over the years, at one or two of the hangers-on. Guinness, eleven years older, had been a friend since the H.M. Tennent days. He had met Burton occasionally, aware that he was no longer an easy man to see. Once, staying at a hotel in Paris, he found that Burton was also a guest. 'I scribbled a note saying, "If you see a balding, ageing, white-haired character sitting around in the bar, you don't have to do a double-take, it's me." Nothing more than that. I had it sent up. There was no reply. Three days later I was sitting downstairs, waiting for somebody, and along comes Richard, does a double-take – "What are *you* doing here?" I said, "I dropped you a note." "Oh, I never got it." Then in New York I sent him a present when he was playing Hamlet. It was never acknowledged. When I tackled him later he said, "Oh, I never got it." I couldn't make it out.' There could have been no wall around Burton without his consent. But filming in Africa in 1967, Guinness found him 'generous' and 'marvellous' to work with, in particular in a long scene near the end, photographed in a single take with one camera, where Guinness is confessing his past to Burton. An actor who has to listen can contribute or withhold his sympathy – how, exactly, it is hard for a non-actor to tell. When the shot, which lasted about four minutes, was over, Guinness told Glenville it was 'the greatest support I've had from an actor, ever in my life'.

The country they were in was Dahomey, a tiny republic, once French, chosen to re-create Haiti, where the novel is set, and where no one connected with Greene's book and its indictment of the Duvalier dictatorship would have been safe, let alone welcome. The film unit, close on 150 strong, made a useful contribution to the national economy. The Burtons, with weekly expense allowances running into thousands of dollars, radiated power and hospitality. 'How could they spend that sort of money in Dahomey unless there were crates of champagne every night?' Glenville was asked. Glenville said, 'There were.' For the first time Burton's fee, three-quarters of a million dollars, was larger than Taylor's, half a million.

His temper was uncertain. The *New York Times*'s senior man in Africa, Lloyd Garrison, looked in to keep an eye on events before and behind the cameras. Early one evening, as the Burtons sat talking over drinks before dinner, someone brought news of the Apollo disaster, when astronauts in a space capsule died in an accident on the ground. Burton, who 'appeared stunned', said, 'Good God. That's horrible. And they got it just sitting there, right on the pad ... not even an honest death.'

The dialogue, here extracted from the article, reads like the script of a black comedy:

Taylor: 'Oh, their poor *children*. What a pity they had to die like that, if only they ...'

Burton (sharply): 'It's not a pity they had to *die*, Elizabeth. And it's got nothing to do with children. It's a pity the *way* they died.'

The *Times* man reported Burton 'bristling', the atmosphere 'suddenly chilled'.

Taylor (eyes blazing): 'Christ, that's what I was *going* to say, what a pity they ...'

Burton (shouting): 'It's not that they *died*. Can't you see that? The poor bastards couldn't even die in *space*! If I'm going to die I want to die in space, or as an old man with my feet up in bed reading philosophy, or even with a gun in my hand fighting another man. But you can't seem to ...'

Taylor (also shouting): 'That's *just* what I was saying, what a pity they were on the ground deprived of ...'

Glenville (arriving to take them out to the honorary British consul's house): 'Ready, everyone?'

The atmosphere returned to normal. An aide, Gaston, a Basque, told the *Times* that such outbursts were not uncommon but didn't last long. Later, at the honorary consul's, Gaston spoke warmly of his employer: 'He was born poor. I was born poor. He worked his way to Oxford, and well, I had to work, I became – how you say it? A *manual*. I tell you, if every *manual* man had a boss like Richard, there'd be no Communism today.' As the night wore on, the *Times* correspondent followed the course of a long argument between Burton and another guest, a young Methodist missionary from Britain who tried to defend the British Conservative Party. Burton asked how old he was, and was told twenty-seven.

Burton: 'Well, then, you don't know what my mother knows. You don't know what my father knows. Perhaps you don't know that we are *Welsh*!'

Missionary: 'I know. Of course you're a socialist. I mean, I know you were a coalminer's son and all that.'

Burton: 'Look. My *stop* year was 1935. My mother was forty-four. I watched my mother die. And *you* killed her. The Tories killed her!'

Missionary: 'What do you mean, *I* killed her?'

Burton: 'You say you're a Christian. What are you, Church of England?'

Missionary: 'No, Methodist.'

Burton: 'Okay, you're a Christian? I am *not* a Christian. I believe that somewhere through the minefield [he was marching up and down] – somewhere through the minefield a man can find . . .'

Missionary: 'So you're an existentialist?'

Burton: 'Existentialist? You must be joking. . . .'

The evening ended with Burton 'a little unsteady, but still articulate, still thoroughly in command', slapping the missionary on the back and shaking hands with him as he left with his party. The missionary looked defeated.

The film, released at the end of the year, was unsatisfactory. Greene the adaptor had lost touch with his material, and in their own ways both Burton and Taylor were larger than life as the story called for it; Guinness's sad Major Jones suggested what the picture might have been if everyone had carried the same conviction.

From a modest failure written by a famous novelist the Burtons plunged into an extravagant failure written by a famous playwright. This was *Boom!* by Tennessee Williams, adapted from his unsuccessful stage play *The Milk Train Doesn't Stop Here Anymore*. Conceived as 'Boom', the film became 'Sunburst', then reverted to 'Boom', then changed to 'Goforth', the name of its central character, a dying rich widow, and finally settled for 'Boom' with an exclamation mark; according to Williams this expressed 'the sound of shock felt by people each moment of still being alive'.

The result was as clumsy and pretentious as these harbingers suggest, despite the expert attentions of Joseph Losey as director. The picture, financed by Universal through its London office, was made in Sardinia in the summer of 1967, providing better opportunities than ever to conjure up visions of the Burtons in paradise. Their yacht *Kalizma*, recently acquired, rode at anchor under the cliffs. Visitors were told that Taylor was wearing real diamonds borrowed from a jeweller in Rome. The project was weighed down with opulence. The principal film set was a cleverly faked villa overhanging the sea, built at enormous expense. Taylor had made two successful pictures from Tennessee Williams material, *Suddenly Last Summer* and *Cat on a Hot Tin Roof*, and wanted to play the widow. Losey, who began by saying 'Christ, it's an old woman's part', came round to the idea. He thought Burton a mistake to play opposite her as the handsome young stranger with a weakness for dying widows who comes ashore on her private island. But 'she wanted him involved and that was that'. Tennessee Williams's concept may have had something to do with male purity and female corruption, but the film, though elegantly set up and photographed, was to emerge as a crippled fantasy. The fact that Burton was too old and Taylor too young added to the difficulties. Tennessee Williams thought them a 'dreadful mistake' in the parts, but has continued to see the film as an 'artistic success'. John Heyman, who was the producer, called it 'a piece of sheer opportunism'. Burton was heard to say that he and Taylor 'only really enjoy working together. It's total comfort for both of us.' People had hinted that 'if we kept on doing films together it would destroy us. But that's rubbish.'

Boom! was poor evidence to the contrary. When it appeared, reviewers made connections between what was wrong with the film and what was wrong with the Burtons for appearing in it. Their achievements in *Virginia Woolf* were put aside; what welled up was irritation. Was it arrogance, the Burtons' or the system's, that gave offence? Visiting Sardinia for the *New York Times*, Mark Shivas, later a film and television producer, was struck by the analogy with a royal court: the 'gaggle of retainers', the favours granted and withheld, the atmosphere of deference. An aide who called everyone 'dear heart' told Shivas that he didn't know why Elizabeth let journalists go there. 'They always ask the same boring questions and she doesn't need them. Every one of her pictures since *National Velvet* [1945] made money, even *Cleopatra*. But Richard is a bit new to all this and says OK, and as his wife, Elizabeth goes along with it.'

The scale of Burton's public life was changing. He was doing things in style; rather, he and his wife were doing things in style together. The big second-hand yacht cost a fortune to run and was soon to be refitted. They owned a company with two or three small jet aircraft. Burton liked to see them hired out to make money, but there was no telling when Taylor would want to make personal use of one or more. Everyone knew about the famous jewels; but the more they were worn and admired, the more they cost to insure and guard. The payroll grew longer; the financial machinery, as far as one can glimpse it, more complex. Burton, always the businessman, was part of an intricate arrangement of trusts and investment concerns, with at least one company, Atlantic Productions, to handle his services as a film actor from a low-tax base in Bermuda. One of his published investments that year was in Harlech Television, a new station for Wales and the West of England. The existing company that served the area was deprived of its licence when franchises came up for renewal, and Harlech, a consortium hastily assembled for the purpose, was appointed in its place. Burton's name as a famous Welshman may have been crucial to the Harlech application; he was recruited by the journalist John Morgan, who visited him twice in the south of France where *The Comedians* had moved from Africa. The Burtons subscribed £100,000. As Burton sometimes pointed out, many people were richer. But they and the media between them made their wealth more conspicuous than most. It was a time of 'growth'. The Burtons were good things made flesh; people could admire and covet. She liked to be seen in her diamonds; he liked, as he said often, the best seat in a plane, the best table in a restaurant. Perhaps it is only the envious and mean-spirited who would complain. But the complaint, in the end, is Burton's; he is the grit in his own oyster, the familiar figure of the 'Welsh puritan', a phrase he has used of himself. Years later, in 1977, when his life had changed again, he told a television interviewer that he wished he was one of those 'quiet, brilliant writers' who 'sit quietly in the corner of a restaurant and nobody knows who they are, and they get bad service, but they watch the bad service of the waiter and they mentally record it. They notice, like Chekhov's Trigorin, that cloud is shaped something like a grand piano. . . . I think to be able to do that in absolute anonymity would be very desirable. But then when you mention your august name, Graham Greene or André Gide or Jean-Paul Sartre, everybody says, "No, it can't be!" You know, that's the kind of thing I'd like.' When the Burtons were in the eye of their public, such desires were hidden under water. In any case, Burton was not exactly renouncing fame in 1977, merely wishing it wore a different hat.

Between 1967 and 1970 his work as an actor took a turn for the worse. It was not easy to spot at the time. Films are released long after the acting is over. Actors themselves may be uncertain while making a film whether they are working well or badly. A performance is compiled in short takes, often lasting no more than seconds, usually out of sequence. As far as the actor is concerned it is a serial spread over weeks or months, and rearranged by director and film editor after he has gone. 'I've had many [failures] in films,' Burton has said, 'but then, it's difficult to know what's going to happen between the cup and the lip' (1977). As for the films an actor chooses to make in the first place, he can easily take the wrong decision. Even the famous and established are afraid of being out of work, of being unwanted. The actor is a man waiting for the phone to ring; he may say yes because he is afraid to say no. Actors end up playing roles they hate. Stewart Granger said he has 'seldom if ever made a film I have really liked or been proud of'. John Heyman, who has pondered the ways of his friend and former client, sees Burton (1979) as someone driven to go against the grain of his talents: 'a man out of his time who has been structured by the shape of the industry. If there had not been movies and TV and mass communication and Elizabeth being the biggest star in the world, maybe it would all have been different.' Given things as they were, 'there is no logic in him doing certainly half of his pictures. Except that it's another job and he can't sit still. He has the actor's basic fear of not having a job. And nobody is capable of judging the final outcome from the script. Ninety per cent of what is made is shit.' Therefore, says Heyman, Burton can be excused for making wrong judgments. 'But not', he adds, 'all his wrong judgments.'

After *Boom!* came a 'cameo' part in *Candy*, based on a satirical novel of 1958 about a young girl's sexual escapades. If this was a mistake by Burton, it was shared by Marlon Brando, Walter Matthau and Elsa Martinelli, who were persuaded to romp through a film that was silly more than anything else. It was filmed in Rome at the end of 1967. Burton played a lecherous Welsh poet presumably intended to be Dylan Thomas. Next came an action movie, *Where Eagles Dare*, another version of how a band of intrepid soldiers raid a Nazi stronghold. It drew big audiences for years and was profitable for all concerned. MGM financed the film as a package that had been put together on paper by a rising young independent producer, Elliott Kastner. This is how an increasing number of films was to be made. Kastner commissioned a script by the British writer Alastair Maclean and sold the idea to Burton while he was filming *The Comedians*: 'I told him he should do a movie that had some meat and potatoes, that it was not a weighty tome, that it was not Graham Greene. It was a good solid action-sweat movie. I talked him into it, based on doing something different.' Later Burton excused himself by saying he made the picture to amuse his children. His compensation was a guaranteed million dollars plus a percentage of profits, with $40,000 or $50,000 for living expenses. He was a star at the height of his commercial power. He could have free first-class travel for eight persons. His name would appear in first position, in letters at least as big as those of the title. His approval was needed for major changes in the screenplay, for the director and for the other leading actors; even Clint Eastwood had to be given the nod by Burton. His presence on the set was not required before nine in the morning. A large car with chauffeur stood by for twenty-four hours a day. He did not have to work on St David's Day.

Burton began to earn his million dollars with location filming in Salzburg, Austria, at the start of 1968. In February he broke off to go to New York with his wife for the US première of *Dr Faustus*, a social occasion followed by displeasing reviews. Then he was back in Britain to begin the studio work, which lasted into the early summer. The Burtons had chartered a yacht – the *Kalizma* was having its refit – and kept it moored on the Thames. Their dogs were on board, unable to land because under British quarantine regulations they would have been impounded; this was supposed to be the reason for the moored yacht. Newspaper coverage of the Burtons made the most of their extravagant ways. The dogs off Tower Pier delighted news editors. So did the first night of Harlech Television's transmissions in May, when a new diamond ring on Taylor's finger threatened to overshadow the rest of the entertainment.

In July Burton began work in London on *Laughter in the Dark*, based on Nabokov's novel. In his role as an art dealer, cameras filmed him bidding at a Sotheby's sale of Impressionist paintings. He bid genuinely for a Picasso drawing and bought it for £9,000; Taylor, who was not in the film, paid £50,000 for a Monet at the same sale. A week later Burton was not in the film either, after a disagreement with the director, Tony Richardson; he was replaced by Nicol Williamson.

In his private life Burton had more than one unhappy episode in 1968. Taylor was ill again. She had a hysterectomy at a private clinic in London in July. The following month Ifor Jenkins, Burton's confidant over the years, and perhaps his conscience as well, was badly injured in Switzerland. The story is that he slipped in snow and broke his neck, but the family will not talk about the accident. He was paralysed, and remained so until he died in 1972. At the time it was said that his death led Burton to drink heavily. 'When he died', Burton told David Lewin in 1977, 'I had vivid dreams. I thought he was there in the room with me, smiling. But it was a fantasy, of course, and it became a nightmare for me to go to sleep because of those dreams.' It may be that the accident itself drove Burton to drink more. Whatever the case, alcohol became a problem.

CHAPTER TWELVE

The Treadmill

WHEN Burton spoke seriously of his drinking (instead of making jokes about the inebriate Welsh), as he did later on, he was explicit. 'Once you have a drink problem', he said on television in 1977, 'you always have one. Once an alcoholic, always an alcoholic. But, er, I'm not quite sure whether I am or not. I think I'm within striking distance of being one. But certainly I've stopped drinking.' In another television interview that year Burton said that 'liquor is a reality ... that little monster', adding, 'I think I'm an alcoholic, actually, but I'm not entirely sure. Nobody's actually defined what an alcoholic is. But from all the various things I've read about alcoholism, I think I qualify. Can't go any more for three days and nights laughing and joking with the ghost of Dylan Thomas or something like that. So I watch it very carefully now.' When the condition was in the making he said less about it. A few clues to the dates are scattered around. In a third television interview in the same year he said, 'I'm afraid for about ten years I went through a sort of – I can only describe it as a sort of male menopause, when I didn't really care what I did. I drank very heavily and did any film that came along.' To Mel Gussow of the *New York Times* he said in 1976 that both taste and luck deserted him. 'From 1968 to 1972 I was pretty hopeless. I was fairly sloshed for five years. I hit the bottle. I was up there with Jack Barrymore and Robert Newton. The ghosts of them were looking over my shoulder.' In the same interview he spoke of the 'nightmare' of making a film called *The Klansman* where 'I started to forget what happened the night before – the classic beginnings of alcoholism.' That was 1974, a climacteric that marked the high tide of his drinking.

Towards the end of the 1960s, then, he was a man in trouble; whether drink was cause or symptom is debatable, as it usually is. Burton said he drank because he was a Celt or to relieve bordom. When he felt maudlin it was 'because the world is so infinitely full of pain and riches, and occasionally you have to kill the pain by drinking'. None of this is much help. He seemed to be coping well enough with the film he was working on late in 1968 with Rex Harrison, *Staircase*. They played a pair of ageing homosexuals in a version of Charles Dyer's stage play. Set in and around a barber's shop in London, it was filmed by Fox in Paris because of Burton's tax position at the time. Taylor was also making a film for Fox, *The Only Game in Town*, set in Las Vegas. Because of her own tax position, and because she wanted to be near her husband, this, too, was filmed in Paris. The company thus had to build expensive sets in France, one to re-create a bit of England and the other to re-create a bit of America, in order to accommodate them. Burton commented unnecessarily that he was 'not even vaguely homosexual' and that 'the most difficult and unnerving aspect of this part is to convincingly overcome one's primitive, atavastic fear of becoming one ... of course, love, we all know it's a foolish fancy.' When the film came out, the critics jeered a little or yawned or damned it with faint praise. Commercially it was a failure, made more painful for Fox by the size of Burton's fee – one and a quarter million dollars, the largest guarantee he had ever received. Taylor's fee was the same, and her film was not successful either.

The following year, 1969, Burton made only one picture, *Anne of the Thousand Days*. This was filmed in England in the summer. Anne was Anne Boleyn. Burton played King Henry VIII. Universal, who financed it, probably hoped for another *Becket*, but were disappointed. Burton plodded through the part, a professional king but no more. An English actor who watched him work at the Shepperton studios was surprised to see him play one close-up scene wearing ordinary clothes on his lower half. The actor had thought highly of him in *Becket*. What had happened since then? 'He seemed to have everything – the woman he appeared to want and was happy with, the entourage, make-up men and secretaries and managers, like a circus going on. If that's what he wanted, he'd got it. He had the Rolls-Royces outside, the plane, the houses in Mexico and Switzerland, so why did he have to be on the vodka at lunch-time – not drunk but not giving a damn if he filmed or not that afternoon? You couldn't get him out of the pub.' And one afternoon, 'He said, "What's the shot? Oh, it's a close up. Well, I'll keep my grey flannels on, I'll only put the costume on halfway." Which is what he did, in his own shoes and his own trousers. But he was Henry VIII!'

Stories circulated that Burton was thinking of taking a rest, even of retirement. At the charity première of *Staircase* in October, Taylor said that she and her husband meant to have a year's holiday. A plan had already been floated for Burton to go back to Oxford for a term in the spring of 1970 and teach Shakespeare. He would take the place of a friend, Francis Warner, poet, Fellow and tutor in English literature at St Peter's College, who was off on a sabbatical; Warner had met the Burtons when they came to do *Faustus*. The teaching project was feasible but it faded away with nothing done, although Burton did take some seminars for Warner. For much of 1970 the Burtons remained in America. There were stories of quarrels, in particular of a scene at a Los Angeles restaurant in January; newspaper columnists said that afterwards he showered her with jewels. The Burton machine was too powerful to be blown off course by rumours. Interviewed on his way from the Beverly Hills Hotel to record a television interview with David Frost early in the year, Burton was as ebullient as ever. He mentioned an article in the *Hollywood Reporter* 'where some producer said that the Burtons and the Waynes and the Pecks, the rest, were finished. All we want is young people, young people. They're the only ones who make money. But I notice in the box office things this year, Elizabeth was still in the top ten and I was still number five.' It was assumed that Burton was in Hollywood and giving interviews because he had hopes of an Academy Award for *Anne of the Thousand Days*, and it was helpful to be seen and heard. He had been nominated for the sixth time,* again unsuccessfully as it turned out. The Frost interview, with both Burtons, touched on Wales (Dic Bach's mangy greyhound), the stage (drunk and caught short inside Prince Hal's suit of armour), and a diamond displayed by Taylor that had cost more than £400,000. Burton looked overweight.

After Hollywood they were in Mexico, in their house by the Pacific at Puerto Vallarta. Burton was seen to sip soda water and heard to say he had given up drink for three months. In July they were in the Mexican desert while Burton made a war film for Universal. He had lost weight

---

* Burton's previous nominations were for *My Cousin Rachel*, *The Robe*, *Becket*, *The Spy Who Came in from the Cold* and *Who's Afraid of Virginia Woolf?* Taylor, who already had one Oscar for *Butterfield 8*, received a second for *Virginia Woolf*.

and admitted or claimed that 'for the first time in twenty-five years I'm seeing the world without an alcoholic haze', adding that it was temporary and only for a bet. In another version he stopped drinking after he saw his puffy face on the Frost programme and thought 'Who is that Chinese gentleman?'

The film in the desert was *Raid on Rommel*, an odd affair. Harry Tatelman, a producer at Universal, had discovered that in the company's vaults were thousands of feet of unused film left over from an earlier war movie, *Tobruk*. A script was developed to use this free footage of dive bombers and blazing landscapes, and it took only twenty days to shoot the new material in Mexico. 'Insurance premiums must be getting bigger all the time on those diamonds,' wrote one critic when he saw the product a year later. 'It's take the money and run time, folks.' Tatelman says that while filming, Burton was 'incredibly professional', and sober all the time. But the studio had been worried. 'I was scared to death, to tell you the truth. You hear these terrible things about people and drinking.' Burton's guaranteed payment was small. Instead he was to receive a larger share of the ultimate profit, if any. They were not the best of times for film stars. As cinema audiences declined, the industry sought economies. Bankers, oil companies and the assorted investors who were putting money into 'package deals' looked carefully at each one. The 'star system' and its big, automatic payments in advance came under suspicion. Younger men were running the studios, and the younger audiences that Burton talked about dismissively to the *Hollywood Reporter* were real enough. As he made one mediocre film after another, Burton was seen to be vulnerable to changing tastes. Years of being a 'personality' with a ready tongue had done more harm than good; overexposure had set in. *Time* included the Burtons among 'the world's prize bores' in July.

As a rich man he had an obvious remedy, to cease work until he found suitable films or plays. He was ready enough to boast that he had 'virtually an absolute choice of any part in the world' (1971). The remark sounded hollow by then. But it might have had some truth in it once and it might have again. He could afford to buy time. Presumably the talk of long holidays and retirement arose from such thoughts. Oxford must have beckoned for the same reason, a way of escape. To Frost on television he was still looking forward to being a don and seeing Elizabeth in a low-cut dress 'give high tea to suitably selected undergraduates'. As usual what he said was pitched in the key appropriate to the audience;

under the varnish of pleasantries he may have been serious. There was his writing, another retreat. At Puerto Vallarta, before *Rommel*, he let it be known that 20,000 words of a novel he was writing 'disappeared when we were in Hollywood for the awards', and he was starting it again. He may have been serious about that, too. But at his back he could hear something that kept him at his potboiling. He was 'one of those weak fellows. I need to keep busy. I go out of my skull if I lie about too long' (1967). He may even have convinced himself that as the husband of Elizabeth Taylor he couldn't afford to stop. In a later conversation, in 1977, he said, 'I've been in trouble all my life, I've done the most unutterable rubbish, all because of money. I didn't *need* it – I've never needed money, not even as a child, though I came from a very poor family. But there have been times when the lure of the zeros was simply too great.' In spite of the potboilers or lapses of judgment or whatever they were, Burton kept clear of the easy money to be made from television advertising.* Leading British actors are or were more inhibited about appearing in advertisements than their American counterparts. The Robert Mitchums and Bob Hopes appear as a matter of course in American commercials. As John Wayne lay dying in 1979, viewers in Los Angeles could see him riding a horse along the seashore, declaring (for a fee of $700,000) that somebody's bank was the one for him. The most esteemed British actor to appear in a television commercial is Sir Laurence Olivier, on behalf of Polaroid, but it was not shown in Britain. Burton said that he was offered and refused half a million dollars from 'a photographic company', presumably the same one, for 'a TV commercial showing me taking pictures of Elizabeth' (1972). In some if not all of his film contracts he refused to let his name be used in 'tie-ups' between the film and associated products.

Burton continued to make pictures that were each a dead end. In September 1970 he and Taylor were in London for him to make a British gangster film, *Villain*, for Anglo-EMI. He played a thug with homosexual tendencies, receiving no fee in advance but only a percentage of profits. 'He did it for his cab fare,' says a producer. In fact he did it for expenses in cash and kind worth around $80,000. *Villain* was good in places in a modest, B-picture manner, but Burton added nothing to it except his name in first place, the same size as the title. It might have been any

---

* Until 1981. Then he accepted a contract reported to be worth nearly a million dollars over three years to use his voice, but not his face, in a series of commercials for an American magazine, *Geo*.

competent actor with raddled features who could snarl in guttural Cockney. The *New York Times* kept watch on him while filming. He was in a hotel thirty miles out of London, suffering from a cold. He had woken at two in the morning, he said, and heard voices saying 'Richard, Richard'. The writer, Bernard Weinraub, noted 'an unmistakable aura of stardom', but Burton sounded tired. 'It seems fairly ridiculous', he said, 'for someone of forty-five or fifty to be learning words written by other people, most of which are bad, to make a few dollars.' There were still challenges. His ego, he said, would force him to play Lear and Macbeth. Nobody asked when. 'Fame is pernicious,' said Burton. 'So is money.' The reporter saw his hand shake when he lit a cigarette, and wrote, 'Despite the bravura voice and style, he appears, at this point, oddly vulnerable, even frail. Somehow, the shadows of the past have deepened. The drinker, the lover, the celebrity, have flickered into a surprisingly weary figure.'

While making *Villain* Burton went to Buckingham Palace with his wife and sister Cecilia on his forty-fifth birthday to receive a decoration from the Queen, a CBE, announced earlier in the year. Honours for actors are not uncommon. From time to time there had been talk in the Burton camp of a knighthood; Commander of the British Empire is the next best thing. Burton said later that he had been offered a knighthood on condition he returned to the UK to live, but that it would have cost him a million or two pounds in back taxes. The Prime Minister's office, which recommends honours, observes coldly that 'the British honours system doesn't work like that'. But it is true that residence abroad for tax reasons is not the best recommendation. The length of time he spent in Britain was governed by a quota of days in each tax year, agreed between his advisers and the Inland Revenue.

In early 1971 he had sufficient days in hand to be able to spend a few of them in West Wales and London making a film of Dylan Thomas's *Under Milk Wood*. Taylor also had a part and so did Peter O'Toole. The budget was small. The film they made was no better or worse than might have been expected of a well-meaning attempt to find ways of illustrating Thomas's 'play for voices'. There was much scenery and demented frolicking. The story put about that Thomas had written the play for himself and Burton was not true. Interviewed on the set by John Morgan, Burton was in good form, telling jokes about the Welsh and confiding that he felt in his bones *Milk Wood* was going to work. 'But of course', he added, 'I've been in films that I enjoyed enormously, and they've turned out to be ghastly failures.' An American critic, seeing the film, wrote that at one point, 'Burton seemed to me slightly drunk. Not the character, Burton.'

Having stopped drinking the year before, he had now started again. This phase lasted until May, by which time he and Taylor had gone back to Mexico and made a film there called *Hammersmith Is Out* with Peter Ustinov, who both directed it and had a part. How Ustinov let himself be involved in such a muddled attempt at satire or black comedy or whatever it was supposed to be is a mystery. Burton played a criminal lunatic called Hammersmith with tired competence; he escapes from detention and roams America doing evil and prospering. Taylor played a waitress who joins him. The film was made cheaply, financed by J. Cornelius Crean, a manufacturer of mobile homes. There seemed no end to these eccentric pictures that Burton should never have needed to touch. As they were released and their effect sank in, friends and enemies began to reappraise him. *Villain*, which had to have voices dubbed in for America because the Cockney accents were hard to follow, dismayed critics there in summer 1971. 'Whatever Became of Richard Burton?' asked a headline in the *New York Times*; the article suggested that the mediocre might be his true level in films.

Burton was now off to Europe to play President Tito as a wartime guerilla, in a film sponsored by the Yugoslav government. He was not drinking; he told a friend that he stopped just after finishing *Hammersmith*, because he 'received a cable saying my daughter Kate from New York was coming to stay with us, and all the kids hate it if I drink'. The Yugoslavs' film was *The Battle of Sutjeska*. The state film makers were said to have been struck by a resemblance between Burton in *Where Eagles Dare* and their President when younger. John Heyman received a telephone call from Burton, asking him if he would negotiate the contract. Had he read the script? asked Heyman. 'No', said Burton, 'but he's a great man.' When Heyman read it, 'it was 250 pages and might as well have been written in Chinese. It was incomprehensible. I rang Richard and said, "Really, you can't do this." He said, "I'm on my way. We're starting in three weeks." ' The Burtons met Tito and stayed with him. Wolf Mankowitz was brought in to write proper dialogue, and photography proceeded until the Yugoslavs ran short of money, when work was suspended.

The next stop was Rome to work with Joseph Losey as director again, in *The Assassination of Trotsky*, financed by a consortium. Burton had a pointed beard and played the Russian in exile, fearing for his life in Mexico, where Losey had already filmed exteriors. This was another part that Burton accepted script unseen. But a film with Losey was in a different category. Serious director, serious subject and serious script-writer (Nicholas Mosley, son of Sir Oswald) promised well. Discussing Burton a year later, Losey said that he was a 'most satisfying actor to direct, although a lot of people don't believe me', an 'extraordinary man of vast talent' with 'a small but distinguished writing ability'. The relationship with Elizabeth was 'very important to him, but he's a perplexed man who is troubled by all sorts of contradictions. He mistrusts everyone, including himself. He has come to trust me as much as he can trust anybody. He doesn't take films or directors seriously and tends not to understand much of what goes into the making of a film.' Burton apparently wrote to Losey about the 'delicacy and frailty' of the performance that the director had persuaded him to give. Perhaps his tongue was in his cheek. No doubt because of its subject, *Trotsky* received a few respectful, even enthusiastic reviews; otherwise it was howled down as 'atrocious' and 'ridiculous'. Burton is often embarrassing and at best unconvincing, merely Burton in a beard chewing on dull speeches. *The Fifty Worst Films of All Time* (1978), though an arbitrary selection with so many to choose from, gives it a place ('A pretentious stinker ... Burton is not to blame for the talky, awkward script but he is to blame for all the instances of misplaced emphasis and shameless overacting').

The Burtons as celebrities remained in business, though film star celebrity in the old sense was on its way out. They were becoming old-fashioned, like a dance band playing on among the pop groups. But there was still some energy left. Taylor's fortieth birthday in February 1972 was to be an event. Burton was filming another potboiler, *Bluebeard*, a co-production with money drawn from three countries, in Hungary, a fourth. The prospect of a birthday party in Budapest, capitalism rampant amid Communism, warmed the hearts of editors. Invitations had gone to European royalty, actors, old friends and even Stephen Spender, the poet. The Jenkinses received telegrams telling them that all expenses would be paid and necessaries provided, down to 'bloaters and caviar'. When they arrived in Budapest, brothers and brothers-in-law found that if they tired of champagne and conversation, they could sit in their private suite and watch films of international rugby matches that Wales had won. It was still customary to write of the Burtons that they were 'never apart'. His present to his wife was a large, lemon-coloured diamond, once the property of an Indian prince, price undisclosed. Burton forestalled remarks about the world's poor by declaring that he would give an amount equal to the diamond's value to a British charity. Similarly the United Nations Children's Fund would receive as much as the party cost. Bigness continued to be the order of the day. Burton let it be known that he would not be playing Nelson in a film but that he would be playing Mussolini. Reporters gathering for the junket saw 'the pale blue eyes narrow into a smile'. They flocked around Taylor and wrote of 'the huge and wide and violet eyes'. Mountains of paperbacks lay around. The pile of film scripts waiting to be read was 'a yard high'. Taylor said the industry had become 'bloody disorganized', and 'I wouldn't dream of asking for a million dollars in front now.' It was not moral, she said, putting a brave face on hard times.

As for the party, a weekend of celebrations, Princess Grace of Monaco came, as did Ringo Starr, Marlon Brando, Nevill Coghill the professor, Frankie Howerd the comedian, Spender the poet and many more. Alan Williams the novelist, son of Emlyn, was involved in an altercation with Elizabeth Taylor, who did not seem as interested as he thought she should be in the Hungarian Revolution of 1956. There were tears and a flurry of henchmen. Williams told a London journalist, Nicholas Tomalin, about it, adding his description of Taylor, 'a beautiful dough-nut covered in diamonds and paint'. Tomalin's sardonic reports from Budapest pointed to changing sympathies. But among those who were fond of Burton, and they were many, there was amazement that he should ever be seen as anything but the good host, the plain man, the generous friend. Victor Spinetti, an actor and friend who comes from another village in South Wales, was in Budapest and says it was 'a riot of fun and nonsense. I was up on the top floor where all the family and the Welsh were. The singing and the carry-on came after Princess Grace and the others had gone to their suites. "*Now* we're going to have the party," he said.' Spinetti, who writes poems, recited one to Burton about a Welsh funeral ('This is the day for gravestones ... the wind blowing flowers over the wet gravel paths'). Burton was taken with it, and recited it at another party where Spinetti was present. When somebody asked who was the author, Burton turned towards Spinetti and said wryly, 'That so-and-so over there.'

A future without mediocre film-making still seemed possible. Burton spoke of giving up acting, of dividing his time between summers in England and winters in Mexico. There was serious talk of Oxford.

14 *Right* Rome, April 1962. Burton greets his daughter Kate as she arrives from London. The *Cleopatra* saga was already well under way.

15 *Below left* Bath-time (i), attended by slave girls in *Cleopatra*.

16 *Below right* Bath-time (ii), fussed over by Rex Harrison in the curious *Staircase* (1969).

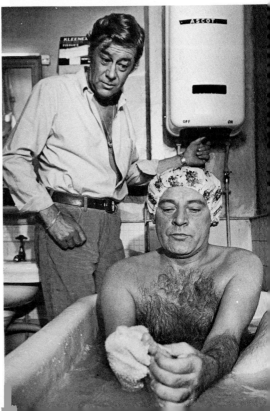

17 *Above* They were husband and wife in *The VIPs* (1963), but just good friends off the set when they visited a pub near the Elstree studios for lunchtime champagne.

18 *Left* Archbishop with cigarette and wife-to-be. Burton was making *Becket* at Shepperton film studios, outside London, in August 1963.

19 *Right* Burton as clergyman, a role he has played more than once, with Elizabeth Taylor in Mexico City, making John Huston's distinguished *Night of the Iguana*, 1963.

20 *Below* Trouble and strife for George and Martha in Mike Nichols' *Who's Afraid of Virginia Woolf?*, the one solid triumph of the Burton–Taylor film partnership.

21 *Left* Backstage at Oxford during the 1966 *Dr Faustus*. Seated is Professor Nevill Coghill, Burton's admirer since 1944.

22 *Below* It never rains but it pours: Burton on location near London Airport making *Villain* in 1970, a gangster movie best forgotten.

23 *Right* Alain Delon, with ice-pick, puts paid to Burton in 1972's *The Assassination of Trotsky*. 'All the clichés of melodrama' wrote the American critic Judith Crist.

24 *Below* The film the Burtons made for television in 1972, the limping *Divorce His ... Divorce Hers*, anatomized a broken marriage. Their own divorces were still to come.

25 *Above* A sombre Burton at the home of his brother David in Sketty, Swansea, after he had remarried Elizabeth Taylor. Sitting next to them is his sister Hilda. David Jenkins stands on the right, brother Verdun left, with other relatives.

26 *Left* Brief interlude: with Princess Elizabeth of Yugoslavia, 1974. Dark glasses were his trademark for a time.

27 *Opposite* A fresh start: Burton with his third wife, Susan Hunt.

28 Burton at fifty-four, New York 1979.

Francis Warner, a guest at the Budapest party, says he took with him the offer of an honorary fellowship of St Peter's. Burton accepted. Warner also discussed with him the college's plan to build a Samuel Beckett Theatre, and newspaper reports (March 1972) suggested that Burton had already given £100,000 towards that project. In fact, no gift was made, though Warner is confident that it will come one day.

Another Burton interest, or rumour, in 1972 concerned the National Theatre in London. Some people believed he had been asked to take over as director when Olivier retired from the post, as he planned to do. Rumours about a successor centred on Peter Hall. But Burton confided in friends that the job had been offered to him. He told Richard Leech a few years later that he had to refuse 'because it would have cost me two million pounds in back tax'. He told another friend in London how sorry he felt for Olivier, who had been 'savagely' shaken when he declined the offer to take over, first in tandem with Olivier and then alone. Philip Burton says that 'Olivier wanted him, but at the same time was honest with him and told him what the difficulties were. I wanted him to take it.' The offer may have been purely informal. Paddy Donnell, who was administrative director of the National Theatre from 1970 to 1975, says that it is news to him: 'There were other names [than Peter Hall's] considered, but certainly not Burton's as far as I am aware.' In practice the London stage was as far away as ever. By the summer Burton was back with the Yugoslavs, completing the film about Tito. This time he was not always sober. Ifor Jenkins had died the month after Budapest. A treadmill of film making stretched ahead. 'I get increasingly disenchanted with acting,' he told the same London friend. 'I'll be forty-seven in November – you might think of sending me a small gold object. As the years totter past I find it ludicrous, learning some idiot's lines in the small hours of the night so I can stay a millionaire.' Perhaps he thought his luck with pictures would improve. Instead it grew worse.

At last he and Taylor were to make a film for Harlech Television, 'their' station in South Wales and the West Country. The project stemmed from John Heyman, who says it was conceived 'because of Richard's obligations to Harlech. He had to do something and she had to do something.' Heyman proposed three films with a common subject, the break-up of a marriage. They would explore it in three ways – his view, her view and 'the truth'. Heyman insists that the theme was unconnected with the Burtons' own marriage, which at the time was 'in no trouble at all'. John Osborne was first approached, and accepted the commission with misgivings. 'The most important aspect of the script', he says, 'seemed to be that most of the locations should be in either Mexico, Acapulco or the south of France, where [the Burtons'] yacht was conveniently moored. I ignored this instruction and followed the presumable premise of the two titles.... When I presented the script of the Richard version a kind of resentful hysteria seemed to break out ... which seemed to imply that I had not followed my brief.' The producers, displeased with Osborne's efforts, turned to John Hopkins, a distinguished television playwright. The three scripts had become two, *Divorce His* and *Divorce Hers*. Most of the money came from Heyman himself (more than half a million dollars) and American television networks (more than a million dollars). Harlech's contribution was perhaps one-twentieth of the total, which meant that the company had little say in what was going on. The director finally appointed was British, Waris Hussein, who already had a good reputation and was to improve on it in the coming years.

These films were to be the worst experience of Hussein's life. He was not at ease with the Burtons' way of doing things. Production problems arose. The films should have been made in Britain, but when planning was well advanced, they had to be moved out of the country for tax reasons: Taylor was already making a film in Britain, *Night Watch*, which over-ran, leaving her with insufficient time. Altogether it was to be another of those occasions when everyone blamed everyone else. The kindest thing to say about the films is that they were a mistake. Once again the Amazing Burtons did their tricks for a restless audience that had seen them all before. Again there was the obsession with affluence. The anatomizing of a broken marriage went on in the unreal context of another glossy 'spectacular', set in Rome, where the separated husband and wife chance to meet and examine their past. The Burtons had never seemed less real. Perhaps they collected more than their fair share of the blame. But the films were constructed around them. Had they been a success, it would have been the Burtons who collected the glory.

Making the films was a strange business for those who saw it at first hand. Like a little *Cleopatra*, it fascinated observers. One of the minor executives who had read the original scripts says they were 'salty and perceptive – I thought we had a bloody winner'. Then he saw some of the rushes. 'I thought they were God-awful and said so. I got an astonished reaction. I was brushed away.' Another visitor to the set likened the atmosphere to 'a fifteenth-century ducal court when the Duke is in a bad mood. There was a guarded, frightened, slightly hateful, exaggerated respect. I don't know whether they liked Elizabeth, but they were certainly shit-scared of her.' He arrived in time to see 'the rather sudden termination of a day's shooting. Burton decided he'd done enough filming. He walked to the edge of the set where a man was waiting with his coat ready, put it on, and walked away.' An actress in the cast, Carrie Nye, wrote a caustic article, widely published. This spoke of Burton's drinking and the long, alcoholic lunches, some of which she attended, 'punctuated by phone calls from the anguished director to inquire when, if ever, work could be resumed'. Burton, said Nye, liked to finish early, 'usually with a magnificent display of temper, foot-stamping and a few exit lines delivered in the finest St Crispin's Day style. My favourite was "I am old and grey and incredibly gifted."'

Waris Hussein, given the unequal task of coping with the Burtons at this stage in their careers, looks back on them with a degree of sympathy. It was a bad time for all concerned:

I think [says Hussein] that a lot of what happened was due to their own personal unhappiness. I first of all met Burton in London, in a house in Hampstead. We got on very well. He made a great show of not drinking – he had Perrier and fruit juices. Then I was summoned to Elstree to meet Elizabeth.

My first encounter was in this incredible dressing-room. She wasn't there when I arrived. Alexandre of Paris had plastered an entire room with drawings of hair styles – coils and plaits and jewels and flowers. I heard her in the corridor saying, 'I don't want to meet him, I don't know who he is, I'm not ready to meet him, what's he want?' The next thing is she came in with a smile on her face, dressed in the costume she was working in, a sort of peach-coloured nightie. She said 'Hello, I'm Elizabeth', smiling very sweetly, and then said, 'I don't know anything about this, I haven't read the scripts. You'll have to tell me.' The project must have been going by now for at least six months. I had been working on it for about two. She must have known for months that she was going to do it. I was asked to give her a summary of the story. I found myself becoming more and more inarticulate because she was busy changing one dress for another. She only had half her attention on the subject. The story dealt with flashbacks, and she said, 'Oh my God, how far do I have to flash back?' I said, 'One of the scenes takes you back to before you marry the character Richard plays, when you're twenty.' 'Well,' she said, 'Alexandre, I guess I can still look the way I did in *A Place in the Sun*.' And then she said, 'Cancel that call to Rome, get me Edith Head in California, she's so good with shoes.'

I sat there listening to all this. She asked one of the producers how long we would be doing it for. He said we reckoned about five weeks. 'You're damn wrong it's going to be five weeks,' she said. 'We've got to be out of this country the minute I've finished this film, otherwise we're into tax for two million pounds.' So the prospect of working in England just vanished. We were using multiple-camera techniques. After scouring Europe the producers found that the only place with studios that were technically feasible was Munich. The story was set in Rome, and I began with a week there, doing exteriors with Burton. He was marvellous and he kept off the bottle. He said, 'Don't call me Dick or Dickie, I hate it. Just call me Richard. I think we're going to get on very well. This is terribly important to me. It must be as good as we can make it because it's our first commitment to Harlech.'

For a week we shot with him and other actors flown out from London. Everything was on schedule. We were expecting Elizabeth on a certain day, and then without warning she arrived two days early. I was doing a night scene with Richard. He had to walk down the street and turn, a very simple shot. It was an old street and just a small crowd gathered. Suddenly there was uproar in the distance, hooting horns, a glare of lights, and she arrived, surrounded by police and *paparazzi*, in a black limousine. She got out wearing a black floor-length mink and said, 'Don't worry about me, Waris, I'll just stand in the corner and watch.' It was pandemonium by now. We couldn't find Richard, and when we did find him, he couldn't walk down the street in a straight line. He had hit the bottle. We had to do the shot about ten times.

The one and only day we did shoot Elizabeth in Rome, she was two hours late, which was routine. I told her where the shot came, and she said, 'It's all right, baby, I've read the script.' She then starts off and walks straight to camera. There was nothing on her face, no expression. So I said, 'Elizabeth, you're remembering things on this walk, and we're going to use it for flashbacks, so it's terribly important. Could you perhaps pause and blow your nose?' She said, '*Blow my nose?* I've never blown my nose on the screen, and I'm not likely to start now. I'll simply flick my scarf or something.' So she flicked her scarf on Take 2. Which is all we got. She flicked her scarf, walked up to the camera, kissed the lens, got into her car and left.

Richard would be sober in the morning but shaking by the afternoon. We broke for lunch at one and weren't back on the set till three. I attended one of the lunches, one only. This was at the height of the terrorism and kidnappings, and security in Munich was such that I couldn't get to their dressing-room at first. Elizabeth I found twirling around in front of a mirror in the most amazing dress which she had found in Munich. Richard came in and said, 'There you are, Waris,' with that extraordinary sending-himself-up air that he has, 'there you are, this is what comes of being married to the world's most beautiful woman.' Then we went in to lunch, which was served by people in white gloves. Elizabeth sat in a dressing gown with a towel around her head, looking absolutely ravishing, much better than when she came on the set later. I, for the first and only time, sat next to Richard. By this time the wine was flowing, and I brought up the Old Vic – more to take Richard's mind off things – because I'd seen him as Hamlet, and he'd been wonderful, absolutely wonderful.

I remembered it vividly. The sort of power that Gielgud or Olivier has is developed. Burton was born with it. It was amazing to be able to stand on that stage and command attention. It was something he knew he had, and he worked at it. Once he went into films, and Hollywood called and all that started, I think he already knew he was making a bad choice. In all fairness to Elizabeth, I think it had started before she turned up. He was on the road which said take the money and run.

Anyway, I said to Richard, 'I saw your Hamlet and I think you were wonderful.' And do you know, he stopped pouring the wine and said, 'Do you really think that, Waris?' And I said 'Yes,' and he said, 'It's very kind of you to tell me.' And I said, 'Do you remember that time?' and he said, 'Oh, vividly.' And then he started telling funny stories about doing a fight scene with Michael Redgrave in armour, about how he'd been pissed the night before, and started to leak in his armour. Suddenly he stopped and looked across the table and caught Elizabeth's eye. She said, 'Come on, Richard, just finish the story.' And he said, 'That's all right, darling, we won't go on.' He said to me, 'Elizabeth's bored by it, she's heard it so many times.' She said, 'Oh no, Richard, I'm always fascinated to know what a wonderful stage actor you were.' And he said, 'No, no. Of course, you know she's the greatest film actress in the world.' It became two people living their lives out in a total world of their own.

Then they talked about their child, Maria, whom Elizabeth had adopted originally. She went to an orphanage outside Munich and picked her out of all the children who were offered. They had almost written the child off. They allowed her to have it for three days, and she said she sat up day and night just holding it, willing it to get better. And it did. They spent a fortune on her in doctors' fees. They even had the orphanage authorities in America checking her out.

In an odd way the scripts echoed their lives, the chaos of their lives. And the interesting thing about it is that they were best in scenes where they were quiet with each other, regretting the past or having conversations about what might have been. Was Hopkins unconsciously reflecting their life-styles? I know that if I could re-do those scripts with two different actors, I could make it a totally different story.

It was two plays of seventy-five minutes each, shot in parallel. It took eight weeks altogether. From early on it was clear it was going to be a disaster. I suppose I should have left then. I couldn't have closed down the production, but I could have walked away from it. When it was over there was a party in Munich for the Burtons. It was Richard's birthday. The set was dressed up and there was a huge picture of them, with 'Happy birthday, Richard, I love you,' coming from her mouth. You know he had this fantasy of wanting to be a don at Oxford, assuring himself that he has an intellectual side? She bought him for his birthday an original copy of Goethe – she said, 'I don't know who he is, but I hope he likes it.' It was a wan effort to get to him and to his mind.

The whole thing was quite an experience. In an extraordinary way I'm grateful because it taught me a lot about myself and my profession. I've never worked with anyone since who's been able to give me a hard time. I say, 'Listen, don't bother, Elizabeth Taylor cut them off years ago.' I had hoped they would get to know me, that they would find out who they were working with. And now I suppose I'm using this to say, 'I'm sorry I didn't get to know you better. I'm sorry for what happened.' Because I admire Burton.

Victor Spinetti happened to be in Munich at the time, working on another film. He telephoned Burton who said, 'Come over for lunch.'

Spinetti, too, had to negotiate the guards. 'They were constantly being threatened with kidnapping. They used to get threatening letters. They were terrified and I don't blame them.' But what Spinetti saw, of course, was a different face altogether. 'I finally get on the set. Richard and Elizabeth are sitting there. The director comes down and says, "I'm going to do a reverse shot of this scene," and Richard says, "Let's go to lunch." ' Spinetti thought the Burtons seemed perfectly happy together. He fell in with their style: the drinking, the stories, the general bacchanalia. 'I went to lunch and we collapsed laughing. "Listen now," he said, "sh-h, sh-h, tell us about that chap in your valley who's seen every film that ever was." This is a chap who always works day shifts down the pit so he can go to the cinema in the evenings. So I say to Richard, "He thinks *Yankee Doodle Dandy* was a fair picture, but the best ever was *Bomba on Panther Island*. It doesn't matter, whatever you do, Billy is going to think *Bomba on Panther Island* is the greatest picture ever, right?" ' Spinetti doesn't remember a cross word over lunch. It was 'just one hysterical nonsense'. The Burtons were his friends. There is no more to be said.

At the beginning of 1973 Burton was back in Italy playing a German Gestapo officer in an Italian production, Carlo Ponti's *Massacre in Rome*. This was based on a true episode, the killing of hostages as a wartime reprisal. Eventually some critics praised Burton highly. But the film was held back – it was not seen in London until July 1975 – and failed to make an impression. After *Massacre in Rome* he was idle for months. There was the usual talk of roles to come – Mussolini, Don Quixote, a paralysed actor cured by a miracle. In May he was at Cortina, not far from Venice, where his wife was making a film, when the young Welsh actor, Keith Baxter, who was in Taylor's film, met him. Baxter walked into the hotel one evening. Burton was sitting alone, reading. He looked up and said, 'Hello, sweetheart. You just did Macbeth.' Baxter had played it at the new Birmingham Repertory Theatre, and Burton had read the notices.

Then and afterwards they talked about the stage. Baxter asked him why he didn't think of playing Macbeth. The usual reason ('It would cost me a million pounds') was produced, but Baxter concluded that he didn't much care for the part in any case. The play that did haunt him was *Lear*. Burton would suddenly veer away from the theatre, saying, 'My friends are not actors, they are scientists, they are writers. My real gift is writing.' He was not at ease. He was not being offered work of the quality he wanted, and he was unhappy with the film that Taylor was making, *Ash Wednesday*. It was about the rich again; later Burton told a friend he had no time for the 'jet set' it portrayed. 'I said to Elizabeth, "I don't like the thought of you doing that kind of thing because it represents the worst kind of people." I was terribly pompous. Anyway, she went ahead with it, and I sat around, loathing every second, with nothing to do except read. We were in Cortina, we were in Venice, and I took to the bottle. I wouldn't have minded if she was doing Lady Macbeth or something. But my soul was affronted. I really don't like the jet set, you know. They offend me. They do funny things, smoke the wrong things, drugs and stuff like that, and I really can't bear them.' By the time he was saying this, the Burtons had twice separated and twice been shakily reunited. His troubles were coming to a head.

CHAPTER THIRTEEN

Film Star at Bay

WHY the marriage of Taylor and Burton ended was much gone into at the time. The severance took three years and was reported on like a war, perhaps a civil war, with battles, truces, peace treaties and fresh outbreaks of fighting. Columnists and interviewers were sympathetic enough, but there were moments when the friendliness seemed to shift a fraction and uncover something else, a delight in seeing them ruined. Then the sentences would shift back again and there would be nothing but solicitude.

Burton's drinking was the favourite explanation of what had gone wrong. Even if true this merely raised other questions. Burton dismissed it, saying 'the problem wasn't drink, it was career' (1975). That statement in turn was cryptic. The picture that emerges is of Burton at the end of his tether, needing to rearrange his life. The books he might write, the theatres he might appear in, were entwined with his hopes, or so it seems from things he said. In theory he could have done whatever he chose while remaining married to Taylor. But if in his late forties he felt he had reached a crisis in his affairs, he may have sought a deeper change of tone and rhythm to free himself from years of compromise. Two or three remarks sound relevant. Burton told a magazine in 1975, 'One day it would be all right, the next day bad - a big explosion. It's been a battle royal. Thirteen years is a long time.' A friend of them both, an American film producer, says, 'I think that he felt he would die without Elizabeth at certain points. And then he realised that it was perhaps better to die than to submit to the relationship again. It was too humiliating for him, it was killing him.' On television in 1974 Burton said, 'I think that my life was changed by a woman who was called Elizabeth Taylor. I am not entirely sure what actually she did to me.' He ended his marriage, then, so that he could be himself again; if so, it is a common enough reason.

The business of separation began early in July 1973. Laurence Harvey, another friend of both, said the immediate cause was 'Richard's temper and thunderous moods'. Burton was at the home of his lawyer, Aaron Frosch, on Long Island; Taylor was flitting between New York and California. She put out a gentle statement about a temporary separation, adding that 'maybe we have loved each other too much'. Burton spoke more tersely about 'mutual love and devotion' and said he did not consider them separated. There was speculation that the way in which critics had scorned the wretched *Divorce His, Divorce Hers*, shown in Britain a few days before (but in America in February), may have added to the problems. A reporter from London, Nigel Dempster of the *Daily Mail*, outsmarted the journalists in Frosch's drive and found Burton in a cottage at the rear. It was 10 o'clock in the morning. Burton was shaving himself with an electric razor and drinking vodka and orange juice. He said he had not spoken to his wife since her 'extraordinary statement', and had no idea what she was talking about. Dempster was given a snatch of the gravedigger's scene from *Hamlet* ('Alas! poor Yorick') and told that Elizabeth was 'a splendid child'. Burton did not sound very anxious. 'She's planning to go back to California to see her mother again,' he said, 'and then to stay with her brother in Hawaii. Am I going to Hawaii? Not on your nelly. It's a terrible place.'

Shortly afterwards he was in Moscow, where *Sutjeska*, the picture about Tito, was being shown at a film festival. Burton or the publicists presented him as a man of the people. 'As the seventh son of a Welsh coal miner,' he was reported to have said, 'I knew hardship first hand.' He came from 'the lower depths of the working class'. At sixteen he worked in the mines for three pounds a week, and had never forgotten the 'emaciated miner' who told him that the new dawn was coloured red. It was true, added Burton, that he now earned one and a quarter million dollars per picture, and 'it sounds strange to say that at heart I am a Communist'. But there was no contradiction because he did not exploit others. *Variety* carried the laconic headline, 'Multi-Millionaire Richard Burton A Red At Heart'.

Moscow was a stopping place on the way to Rome, where he was to make a film with Sophia Loren, *The Voyage*, produced by her husband, Carlo Ponti; he stayed at the Pontis' villa. By 20 July Taylor had arrived in Rome – she too was making a film there – and they were together again, but not for long. For much of the summer he was in retreat at the villa. His children came to see him; now and then he went into Rome and met his wife, who had acquired a new escort, a Los Angeles car dealer and businessman, Henry Wynberg. Every morning he wrote early and then swam in the pool. 'Tell me you suffered,' begged a privileged woman journalist later. 'Well ...' he said amiably, letting a doubt remain. 'Arrogant bastard,' she said. 'I've not come all this way to be told you had a lovely time in the swimming pool.' 'Well,' he said, 'you can swim in a pool and still suffer.' The Pontis had a private viewing room in their villa. Among the films he saw with them there was *Last Tango in Paris*, which so 'absolutely revolted' and embarrassed him, he said later, that 'I didn't know where to look. . . . I said, "I'm sorry, I can't stand it, I have to go." It did not turn me on, it turned me off. For a month I was asexual.'

Among his visitors that summer was Jack Le Vien, the producer with the television rights to Churchill's memoirs, who had used him in *The Valiant Years* at the time of *Camelot*. Since then he had found Burton a difficult man to get hold of. He wanted him to be Churchill's voice in a 1964 film, *The Finest Hours*: 'We sent dozens of letters and phone calls to him, to his agents, to his aides. There was no reply.' A few years later Le Vien was planning a film about Orde Wingate, the British general who operated in wartime Burma. 'One of Burton's people rang and said he wanted to play him. I said "Fine." I sent cables and letters but that was the last I heard.' Le Vien was now making a short film about Churchill to help raise funds for Churchill College. Lord Mountbatten was to narrate it. Burton was asked to be Churchill's voice again. Suddenly all doors were open. 'He said he'd love to do it. He is so contradictory. He couldn't possibly have been more co-operative and kinder, and he wouldn't take a penny for his work. We spent hours and hours doing it at the expense of the film he was making with Sophia Loren.' While Le Vien had Burton's ear, he asked him if he would play Churchill in a film to be made in 1974 for British and US television. Burton accepted at once. Le Vien was left to ponder how it was that he could be such an enigma at a distance, so straightforward when close to.

The Voyage did not turn out to be much of a film, despite its director,

Vittorio De Sica. It was his last picture, a mannered account of a love affair at the start of the century. A New York audience hooted the dialogue when it had a rare showing there in 1978. 'Never have I seen such beauty,' Burton tells Loren, as if repeating words in a foreign language. 'It's very becoming. Turn around.' Filming moved to Sicily later in the year. Before this he was briefly in New York, where the gossip writers spoke of a new girlfriend or two, and also of a reconciliation with his wife. But she was not in Sicily.

Burton was to be found living on board the *Kalizma*, anchored off Palermo. He drank white wine with visiting journalists, asked eagerly about what was happening in Britain, and said that he planned to return to Shakespeare on Broadway the following year. Sydney Edwards, a London journalist who was on good terms with him, asked if it was true that he might succeed Olivier at the National Theatre. Burton said abruptly that he didn't want to discuss the matter. To Edwards he seemed ill at ease, cut off, enclosed in the little bubble of the entourage. Taylor was in Los Angeles, ill again, and he was afraid she might have cancer. One evening Edwards was in a Palermo hotel with Burton and his aides. Burton was expecting a call from the hospital. When it was put through to the bar where they were drinking, he had to be led upstairs lest Edwards overhear. By the time someone had found a secluded telephone, the switchboard or the Italian telephone system had lost the call. They failed to get Los Angeles back. 'He stormed out into the night by himself and went back in the motor-boat they kept in the harbour. I was left buying drinks for the rest of them.'

In a day or two, word came through that, after surgical investigation, Taylor was all right. She asked Burton to visit her and he did, flying via London and over the Pole for a few hours in California. Their greetings went on record, 'Hello, Lumpy.' 'Hello, Pockmarks.' The car dealer faded into the background. They were to be reconciled. And what had Burton learned from the experience? asked Romany Bain. 'Never again to take anything for granted,' he replied solemnly. 'I assumed too much about my relationship both with Elizabeth and other people. I assumed they all loved me.' It was time for a confession or two. He spoke about infidelity: 'I am not excusing myself. I am very puritanical about sex outside marriage. I believe in fidelity. I don't believe it doesn't matter if you are unfaithful. It's torture because you betray both yourself and her. Elizabeth was never unfaithful to me, but I cannot say the same.'

For a while they travelled about the world, keeping out of the news. They were in Italy, they were in Switzerland, they were in New York, they were in Puerto Vallarta. They were even in Hawaii, where Taylor had a brother and a grandchild. Or perhaps Hawaii was only where they meant to go. They were certainly in Oroville, northern California, in spring 1974 for Burton to make *The Klansman*, a Paramount film about the Ku-Klux-Klan, co-starring Lee Marvin. The film was based on a novel by William Bradford Huie about racial and sexual violence in Alabama before a civil rights march. Rape, castration and murder were promised, but visitors to the set were more interested in Burton. Word had got around that he was drinking recklessly. A public relations person on the set was telling journalists, 'If you want to come up here, OK. If you want to interview a drunk and watch a drunk fall in the camellia bushes, come ahead.' His wife had departed, supposedly outraged because Burton had given a ring to a waitress aged eighteen who worked at Sambo's coffee shop.

A press party arrived the day after Taylor left, scenting disaster. Asked where she might be, Burton gave a series of answers, any of which could have been true. She 'fell off her sandals and sprained her ankle', she 'had to attend to some matter involving the Academy Awards', she was 'in Los Angeles being examined because she had an operation five months ago and had her exquisite stomach ripped open, and they want to see if it's all better again', she had 'gone to Hawaii to visit her brother'. In his hand was a glass of vodka and ice. Reporters began to bait him and he baited them. What about the girl of eighteen? 'Nonsense,' he said. He had noticed her across the street and suggested her for a part in the film. What about the ring, price $450? 'Ah, well, that was a drunken night. I was looking for a present for Elizabeth, and the little girl was very sweet, so I bought her a ring.' He quoted grandiloquently, 'Can I do all this, and cannot get a crown?' Somebody shouted, 'Tell us something about Wales.' Burton sipped his vodka and said, 'Well, in Wales we subsisted mostly on trout, which we poached from a stream. We would take an enormous grand piano down and place it on the bank, and then someone would play the Moonlight Sonata which, of course, makes trout rise to the surface. Then we would bash the buggers on the head with a banana. One Welshman became so stout on trout and bananas that when he died they couldn't get him out of his cottage to bury him.'

Other journalists on other days had him to themselves for an hour or two. Just before Taylor left, Merv Griffin had interviewed him for his television show (the programme was transmitted later). Burton said, 'Elizabeth criticizes me. She's very dogmatic about what to wear, what stories to tell.' Griffin asked, 'How long will you take it, Richard?' Burton replied, 'Oh, I suppose forever.' Asked who his heroes were, Burton said, 'If I had any, which I doubt, they'd be Socrates, Plato, Aristotle, cleanliness. There's no point in talking about Shakespeare and Dr Johnson because they smelled. Did you know that Dr Johnson had only one bath in his life?' He sounded like a man who had had his fill of talk shows. The astronauts who had reached the moon were 'idiots . . . no man who got on the moon ever said anything of interest. "One giant step" is rubbish.' It was the film star at bay. Griffin asked a stock question, did he have any personal prejudices? 'Yes,' said Burton, 'I hate talk shows. When you think, sweetheart, that I've played Hamlet, Henry v, Iago etcetera, and you're more famous than I am. Because all those idiots down there watch you.'

Words poured out of him. Was it that he said more or that he was more listened to? He told a writer for *Playgirl*, Judy Stone, that he was 'insulted by the lies about my taking people off the streets. I was supposed to have gone to bed with a fourteen-year-old. Then this story about Lola [a young actress in the picture]. I said, "What the hell, Lola! If they say it about us, we might as well do it." I don't *want* to. Her husband called and asked, "What's all this?" She told him, "If you don't believe me, baby, you get a lawyer." A very curious child, Lola. Remarkable intelligence. She talks like an angel. She has been here working all the time. I never touched the baby. She has nothing to do with me at all.' His listeners fed cassettes into their tape recorders and settled down to that safest of reporting, where the subject says it all himself. No doubt much of it was an act by Burton, but the act itself was part of the reality. 'As Lee Marvin says,' he told Judy Stone, 'who gives a shit? We're born, we come staggering out of the womb, we come searching for death. My father was a Welsh miner, a remarkable man. Tough, powerful. Obese. Short. I come from an enormous family – thirteen children.' He was groping back into a real past. 'My eldest sister was having a baby. I didn't understand it. I said, "Will she be all right? Will she live?" My father – he was massively drunk – was worried too. "Never mind," he said, "we're all dying." He talked like an angel. "Even your growing pains are reaching into oblivion".' Now he was quoting from his own *Christmas Story*. 'There's a poem,' he said presently. 'Would you like me to recite you a poem? It's by A.E. Housman.' He recited,

The night is freezing fast,
Tomorrow comes December;
And winterfalls of old
Are with me from the past;
And chiefly I remember
How Dick would hate the cold.

In photographs he was drawn and tired. Robert Kerwin of the *Chicago Tribune Magazine* described thin wrists, a pallor, and eyes where 'the irises are bright blue, but the whites are deep red, with only flecks of white. On his face is a dazed grin, as if he's been shocked awake under these heavy lights in the midst of surgery.' Kerwin watched them do a night scene, Burton 'falling over like a sack of potatoes as he leans myopically toward the script table to commit a single line to memory'. Burton played Stancill, a 'Southern aristocrat'. The line, not memorable, was 'I don't mean to be contrarying the country people's feelings.' It was some time before the British director, Terence Young, could get him to say it.

'*Burton:* "Well, ahhh ... Ah don't mean to be, ah, offending ..."'
' "Cut! Let's go again, Richard ..." '

For the next five takes, 'Burton plays with synonyms, a perverseness creeping into his eyes. "Don't mean to be quarrelling with ... getting on the wrong side of ... rubbing the country people's feelings the wrong way".' Kerwin saw it as a game: after each of the cuts, 'Burton grins and points a finger at Young: got you, Terence, old man.' The voice was 'raspy and weak; he's hoarse and coughing, but when he speaks he is the *centre* of the room. Finally he says the right words, but this take he pronounces them not in Stancill's Southern dialect but in Shakespearian British. When Young cuts him, Burton gives him the wicked smile, then suddenly – almost as if he's going to begin to cry – he says, "I'm sorry, Terry. I'm terribly sorry, everybody. Can we do it again?" The next take works, and they break while lights are changed.'

Later that night Lee Marvin remarked that Oroville was enough to drive anybody to drink. 'The man's suffering. Who knows what it is? He has to fend off so many people that his mind is hardly his own any more.' The producer, William Alexander, was heard to say, 'It's not something you get mad at about. He's to be pitied.' An unseen person in the production office said, 'He's committing physical and professional suicide.'

But Burton survived. As soon as his last scene had been shot, he went into hospital, St John's at Santa Monica, beyond Los Angeles, by the Pacific. This was in mid-April; 'bronchitis' and 'influenza' were given as the reasons. In his own account on television in 1977 Burton said that by this time he was 'into my third bottle a day' of hard liquor, and was told he had two weeks to live. He told the same story to David Lewin in 1975, with more detail about the drying-out that he underwent. When, after four days, he was taken off alcohol altogether, 'I had to be fed through a tube, I would shake so much.' This was a time of more nightmares about Ifor. While he was in hospital he had a chance encounter with Susan Strasberg, who had been in love with him sixteen years earlier. By now she had married and divorced, and was visiting her daughter at the hospital. Burton was taking a walk, helped by two aides. At first he didn't recognize her; she saw that his hands were shaking. It was a brief, awkward meeting. 'The years had reduced us to small talk,' she wrote.

When he had been two weeks in hospital, news came that he and Taylor were to seek divorce because of 'irreconcilable differences'. London papers quoted Los Angeles papers which quoted anonymous informants on the trials and tribulations of their marriage. There was not much information to be had. After the manic weeks at Oroville, Burton retreated into the shadows. Discharged from hospital in the second half of May, when he had undergone five weeks' treatment, he went to Puerto Vallarta to recuperate; Taylor was elsewhere. Soon after, Jack Le Vien went there with two colleagues hoping to confirm his tentative deal with Burton for the new television play about Churchill. This was to be based on Churchill's memoirs of the years leading up to the Second World War, and had the title *A Walk with Destiny* in Britain, *The Gathering Storm* in the US. The BBC, which would make the film, was putting up part of the money, along with an American sponsor, Hallmark Cards Inc. of Kansas City, whose 'Hall of Fame' produced plays for the NBC network.

Despite Burton's agreement in Rome the previous year, his agent in Los Angeles seemed to know nothing of the project. Scripts had been sent to Burton while he was in hospital, without response. Le Vien and his colleagues – a man from an advertising agency, representing the Hallmark interest, and Herbert Wise, who was to direct the film for the BBC – arrived in Los Angeles to be told that Burton was out of reach in Puerto Vallarta, and that it was impossible to phone him. They sent a telegram to say they were coming, and flew to Mexico, where they found him being looked after by a nurse and her husband. Wise, who had already suggested that because of the difficulties of contacting Burton they should think of using someone else, was not encouraged by what he saw. He wondered if Burton was fit to play such a demanding part. But Hallmark was determined it should be Burton, and Le Vien got his agreement to film in England in August. On their second night in Mexico they were invited to dinner. The house was built on several levels into the side of a hill. From a terraced room at the top verandahs looked over village and hills. The American consul and his wife had been invited as well. They sat in the terraced room with drinks while Burton entertained them by acting out portions of the Churchill script. Wise was embarrassed. 'And then,' he says, 'in mid-sentence, Burton went to sleep. I think it was the consul's wife who said, "We'd better be going." We all left. I was the last one to go. I thought, I must get this in a film one day. There were steps set in the floor, and as I looked back, there were the hills, and a purple sky, and Burton with the nurse in silhouette. That was the last time I saw him until we started filming.'

Before Burton left for Europe, travelling by sea from New York, the divorce was granted in Switzerland. Taylor was in court to say, 'There were too many differences. I have tried everything.' Amicable agreement about property and funds was reported. Burton went to Switzerland for more holiday, but was asked at short notice if he could fit in another film to be made in England for Hallmark's 'Hall of Fame' before the Churchill. This was a remake of *Brief Encounter*, a reckless venture given the quality of Trevor Howard and Celia Johnson in the original nearly thirty years before. Robert Shaw was to have played the ordinary doctor who meets the ordinary housewife at a railway station, but had not been released from work on *Jaws*. The ordinary housewife was Sophia Loren. Filming by Associated Television had begun in Hampshire before it was certain that Shaw would not be free in time. The director, Alan Bridges, thinks it was Loren who suggested Burton as a last-minute replacement. Bridges flew to Switzerland with the script, and Burton read it in the garden while he waited. He was charming, sober, emaciated; 'his body', says Bridges, 'looked worn.' The director failed to achieve much rapport with the actor, who seemed withdrawn, both then and when he arrived in England a week or so later. His fee was probably similar to the one negotiated for *Walk with Destiny*, £200,000, with a large expense allowance, salary for two aides, and a Rolls-Royce always available.

On his first day, he and Bridges sat in a hotel room in Winchester, where the unit was based, discussing costumes. Bridges would have liked a positive response, even if it was only about something as trivial as suits and ties. Instead he felt that Burton would say yes to almost anything. When they were filming, 'I had the feeling that when I discussed the concept, his thoughts would wander. He wasn't rude but I felt he might easily have been saying, "Never mind the philosophy, let's get on with it." ' No doubt this is what Burton meant. Bridges thinks that the one scene in which Burton took real interest was where he says goodbye for the last time to Miss Loren, the ordinary housewife. The producer, Cecil Clarke, was worried by stories from America about drink. Some of the film crew had worked with Burton before. They winked and prophesied trouble. In the event he was reliable and sober throughout the few weeks of photography. He was known to be doing exercises and keeping fit; townspeople saw him pedalling around Winchester on his bicycle in the early morning. But everyone was so nervous lest he fall into his old habits that when press reports began to appear that Taylor was thinking of marrying Henry Wynberg, the businessman, there was talk of keeping newspapers from Burton in case he was upset. In the interviews he gave while filming he spoke cordially of Taylor and affected not to be sure how Wynberg's name was spelt or pronounced.

In a bizarre conversation over lunch with a journalist, Roger Falk, he wrote out an 'advertisement' which said, 'Intelligent, well-to-do actor, aged 49, twice divorced, seeks nice lady aged between 28 and 38 to have baby by him. Will pay £20,000 ($50,000) if it is a boy child or £10,000 ($25,000) for girl child. Mother will then legally surrender all rights over child. Apply: Richard Burton, CBE.' He also told Falk, 'You think women have been my passion? The real passion in my life has been books.' Falk noticed that he drank nothing but soda water. Italian photographers, anxious for shots of him with Loren, were in the offing. Burton was in a charitable mood. 'I'm fair game,' he told Falk. 'Anybody who can make a spare penny out of me is entitled to do so when I make so much money out of other people.'

From *Brief Encounter* he went to *Walk with Destiny*. While making the first film, he was often heard talking about the second. Cecil Clarke, who had met him when he arrived in London at Victoria Station, en route to Hampshire, was told that the most important item in his luggage was a bust of Churchill. The prospect of playing the part and not merely using a Churchillian voice as narrator, which is what he had done in

The Valiant Years, seems to have worried him. He was reported to have said that 'I may have bitten off more than I can chew' and that he was 'scared witless'. He was drinking again during rehearsals, causing problems for Le Vien and Wise. His friend from earlier days, Richard Leech, was in the cast; they had been out of touch for many years, and Leech watched from the sidelines. Shortly before filming began, a studio rehearsal was called for 9.30 am. Nothing happened for an hour; there was no Burton. 'Then we were called in and told we wouldn't be rehearsing. The director said, "The technicians want it, I want it, the cast want it, but we can't do it because our star is, I am afraid, not with us. Good morning."' Most of the picture was shot on videotape, a technique that uses more than one camera and involves recording whole scenes, or long sections of scenes, without interruption, unlike photography on film, where lenses and the camera position are changed frequently, and shooting proceeds in small instalments. Burton had trouble remembering lines, though Wise believes he was sober during the actual production. Wise, like Bridges, failed to strike any spark. 'I don't think he liked me,' he says, 'and I didn't like him. I didn't find him creative in any way. I found I couldn't reach him, maybe because of the drink.' Le Vien says that Burton was at his best with Churchill's darker moods. Colin Morris, who had written the script, noted the same thing, and later wrote that because of Burton's 'sourness, gloom and lack of humour' in some of the early scenes, 'several incidents depicting the lighter side of Sir Winston had to be removed from the final TV play'.

American viewers were to see it first, on 29 November 1974, a Friday. Over the previous weekend, two articles by Burton appeared in America in which he wrote harshly, even derisively about Churchill. These caused an uproar, and Burton in turn was dealt with harshly. It was an odd episode. Instead of the garrulous film star with drink and marriage problems, he showed himself again as a serious writer. But this exposed him to serious judgments, especially when he dared set himself up as an authority on such a revered subject. No doubt there are clues to his state of mind in what happened. Did his attack on Churchill reflect some feeling of his own inadequacy beside the great man? Colin Morris thought so. There was, too, the matter of how a working-class Welshman, brought up to dislike arch-Tories, felt in his heart about a man like Churchill, who was much hated in the coal valleys. Burton was no longer a working-class Welshman. But he may have found comfort in acting the part of a Jenkins from long ago.

The original proposal involved a public relations consultant to Hallmark Cards, Jack Meelan, who watched the film being made, and who says he suggested that the *New York Times* might use an article by Burton on what it was like to play Churchill. The *Times* say it was their idea. Wherever it came from, Burton agreed to write an article, the *Times* agreed to print it, and a deadline was set, some time ahead. While Meelan was on the set, he took notes of things that Burton told him. These included the familiar anecdote about Churchill and Burton's Hamlet at the Old Vic, and a mixed bag of comments. Churchill was 'the best actor of our time – playing himself, of course. But then, most actors play themselves.' In the past year there had been 'a rash of new writings' about him, including the theory by a psychiatrist that Churchill was 'tremendously timid and puny as a young man, which explains why he over-reacted by taking great physical and intellectual chances'. Burton added, 'They're beginning to attack him now in articles, but many of the authors enjoy the luxury of hindsight. He was a formidable man and a great statesman.' Meelan also noted Burton's remark that 'after weeks of study and research I'm beginning to feel as though I am Churchill'.

The article arrived in New York by teleprinter, forwarded by a Burton secretary from Rome. Burton was either there or in North Africa with a new friend, Princess Elizabeth of Yugoslavia. She was the daughter of the exiled Prince Paul, and their affair had been public knowledge for a month or so. They were supposed to be getting married as soon as possible, although at present she was married to a British banker, Neil Balfour. The new liaison gave the Burton industry a busy time, especially since the princess was related to the British royal family, and Balfour had been trying to enter Parliament as a Conservative MP. It was later suggested that Princess Elizabeth, whose father was not favoured by Churchill during the war, might have had something to do with Burton's outburst, but this seems unlikely. The article breathes conviction. Meelan says that when he received it, he phoned the *Times* and said, 'I don't think you're going to want this, it's irrational.' The *Times* said they were the best judges of that. They were delighted when they saw what they had, and ran it prominently under the headline, 'To Play Churchill Is to Hate Him.'

Burton's thesis was simple: Churchill was a world figure but at the same time he was a monster. He said he had 'realized afresh that I hate Churchill and all his kind. I hate them virulently. They have stalked down the corridors of endless power all through history.' Burton called him a 'vindictive toy-soldier child', spoke of his 'merciless ferocity', and drew comparisons with Attila the Hun, Hitler and Stalin. The wartime bombing of Dresden was cited as evidence that Churchill favoured genocide. For good measure Burton brought in the theory, which he expressed as a fact, that Churchill was essentially a coward, compensating for his timidity by being bold. He didn't hide his own feelings of awe. Churchill was 'one of the few people – two others were Picasso and Camus – who have frightened me almost to silence when we came face to face, a difficult task in my case.... Was I apprehensive because he was such a towering world figure and already a myth and legend and destined to be a part of England either as a hero or a joke, or was it because I knew I already hated him and knew that he was just an actor like myself but had a wider audience?'

While it was their article that gained the publicity, the *Times* were displeased to find that Burton had written a second article, though it was briefer and milder, for *TV Guide*. In this, too, Churchill was 'power-mad (and for a time at least almost insane with power)'. But far from calling him a coward, Burton said here that he was 'afraid of nothing either physically or morally'. The valley Welshman could be heard for a moment, when Burton described meeting him. 'The shock of his presence was like a blow under the heart,' he wrote. 'I cannot pretend otherwise, though my class and his hate each other to seething point.' A few days later he elaborated to reporters in Rome, where he was riding out the storm of protest. He withdrew nothing and added that 'Churchill has fascinated me from childhood – a bogey-man who hated us, the mining class, motivelessly. He ordered a few of us to be shot, you know, and the orders were carried out.'*

The article was an embarrassment for some; it was also publicity for the film. Meelan could only repeat that he, like everyone else, had assumed that Burton was 'a great admirer'. The president of Hallmark Cards wrote to the *Times* to dissociate his company from Burton's views. Colin Morris wrote to it to say that Burton 'told me he was in awe of Churchill in life and terrified at the prospect of playing the part. It would now appear this awe surfaced during

---

* This is a travesty. The event for which Churchill was excoriated in the valleys occurred early in the century, when striking miners attacked a pithead at Tonypandy in November 1910. Churchill was Home Secretary. After hesitating briefly, he sent units of cavalry and foot soldiers to the Rhondda. They did nothing; it was police reinforcements, sent from London, who left broken heads and bitter memories – but no corpses.

the evolution of his performance.' Jack Le Vien wrote that in all the years he had known Burton – 'indeed up until a month ago when he and I had tea with Lady Churchill' – the actor had 'expressed only the greatest admiration for Sir Winston'. It was a nine-day wonder. Politicians – mainly Conservatives – and old soldiers told Burton he was a disgrace. 'If there were more Churchills and fewer Burtons, we would be a better country' was a popular line of attack. A columnist in the London *Times* thought he had 'damaged himself in the eyes of the British people' and 'does not deserve to recover'. The boot went in: 'He is now more clearly seen for what he is: an actor of talent, though not a great one – and a fool.' The Churchill family was deeply offended. Meanwhile the film was shown in America, where the critical response was mixed, though it attracted a large audience. Burton continued to hold the same views. When a journalist asked next year about the comparison with Attila and Hitler, he said, 'Well, they were all killers. Perhaps we all are.' He added that the article raised the viewing figures. Jack Le Vien continued to produce films about Churchill. Burton was not offered the part in his *Churchill and the Generals* five years later.

The affair with Princess Elizabeth meandered on. An air of anti-climax attended news of Burton, his women, his drinking, his plans to teach in Oxford, his plans to return to the theatre. It had all happened before. In newspaper photographs his eyes were invisible behind dark glasses. One minute the princess was supposed to be back with her husband, the next she was back with Burton. It was months before she faded from the papers and a new 'romance' was confidently reported. By this time, February 1975, Burton was in the south of France, working on a film called *Jackpot* that had trouble with money. He and others were intermittently employed into the early summer before work finally stopped. Among the interviews he gave between times on the set was one to his friend David Lewin. The two of them talked alone at an hotel in Nice. Burton still seemed as keen as ever to explain his life to the public. His interviewer noted that he was 'bronzed' and 'very fit', smoking heavily but drinking only wine. Burton wondered aloud why he drank. It was on this occasion that he said it was 'not natural to put on make-up and wear costumes on stage and say someone else's lines': one drank to overcome the shame. (This was the remark Burton shrugged off on television later, saying he was 'probably on the fourth bottle that day when I said it'. See Note to p. 110). Burton had an odder theory. He had been reading a book by Jean Renoir, the French film maker, about his father, the painter. 'He quoted his father as saying that all actors were homosexuals,' said Burton. 'That is nonsense, of course. But perhaps most actors are latent homosexuals and we cover it with drink. I was a homosexual once but not for long. But I tried it. It didn't work so I gave it up.' Lewin says that Burton was talking seriously as far as he could tell. He didn't like to press him.

For the remainder of 1975, Burton did no more film work, and he might have dropped out of sight if his relationship with Taylor had not started up again. They were reconciled in August and soon attracting as much attention as ever. Victor Spinetti saw them in Switzerland in September at a film première. Next morning he was to go to their house to lunch. At 10.30 Burton was already at the hotel, telephoning from the lobby to see where he was. 'I said, "You reformed drunks, you don't know what to do with yourself in the day." He said, "What else have I to do? I might as well come down here." He didn't go into the bar or the lounge. He just sat.'

That autumn the Burtons came to rest to South Africa. Here, as described by Taylor later, they were caught up in October in another of her medical dramas. An X-ray of her chest, taken for a suspected rib fracture, showed two spots on the lungs. 'I had about twelve hours to contemplate death,' she wrote, 'and a nasty one at that – cancer of the lungs.' Her egregious account, published in magazines all over the world, describes how they 'held each other with a kind of awe'. She gave him a Valium and he whispered poetry. Next day she was told it was not cancer after all. How the disease could have been suspected and then excluded on the basis of X-rays studied overnight is not clear. But perhaps it was meant to be symbolic. Burton proposed marriage. They went from Johannesburg to Botswana and were married in the remote bush by an African district commissioner. 'My beloved is as stout as a Welsh chicken' wrote Taylor, who strewed the account with endearments. She sent him a note to say they were 'stuck like chicken feathers to tar', not the happiest simile. Burton wrote back, 'Without you I was a ghost'. It was observed that he didn't seem himself. On 10 November he had his fiftieth birthday and celebrated in London with a party at the Dorchester. Sober, drawn and quiet, he was described as looking 'shaky', 'lost' and 'like a man who wasn't really there'. Later in the month they were in Wales on a family visit. At the home of his brother David, now retired from the police, in a suburb of Swansea, a photograph of a family group in the sitting-room shows smiling faces around Burton's harassed stare; his eyes look through the camera, not at it.

The second marriage was 'disastrous', Taylor said later. She was finally ousted by Susan Hunt, the wife of the British racing motorist James Hunt. Mrs Hunt was about twenty-nine, a former model. Her smile of sculptured teeth for the cameras made her look as fresh and clean as a television commercial for minty toothpaste. She looked what she was, English middle class with a spot of money in the background. According to Burton they met in a ski-lift in January 1976 when he and Taylor were at Gstaad. She seems to have been the capable young beauty who can appear on a gloomy scene and produce the illusion or even the reality of a fresh start. Once established and married to Burton, as she was by the summer of 1976, she helped reorganize his business affairs. Personal connections with the past were not always popular. Friends winked and talked about a new broom. Burton talked about having his life saved. Taylor went off and married John Warner, who had been Navy Secretary to President Ford and was trying to rise in politics.

For fifteen years the Burtons had publicized one another with great success; together, they were more than the sum of two film stars. Taylor, a phenomenon even by Hollywood standards, was also the womanly woman with a weight problem, gobbling hamburgers and puddings when she weakened, cheered up by diamonds and clothes, demanding his fidelity with a prudent smile (' no more girls, not unless you want a knuckle sandwich'), dutifully learning Welsh folk songs, trying to keep up with him intellectually, mooning over his socks when he was away.

Burton liked to play the old-fashioned male who knew what was best for a woman, who wasn't afraid to make jokes about her double chin and large breasts, who told a thousand reporters how wonderful she was ('a wonderful new toy on your pillow every morning') but was capable of irony when he felt like it ('How can you conceal a love for the world's most beautiful woman, earning a million dollars a picture?' If it was irony, that is). He admitted he had been unfaithful to her. After their first divorce and before their remarriage he told a magazine (1974), 'I have a fair choice of women myself if I wish. But I don't wish it. Since Elizabeth, I have seen two. I've a fundamental and basic loyalty. Next year I'll be fifty and I've only been married twice. Yes, I betrayed them both a couple of times, but not mentally, only *physically*. You see, I may fall in love and it may last six months, but then the affair breaks up.' It has been one of his lifelong themes. Aled Vaughan, visiting him in

Geneva for the BBC in 1959, saw him respond angrily to someone's wink or nod about his sex life. They were with other men in a bar. Burton asked each one in turn if he was faithful to his wife. All said 'Yes,' somewhat intimidated. Finally Burton stabbed a finger at himself. 'So am I!' he declared. No doubt he could have sworn on a Bible that mentally he was.

As for his life as an actor, it is possible that if they had never met, his career would have been different. But it is more likely that he was driven to look for someone of that kind, just as he was driven to make money and be famous at the expense of the other career he might have had. At the start Taylor was a conquest, a bare-shouldered beauty to cover with jewels and prove how potent he was, the miner's son. Fifteen years later the point had been made, his needs had changed, and he turned to the business of shaping the last third of his life. On his deepest needs from women (or from anything else) Burton has wisely kept quiet most of the time – the fact that he has talked so often to so many people armed with notebooks and tape recorders can make it appear that every possible personal topic has been exhausted, but much of the talk is repetitive, and has to be scrutinized for the odd insight here and there. A couple of conversations about women seem to point to a dependence on them going back to his earliest years. Both date from after he and Mrs Hunt were married and he was leading a quieter life. In the first, interviewed by Barbara Howar in 1977 on CBS television in America, he was asked why he preferred the company of women to men, and answered, 'Well, possibly because – I don't know. I – I don't believe in that Freudian analysis. I always wanted to call his name Fraud, didn't you? But anyway, my mother died when I was two years old, and I was brought up with four sisters, who naturally – because I was very small and they were older – spoiled me, I suppose the word is. And I suppose because my childhood was so dominated by women that I sort of understood women, as far as a man can possibly understand somebody from such an alien race, ever since.' In the second, in 1978, he told a British journalist, Alex Harvey, another old acquaintance, that 'although I like to be thought of as a tough rugby-playing Welsh miner's son, able to take on the world, the reality is that this image is just superficial. I am the reverse of what people think.' His wives had always saved him, and now, 'Suzy is a crutch to me.' It was not the kind of admission that Burton had been accustomed to make. He talked about his childhood, again implying an awareness of Dr Freud or at least of Dr Fraud. 'Women do cling to me a bit,' he said, 'but for the most part I do the clinging. After the death of my mother when I was two I hid behind my older sister Cecilia. She protected me and even lied for me. It has been the same with all the women I have loved since.' It is the voice of a different Burton.

CHAPTER FOURTEEN

The Past Revisited

WHEN, in 1976, Burton began to emerge from the shadows, he gave three signs of the change. He married Susan Hunt, he drank less and his interest in the theatre revived. He said his return to the stage was crucial, that he did it 'to discipline myself' and to demonstrate that 'I actually wasn't the falling-down drunk.' In the end the idea of a return to the theatre seems to have counted more than any achievement once he got there. It had remained his touchstone, although he had not been in a play (apart from a week of *Dr Faustus* at Oxford) since the Broadway *Hamlet* twelve years earlier. Before that he had been in no plays except *Camelot* (1960–1) and *Time Remembered* (1957–8) since his last Old Vic season ended in 1956. For years he had been heard to deny his gifts as an actor of any kind, on the stage or in films. He was in the profession by accident, he was bored with learning other people's words, he was going to give it all up. He was unlike those other actors with vocations, the Gielguds and Scofields. 'I'm not dedicated, I never was,' he said in 1970. 'In a sense I'm totally alienated from the craft that I employ so superficially and successfully.' He did not deny that there exists a serious art or craft. Sometimes he conceded that it embodies a mystery, as when he wrote in 1964 that 'once or twice in a lifetime' acting could become 'something odd and mystical and deeply disturbing'. He said on television that it was 'very difficult to know exactly what the actor does. He's a very odd being and I watch him with fascination' (1964). And 'You can, in a sense, understand the greatness of a painting. Certainly you can understand why a piece of writing is remarkable. But the mystery of the actor is the ultimate mystery, because no one even begins to know what it is' (to a reporter, 1966).

This view of acting, seeing it as something that the actor himself cannot understand, is a clue to Burton's rejection of the craft, when he is forced to take it too seriously. It is beyond his will, outside his control. It makes him vulnerable. He told Anthony Quayle in 1951 that he was frightened of his 'gift': it was a knack, and to understand it might be to lose it. Safer, then, to treat acting as a trade or even a joke. By so doing he may not rise so high. But he knows that the gods who casually bestow a gift may just as casually take it away again.

Yet Burton has never been able to shake off the theatre and its mixture of threat and promise. He told Kenneth Tynan that although he was frightened of the stage he must return to it. His obsession with playing Lear, that troublesome part, is surely an echo of his distress at having failed to attempt more than he has. The word was on his lips year after year. He was anxious to do it as early as 1959. Sometimes he said he was too old for it, sometimes too young. In 1976 the play that he used as his vehicle for a return to the theatre, in New York, was *Equus*, Peter Shaffer's cruel encounter between the boy who dreams of horses and the doctor who has lost his faith. But for the next year or two Burton made it plain that his eyes were on *Lear*. Plans were made for a New York production directed by John Dexter, who had directed *Equus*. It was discussed when Burton and his new wife stayed with Philip Burton at his home in Key West in September 1977. The older man was in his seventies now, still the upright, kindly pedagogue, his speech as exact as it had been in the Port Talbot classrooms and Ma Smith's front parlour. He wanted his pupil to 'feel his way back into Shakespeare with *Richard III*, which he's never played, which would have been marvellous for him. But it had to be *Lear*.' At the end of the year came an announcement from Alexander Cohen in New York that Burton's *Lear* would alternate with *Romeo and Juliet*, with Burton playing Mercutio; rehearsals would begin in April 1978. But before April came the project had fallen through. Dexter complained of indecisiveness; he later refused to talk about Burton, 'who has already wasted so much of my time'. Cohen turned to a new director, Elia Kazan. This plan foundered too; according to Cohen it was because he insisted that seven performances a week were needed to recover the investment, and Burton was not prepared to do more than six. But the word *Lear* continued to crop up in interviews with Burton like a message in code. He told a friend in London that he knew the play by heart.

The part that Burton used to show he was a changed man, Dysart the psychiatrist in *Equus*, seems to have been offered him late in 1975. Three actors had already played Dysart on Broadway. Burton was to be in the play for three months, replacing Anthony Perkins, who had replaced Anthony Hopkins, who had replaced Alec McCowen, who had played in the original Old Vic production in London, which Dexter directed. When he accepted the part he was still in Switzerland with Taylor. 'I walked through the snow in the wood thinking about Dysart, muttering Dysart, spouting Dysart.' By February 1976 he was rehearsing in New York; Susan Hunt was there as well as Elizabeth Taylor, and the Burtons parted for the last time. He took over at the end of February, declaring that 'I thought, if I don't take the plunge now, I probably would never go back,' and 'I've never been so bloody scared in my life.' He said later that it was 'the first time in my life I'd ever been on the stage without a drink, and I shook and shivered'. His reviews were mixed. Walter Kerr in the *New York Times* called it 'the best work of his life'. Clive Barnes in the same newspaper said that although it was 'unabashedly a star performance', and Burton was not his idea of what a failed psychiatrist should be like, 'yet somehow his larger-than-life approach works ... [Burton] is the most promising middle-aged English-speaking actor of his time', a phrase that Burton seized on and repeated with glee, adding no more than a superlative or two ('unquestionably the most brilliantly promising middle-aged actor now alive'). Martin Gottfried in the *New York Post* found him 'implausible', 'obsessed with the resonance of his voice', using 'Shakespearian cadences' that were irrelevant: 'What he has lost, through lack of use, is the ability to interpret a character and play him.' Visitors to Burton's dressing-room saw 'You are fantastic, love,' scrawled on a mirror with eyebrow pencil, and were told that his estranged wife had written it there.

An actress in the cast, Marian Seldes, who published her autobiography two years later, wrote that at first Burton 'seemed as apprehensive as a young actor with his first important role'. She was told he was being paid $10,000 a week; noted that 'the audiences adored him'; listened to him at a party tell stories about his two fathers, recite poetry and apologize for drinking so much wine; rode in a limousine with him and Mrs Hunt, heard her scold him for being rude, heard him groan 'I'm bored, I'm *bored*.' According to Burton's account (1980), he was still fearful of drink during *Equus*. Without Susan Hunt, 'I might very easily be dead … the audiences were fantastically kind, and they gave me standing ovations and all that, but every night we never knew if I'd crack.'

The film of *Equus* that Sidney Lumet was to make later in the year was being planned. Burton was far from being the inevitable choice. His last cinema film had been the ill-famed *Klansman*, released eighteen months earlier. 'The community felt he was in too many pictures that failed,' says a film producer who was in touch with him at the time. 'The community tires. The community says, "Forget it, he's out to lunch."' Marlon Brando was talked of to play Dysart. So was Jack Nicholson. Eventually the part went to Burton, at a fee of half a million dollars. Times had changed. But Burton was moving steadily to recover the ground he had lost. The same producer says that 'he threw a lot of armour in front of him to get through the days'. His divorce from Taylor, which eventually took place in Haiti, was being arranged; so was Susan Hunt's divorce from the racing motorist. They were married in August, in Virginia, and Burton managed to tell the *National Enquirer*'s man that he would soon be playing Lear on Broadway. His new wife said little in public, then or later. By all accounts she was tougher than she looked, familiar with the rich and their funny ways, but self-effacing, making a virtue of discretion: more of a Sybil than an Elizabeth. Burton, who was coming to enjoy the idea of being saved, was soon telling people that before she had appeared, 'I was on the edge of self-destruction', that 'Susan saved my life. I met her just when I was putting my hand up for help for the last time.'

His friend Stanley Baker had died in June of lung cancer. Burton said in 1977 that he was 'profoundly shocked', adding that 'it wasn't unmixed naturally with a little fear, because Stanley was two years younger than I'. This intimation of mortality prompted him to offer *The Observer* in London an article, 'Lament for a dead Welshman', which proclaimed his affection for Sir Stanley Baker (he was knighted shortly before his death) and the South Wales background they shared. 'Stanley was inwrought with his valley,' wrote Burton, 'and so am I with the *idea* of the valley.' A phrase carried an echo of a Dylan Thomas poem – 'and whose tears are burning my cheeks and whose heart is shifting uneasily in mine?' The article, over-written but heartfelt, offended Baker's family, and in particular his widow, Lady Baker. In 1978 she talked to me about Burton on the telephone, in anger, for half an hour, explaining why she couldn't bring herself to talk about him. She was a young actress in London after the war, when she fell in love with Baker and met his Welsh friends – 'I was dazzled by them all,' she said, 'they were all so different' – so that her acquaintance with Burton and his circle went back thirty years.

'I was always very guarded with Richard,' she said. 'Stanley loved him and forgave him and forgave him and forgave him.' The *Observer* article seemed to enrage her because she felt it was being written at the expense of Baker. She read it sitting in the garden on a sunny Sunday morning. 'I heard Stanley's voice, though I don't believe in voices. He was laughing very gently....'

There were further trials for Burton in 1976. Between appearing in *Equus* on the stage and *Equus* for the screen he had a leading part in a film that was meant to be a sequel to *The Exorcist*, which made a fortune from occult nastiness in 1974. Warner's *Exorcist II: The Heretic* seemed to mark another turn for the better in his affairs. He and Susan Hunt were married during a break in the filming. The capable director, John Boorman, whose previous pictures included *Deliverance*, was expected to treat the supernatural in intelligent new ways. The result was baffling. Burton, who played a priest battling against evil and one of the silliest plots ever seen in the cinema, said later that after a few weeks of filming, '[Susan] could see I was very unhappy about it. She said to me, "You must never do anything like that again, even to get a million dollars." ' After *The Heretic* there were signs that Burton did become more careful, although even with that film it is fair to say that he, and everyone else involved, were caught unawares. Released in the summer of 1977, it was probably the worst major film of his career. *Variety* said it was 'guaranteed to keep audiences on the edge of their seats, wanting to go home'. *New York* magazine wrote, 'Whereas it is impossible to designate even approximately the worst film one has ever seen, there is a very strong probability that *Exorcist II* is the stupidest major movie ever made.' Booed and laughed at in Los Angeles and New York, the original version was recut in an attempt to improve matters. Boorman had meant to give the film a 'visionary quality', but had misjudged either his material or his audiences. He admitted that 'theatre managers didn't want to wear their tuxedos. They were afraid of getting lynched.... I basically made the wrong movie.'

There were delays in filming *The Heretic* in the summer of 1976, but Burton was free in time for Lumet's *Equus*, which was shot in Canada.

As the psychiatrist, he had seven or eight long speeches, designed to punctuate the film, where he soliloquizes to the camera. All were shot in a single day. Burton was as capable as ever. The film was only modestly successful when it appeared. His last piece of work that year was in London, where he returned to Broadcasting House to record the narration for twenty-six episodes of a radio 'chronicle of the English crown', based on the works of Shakespeare and others, under the title of *Vivat Rex*. The fee was £4,000 for two days' work; he was not the BBC's first choice. Sitting in studio B10 amid half-empty cups of coffee and crumpled scripts, he said, 'This is home. This is where I started professionally.' He was revisiting the past. His new wife was taken for brief trips to Wales; on one they arrived in a black Rolls-Royce, on another in a white helicopter. The BBC in Wales filmed an interview with him in a pub without customers near Pontrhydyfen. He said that the village, 'apart from the knocking down of a few houses and the erection of three or four others, is stick for stick, stone for stone, blade of grass for blade of grass, virtually as it was when I was a child'. A glass containing a colourless liquid stood in front of him. 'I can't believe that I've been in Wales for thirty-six hours and I haven't had a drink yet,' he said. 'This by the way in case my sister is looking is *water*.'

Apart from presenting the obvious difficulty, a biography of somone still alive is liable to lose focus as it approaches the present. All lives are conditional until they are over, and it is dangerous to draw conclusions from what happened yesterday. The last film-making where I can see Burton with some clarity through the eyes of others is *The Medusa Touch*. He worked on it for three weeks in the early summer of 1977, for a fee of half a million dollars. This is rather more than a dollar a second, good even by Burton's standards. The film was another of Elliott Kastner's successful packages, made at the Pinewood studios outside London. The screenplay was based on a 1973 thriller by Peter Van Greenaway about a man who has discovered that he has 'a gift for disaster'. He practises telekinesis: he can will physical events – a fire, a plane crash, the destruction of Westminster Abbey. Kastner says that he 'wasn't crazy about the book', but Jack Gold had said that he would like to direct it, and Kastner wanted to make a film with Gold. Gold was not crazy about Burton in the part; he would have preferred Nicol Williamson, but Kastner thought the money for this particular film would be easier to raise with Burton. Burton himself was not crazy about the script. 'But,' says Kastner, 'I told him it was a nice piece of change for a short period of time. It wasn't negotiated. I just came up with a figure.'

Gold had his first meeting with Burton at a hotel in Geneva: 'He had come in by train from his house. He tends to go into Geneva on the suburban line and buy the British papers.' They ate lunch. His wife was present. Gold, like other directors who had sat around a table with Burton to discuss a script, 'almost had the feeling that he was somewhere else. I had heard about him that there was always the one step backwards, two steps forward. I thought he didn't want to do it, that it was a reluctant acceptance. From things he said, I felt he would rather be writing or acting on the stage. He said he had checked me out with other directors. He asked why I wanted to do the book, about which he was sceptical, because he didn't want to be caught doing another *Exorcist II*. Was it a film Elliott wanted to do, and I'd been pulled in as the director, or was it a film that I wanted to do myself? Suzy left after lunch, and we went to my room in the hotel and went through the script. A script is no difficulty to him whatsoever. After the reading he knew exactly what it was going to be – twelve or fifteen days of not difficult work. He didn't suggest changes.' In the evening they met for dinner at a bistro. His wife was there again, and one of his daughters. 'We had a fondue and that was that. He was still quite high on *Equus*, and there was talk about whether he might get an Oscar the following year.'

At Pinewood 'he did it all as expected. Technically he's very good. When I said, "I'm going to do a long tracking shot with your eyes in close-up, lasting forty seconds, as you're bringing down the plane, so don't blink", there was no problem. I saw no overt acts of ego. If we both spoke at the same time, he'd stop. It was the same with the crew. Some days he was full of anecdotes. Other times he'd go back to the caravan and Suzy would make tea for him. There were occasions he was moody. Stanley Baker had died. I think he'd become aware that life was finite.' And did Gold like him? 'There wasn't much to like or dislike.' Journalist friends visited the set. Sydney Edwards heard him talk about a new biography of Dylan Thomas, pouring scorn on the suggestion that Thomas had brief homosexual experiences as a young man. 'That made me laugh,' he said. Edwards was with him in the canteen at Pinewood when Elliott Kastner came in. 'Richard came alive instantly. I suppose, because Kastner represents wealth and comfort.' Romany Bain noticed a refrigerator full of Fanta, a non-alcoholic fizzy drink. 'Richard had a bib around his neck to keep the make-up off his clothes. He was sitting low in a chair, looking about sixty-five.'

Despite its bizarre theme *The Medusa Touch* turned out well, an agreeably compact movie. A second film that Burton made in 1977 was even more straightforward, *The Wild Geese*, in which he played the leader of a band of white mercenaries in Africa. It is full of bravery and explosions. The producer, Euan Lloyd, says that Burton's agent was looking for an 'adventure script' on his behalf. He was paid three-quarters of a million dollars for twelve to fourteen weeks' work. The director, Andrew McLaglen, says he was reliable and hard-working throughout. The new Burton, in love with his wife and sober, was being emphasized in many interviews. On British television at the end of 1977 he talked to Ludovic Kennedy about his drinking, his past and his future. He said that he feared crowds, and in the past twenty years had 'very rarely gone out, except when commanded to, in a sense'. Having stopped drinking, he was trying to stop smoking; he admitted he got through between sixty and a hundred cigarettes a day, 'especially when I work'. In 1978 he would play Lear. As for the past, 'since I can't change it, I don't regret it'.

Early in 1978 he was in Los Angeles, available for interviews, waiting as he had waited before to see if he would win an Academy Award. *Equus* was his seventh nomination. He was passed over again. His next picture, *Absolution*, was due to start filming in Britain, with Elliott Kastner as producer. The screenplay by Anthony Shaffer was set in a Roman Catholic boys' school; Burton was a schoolmaster priest who hears the confession of a boy who has committed a murder. According to Burton it was based on a true event in Germany; he had been interested in the project since 1970, and there had been earlier attempts to finance it. Now he began to make difficulties. A cable from Kastner's office to his agent in April warned that time was ticking by, half a million dollars had been spent already, and each day added twenty thousand to the total. The film was duly made, at Pinewood and on location in Shropshire, though three years later it was still on the shelf, without a distributor. Later in 1978 he made a war film in Germany with Robert Mitchum and Rod Steiger, *Breakthrough* (also called *Sgt Steiner*), directed by Andrew McLaglen; this, too, has been slow to appear. If the plans for *King Lear* had come to fruition, he would have been doing that instead.

It was time perhaps for friends and critics who had known him for years and followed his career to make the assessments that begin to settle on people like dust once they enter their fifties. A director who has worked with Burton summed him up in 1979: 'What he isn't is a daring actor. It's all based on variations on his own rather strong, full-throated Welsh personality. He'll never do as Olivier would, put on a mad nose or try a different voice or play it as a negro. He always respects his rather conservative vocabulary, which is an effective one, because he has a strong personality, a good appearance and a very fine voice. His Henry V, his Prince Hal, even his Petruchio in that extravagant film, were based on the roistering moments of Richard Burton. He takes direction very very well, but he's always a little empty. Often very good, too. But if you say, "Go to a window and then throw it open" – physical, extrovert acting – he'll say, "Can't I do the expression and then *slowly* open the window?" – that sort of thing. He's nervous of external acting. It's always well done, but done with prudence, not daring.'

In November 1978 I was in Key West, at the tip of the Florida Keys, staying with Philip Burton. We talked for days, off and on, sometimes in the small garden with iced beer on the table, sometimes in the house, which smelt of polished wood and books. Until my visit we had met only once, thirty years before in his office at the BBC in Cardiff, when I nervously showed him a script. He had forgotten the occasion. He told me some of what he knew about Richard Burton, though long silences were liable to fall. Photographs of Richard were everywhere. Philip thought he was in Mexico, in the house at Puerto Vallarta that he had bought for his new wife. He promised to forward a letter, but held out no hope of a response.

Burton seemed to be growing more elusive, even Burton the celebrity. In New York a week later I talked to the editor of *Photoplay*, who let me look through the files for articles about Richard and Elizabeth from their hectic years. At random I pulled out *Liz Screams! Mob Beats Up Burton* and *We Find Burton's Two Girlfriends and They Tell It All!* The editor said, 'It was Taylor had the charisma. She was crazy. You never knew what she'd do, if it was only get rushed to hospital because she'd swallowed a chicken bone. She's still potentially interesting.' And Burton? The editor shook her head. 'He's married to Susan Hunt. She's straight and not very exciting.'

Clearly Burton belongs somewhere else. But it is difficult to place him. Fame inspires a kind of lunacy on the part of the unfamous. Sir Alec Guinness told me an odd tale in May 1979. He and his wife had been with Burton and Susan in London, having a late dinner at Langan's

Brasserie, off Piccadilly. 'He was the Richard of the old days,' said Guinness. 'Funny, very companionable, considerate, generous in his assessments. Years of tortured difficulty had slipped off him.' A party was celebrating noisily elsewhere in the restaurant. Presently a man came over and asked drunkenly if Richard Burton would go across to the party and say, 'Happy Birthday, Chris.' Burton indicated that he might do so when he had finished eating. 'Twenty minutes later the chinless wonder came lurching back,' said Guinness, 'and Richard told him he would go over in about three minutes. I said, "You really can't, you're opening yourself to insults and embarrassment," and Richard said, "What do you do?" So he went across, and one heard a kind of astonished silence. A minute later he was back. He sat down very quietly, and we all said, "What happened?" "Oh well," he said, "I went over, and they stopped speaking, and I said, 'Happy Birthday, Chris,' and the drunken man said, 'Fuck off, Richard Burton, we don't want you at our party.' I'm used to it." And that was the great joke. I would have been trembling with rage. He took it all absolutely calmly, in a way admirably, but also a bit sadly, I thought. I felt awfully sorry for him.'

That summer, 1979, Burton was making a little-publicized film in Ireland about Tristan and Isolde. In the autumn he was to have been in India to play the lead in another wartime adventure, *The Sea Wolves*. When it was filmed he was 'unavailable', according to the producers, who used Gregory Peck instead. Was he planning some dramatic change of direction? Had he decided to mend his ways and go back to the theatre that made him? Such a question, often asked, implies that he has somehow misbehaved. But he was under no obligation to follow a different career. He has done what seemed best to him at the time. If there was any treachery, it was hardly to others. Mankiewicz's script for *Cleopatra* put a possible epitaph into his mouth: 'The ultimate desertion: I from myself.' Even that may be ridiculously overstating the case. Why should he not be like dozens of film stars who keep the old bicycle wheels turning with a succession of forgettable pictures, lending their faces to advertise products on television, having their sanitized memoirs ghosted? In the end, though, it is Burton himself who has invited censure of his career by talking with such grandeur and pride and with so many hints of the unachieved, as though he knew in his heart that he was cut out for something better. His style as a film actor – pretentious, contempt-uous, rarely at ease – has been suggesting it all his life.

What he did in 1980 was to go back to the stage, but in a revival of

Camelot, which he had left behind nearly twenty years earlier. Nor was it a token reappearance as King Arthur – beginning in Toronto and New York, he played for weeks or months at a time in half a dozen American cities, ending with a long season on the West Coast. Theatres were sold out and audiences enthusiastic. Playing in New York in July he was ill on the stage at one performance. Suggestions that he was drunk were denied, and the episode was put down to 'nausea and exhaustion'. In November 1980 he was a month at Miami Beach, telling reporters he had gone there so that Philip Burton could travel up from Key West and see the show. The old teacher, who says he had sworn never to spend another night away from his home, let himself be persuaded, though he refused to let a car be sent for him. He took the bus and stayed with Richard and Susan for a week in the house they were renting at Golden Beach, a wealthy resort community. Richard was an older King Arthur but a better one, according to his mentor. They talked, too, more than they had done for years. He was there for the party on Richard's fifty-fifth birthday, given for the cast, and went back on the bus a happy man, which is no more than he deserves.

As for Richard Burton, a year on tour with *Camelot** was a singular venture for someone who has complained so much about the drudgery and boredom of the stage. But the salary was large and *Camelot* sounds like a compromise between the drive to go on earning and his nostalgia for the theatre. In Pontrhydyfen they were kept in touch by means of fat envelopes of press cuttings from his agent. One or two of the family did wonder why Rich had chosen so much hard work, even at £20,000 a week – or was it £30,000 or £50,000? There were still the rows of noughts. But when it came to motives, the family had always accepted that Rich was a law unto himself. It was the same with the television commercial that he agreed to make in 1981. If he did it, that was good enough for them.

One of the last people I interviewed, when this book was already begun, was Robert Hardy. He lives in a farm at the end of a broken road at the side of a wood on a ridge above the Thames Valley. He talked about Burton all day, lingering over Oxford and Wales. 'Beware

---

* Before the tour finished, Burton was taken ill and had to leave the show for an operation in April to ease a chronic spinal condition that was causing pressure on nerves affecting his right arm. Hilda Owen, who saw him in Los Angeles, said afterwards that her brother's 'nausea and exhaustion', on stage the previous July, stemmed from painkilling drugs that he was already receiving.

of me as an impartial source,' he said. 'I think Richard a great figure. There was something so enormously aristocratic about his attitude. When one met his brothers, there was something extraordinary about *them*, too. None of them was the cavalry leader that Richard was. But they all had an amazing dignity.'

Hardy was very hospitable and we were still drinking at four in the afternoon. A brilliant idea occurred to him. He would be in America soon, in connection with a series of television films in which he was playing, of all people, Winston Churchill. If I could discover the theatre where *Camelot* was on now, he would send a long telegram suggesting that he bring me to meet Richard in the near future. I demurred but he insisted, so I found the whereabouts of his old friend. He was in Chicago. Hardy sent off his telegram and I got on with the book. No answer came.

Notes

'IN conversation' means a conversation with the author. Subsequent quotes from that person can be assumed to come from the same interview. 'In a letter' means letter to the author. 'USC' is the University of Southern California.

CHAPTER ONE: JENKINS, ARISE

p. 1   'Bare-shouldered beauties': *A Christmas Story* (Heinemann, 1965).

p. 2   Family origins: 'Miles Jenkins, Miller' is shown as the father of Thomas Jenkins, Richard Burton's grandfather, on Thomas's marriage certificate in 1875. Thomas's age is given as twenty-seven, but I failed to find his birth certificate among dozens of possible Thomas Jenkinses born around 1848. However, a search for his parents' marriage, from 1848 back to September 1837, when central records were first kept, shows (fortunately) that only one Miles Jenkins was married during that time. This I take to be Burton's ancestor.

p. 2   Origins of Pontrhydyfen: Arthur Rees, Port Talbot Historical Society *Transactions*, Vol. II, No. 3 (1974).

p. 3   Burton on his father: *Listener*, 9 September 1970, reprinting a television interview by David Frost.

pp. 3-4 Edith's marriage (and many family details throughout): conversations with Cecilia James, Hilda Owen, Catherine Thomas (Burton's sisters) and Will Jenkins (brother).

p. 6   Burton's story: 'A Story of Christmas ... in the Twenties', *Daily Mail*, 23 December 1971.

p. 9   The 'coffin' story: 'Richard Burton, the streetfighter who'd skip class to hunt rabbits', *National Enquirer* (US), 28 July 1974.

p. 10   The Dummers: Dillwyn Dummer, in conversation.

p. 11   The teacher: Tom Howell, in conversation.

p. 11   In the snow: *Listener*, 9 September 1970.

p. 12   Burton on Jones: 'The magic of Meredith Jones', *Sunday Times*, n.d.

p. 12   Contemporary at school: David Williams, in conversation.

p. 13   Trevor George, Tom Mainwaring: in conversations.

CHAPTER TWO: THE OTHER BURTON

p. 15   In charge of rugby: Jack Nicholas, in conversation.

p. 15   'Boxing poet': in *An Actor's Profile*, BBC Welsh Home Service (radio), 10 March 1961.

p. 16   The gas mask story: Trevor George; on the train: Eric Lamborn; both in conversation.

p. 16   Third friend: anon, in conversation.

p. 17   Philip Burton: most of his story, here and later, is from a series of conversations. His autobiography, *Early Doors. My life and the theatre* (Dial, US, 1969) has also been used.

p. 18   The radio profile: *An Actor's Profile, op. cit.*

p. 18   'Wild ambition': *Sunday Graphic*, 19 June 1955.

p. 19   Rugby reminiscence: an article in English with a Welsh title, 'Le ma'r blydi film star 'ma?' in *Touchdown* (Rugby Football Union, 1970).

p. 19fn.   Stanley Baker's brother: Anthony Storey, *Stanley Baker. Portrait of an actor* (W.H. Allen, 1977).

p. 19   Hollywood article: 'The wild Welshman', *Look* (US), 8 September 1953.

p. 20   Emyr Humphreys: in a letter.

pp. 20-1   Return to school: conversations with Evan Morgan, Trevor George, Brian Tashara, Jack Nicholas, Philip Burton.

p. 21   'I discovered him': 'Angriest star in Hollywood', *Saturday Evening Post*, 3 October 1953.

CHAPTER THREE: DIFFICULT ROLES

p. 25   Promise to be a teacher: Llewelyn Heycock in *An Actor's Profile, op. cit.*

p. 27   'Out of the gutter': *Newsday* (US), 6 February 1968.

p. 28   'Great man's socks' and 'rivals': Brinley Jenkins (who came first in the verse speaking competition), in conversation.

p. 28   Girl in class: Mair Jenkins, in conversation.

pp. 28-9   Burton on his adolescence: interviewed by Romany Bain, *Sun*, 3 July 1972.

p. 29   'Gate', not 'gairt': Brinley Jenkins.

p. 29   'Twenty-eight bloody little Burtons': reported by Jack Nicholas, who adds, 'I didn't regard it as a criticism: it was a tribute.'

p. 30   'We all do that': the reporter was Alan Road, in conversation.

p. 30   On location: 'The drama the cameras missed', *Saturday Evening Post*, 11 July 1964; the film was *The Night of the Iguana*.

pp. 31-2   How Jenkins became Burton: the information is from Philip Burton.

p. 32   'Split personality': Burton interviewed by John Morgan, *Panorama*, BBC TV, 12 September 1966.

p. 32   Cardiff newspaper: *Western Mail*.

pp. 32-3   The *Druid's Rest* audition: Philip Burton; Emlyn Williams, in conversation and in *An Actor's Profile, op. cit.*, which also has Richard Burton on the subject. Daphne Rye on Burton: Anthony Storey, *op. cit.*

p. 33   'Half success': *Actor's Profile*, BBC, *op. cit.*

p. 33   *New Statesman*: 2 February 1944.

p. 34   'Birds and booze': the late (Sir) Stanley Baker, quoted in John Cottrell and Fergus Cashin, *Richard Burton ... a Biography* (Coronet, 1974).

p. 34fn.   Baker and Morse: Anthony Storey, *op. cit.*, and Glynne Morse in a letter.

p. 34   The Liverpool girl: one version of the story is by Lynda Lee-Potter, *Daily Mail*, n.d.; another, in Lester David and Jhan Robbins, *Richard and Elizabeth* (Arthur Barker, 1977).

pp. 34-8   Burton at Oxford: the account is based on conversations with Philip Burton, Robert Hardy and Nina Bawden; Nevill Coghill in *Actor's Profile, op. cit.*; BBC transcripts of a television interview, 'Burton and Taylor at Oxford' ('filmed in the Mure Room at Merton College, Oxford, Saturday 14 October 1967'); a BBC TV interview of Burton by Kenneth Tynan in 1966, transmitted 1 April 1967, subsequently published in *Acting in the Sixties*, ed. Hal Burton (BBC, 1970). Some of Coghill's remarks are from Cottrell and Cashin, *op. cit.*

CHAPTER FOUR: AN ACTOR'S LIFE

p. 40   Burton's fellow Welshman: Harold Griffiths, in conversation.

pp. 40-1   BBC letter: from the play's producer, John Glyn-Jones, 13 August 1946. BBC Written Archives.

p. 41   Cleverdon on Burton: in conversation.

p. 41   Burton on Thomas: *Book Week* (US) 24 October 1965.

p. 41   Grainge on Burton: 'Richard Burton's War', *Sunday People*, 1 December 1974.

pp. 41-2   Port Talbot actor: Evan Morgan, in conversation.

p. 42   Eleanor Summerfield: in conversation.

p. 42   'Came out of the RAF ...': 'A visit with Richard Burton'. *Theatre* (US), May 1961. Burton was appearing in *Camelot*.

p. 42   At H.M. Tennent: John Perry, administrator of the Company of Four, in conversation.

p. 42   Richard Leech: in conversation.

p. 44fn.   *Variety*, n.d.: the review is datelined 'London, April 20'.

p. 44   Emlyn Williams on Burton: in conversation. An account by him of the filming in the village of Rhydymain is in the *Listener*, 23 June 1949.

p. 44   *Dolwyn* notices: 'impeccable acting', *Sunday Graphic*, 24 April 1949; 'very promising', Dilys Powell, *Sunday Times*, same date; *News of the World*, same date, by Ewart Hodgson.

p. 45   Television interview: Tynan, *Acting in the Sixties*, *op. cit.*

pp. 46-7   Sybil Burton: biographical information chiefly from Robert Hardy; Hilda Owen; anon; and an article by Elaine Dundy, reporting one of the few genuine conversations with the former Mrs Burton after her first marriage broke up, 'Can a simple Welsh lass of thirty-six find happiness with a Macedonian rock-and-roll star of twenty-four? Yes, says Sybil Burton Christopher. Hear, hear, says the author. (Yeah, yeah!)', *Esquire*, December 1965.

p. 47   'Posh Welsh': *American Weekly*, 13 May 1962.

p. 47   'She thinks I'm a genius': Sheilah Graham, *Confessions of a Hollywood Columnist* (William Morrow, New York, 1969).

p. 47   'Giving me confidence': Elaine Dundy, *op.* cit.

p. 48   Peter Glenville: in conversation.

p. 48   Noel Willman: in conversation.

p. 48   Burton on the sacking: 'A candid look at "Becket" and myself', *Life*, 13 March 1964.

p. 48   Frank Hauser: in conversation. His colleague was Archie Harding. Burton was paid thirty guineas (£31 10s).

p. 49   Christopher Fry: in conversation.

p. 49   Burton on Gielgud: 'profound' influence, *Listener*, 9 September 1970; 'vast differences', *Life*, 13 March 1964.

pp. 49-50 Reviews: 'sturdy and forthright', unidentified; 'industrious apprentice', Anthony Cookham, *Tatler*, 25 May 1949; Richard Findlater, *Time & Tide*, n.d.

p. 50   Alec Guinness: in conversation.

p 51   Reviews: *News of the World*, 29 May 1949 (Ewart Hodgson again); C.A. Lejeune, same date; *New York Times*, 19 June 1949.

p. 51   Burton's broadcasts: BBC Written Archives.

p. 52   Phyllis Calvert: in conversation.

p. 52fn. Sir William Jenkins: his father was a Miles Jenkins, son of Miles the Miller, and brother of Thomas. This second Miles Jenkins ran a small business hauling coal. Information from Sir William's daughter, Mrs M. Davies.

p. 52 *Waterfront*'s cast also included Robert Newton. The screenplay was from a novel by John Brophy. Released in Britain in 1950, it reached America in 1952 as *Waterfront Women*, with desperate publicity stills of girls doing up their suspenders and lying in rumpled beds.

p. 52 *Green Grow the Rushes* was made by ACT Films, set up by the Association of Ciné Technicians, and was described as 'the most exciting venture in the history of British film production'. No one wanted to distribute the result, and few people ever saw it in the cinema. The executive producer: Phil Samuel, in conversation.

p. 53 Anthony Quayle: in conversation.

p. 54 *Time*: 20 November 1950.

CHAPTER FIVE: WELSHMAN AT LARGE

p. 56 'Nearly fired': Tynan interview, *Acting in the Sixties, op. cit.*

p. 59 American television show: an interview on ABC, transmitted 9 April 1964, quoted in *Playbill* (US), April 1965.

pp. 59-60 To Kenneth Tynan: *Acting in the Sixties, op. cit.*

p. 60 Tynan's review: reprinted in *A View of the English Stage* (Paladin, 1976); original publication unknown.

p. 60 Sybil in 1951: Elaine Dundy's *Esquire* article, *op. cit.*

p. 61 Burton on his Ferdinand: Tynan interview, *Acting in the Sixties, op. cit.*

p. 61 Radio documentary: *Birth of a Giant*, broadcast 15 July 1951. The BBC producer: Elwyn Evans, in conversation.

p. 61 Burton on acting: *Life*, 13 March 1964.

p. 62 'Old ones, young ones ...': *Evening News*, 10 June 1977.

p. 62 *Los Angeles Times*: 26 August 1951.

p. 62 'After Shakespeare ...': *New York Post*, 26 December 1951.

p. 63 *New York Times*: undated cutting, about October 1977.

p. 63 Former friend: Trevor George.

pp. 63-4 Burton's early film contracts: Korda is variously reported to have failed and succeeded in persuading Burton to sign a long-term contract as early as 1950. David Shipman, *The Great Movie Stars* (Angus & Robertson, 1980) says he signed a five-year contract with Korda, starting at £100 a week, in May 1952, and that Fox negotiated to borrow him for *My Cousin Rachel* and two further films. Burton probably did have a contractual link with Korda, and Korda had connections with Fox. But Fox were talking about parts for Burton at least by April 1952, a month before the alleged contract with Korda.

p. 64 Cukor and the play: in conversation.

p. 64 Zanuck's memo: USC, Fox file on *The Desert Rats* No. 2528/4. Zanuck's other candidate for the part was Richard Todd.

p. 64 Cheering at the *Lyric*: Noel Willman; *Daily Mail*, 9 April 1952.

p. 65 Zanuck's biographer: Mel Gussow, *Don't Say Yes Until I Finish Talking. A biography of Darryl F. Zanuck* (Doubleday, US, 1971).

p. 65   Cukor's departure: J.R. Parish and D.E. Stanke, *The Leading Ladies*, on Olivia de Havilland (Arlington House, US, 1977).

p. 65   Henry Koster: in conversation.

p. 65   Censorship problems: USC, Fox files containing *Rachel* scripts and correspondence, No. 2514.

p. 65   de Havilland's biographer: Judith M. Kass, *Olivia de Havilland* (Harvest, US, 1976).

p. 65   Burton bangs his head: the version here is Koster's. 'Angriest star in Hollywood', *Saturday Evening Post*, 3 October 1953, says he lost his temper because he forgot his lines: 'The actor ground his teeth and kept groaning in a voice of furious agony, "Why can't I say my lines, why can't I?"'

p. 66   Getting on badly: Shipman, *op. cit.*

p. 66   Burton's *Rachel* earnings: Shipman says $50,000, *Saturday Evening Post*, 3 October 1953, says $60,000. Henry Koster says $50,000 was about the going rate for a leading man who was still a long way from stardom.

p. 66   Ten-picture contract: *New York Herald Tribune*, 7 October 1952.

p. 66   Zanuck and the scripts: USC, folders on *The Desert Rats*, No. 2528.

p. 66   Robert Wise: in conversation.

p. 67   'Someone was guiding us': quoted in an article in an unidentified movie magazine, 'by Liza Wilson, Hollywood editor', *circa* 1953.

p. 67   Louella Parsons: syndicated article in unidentified magazine, 1953.

p. 67fn   The detective: Mel Gussow, *op. cit.* CinemaScope publicity: eg an advertisement for *The Robe* in *Motion Picture Herald* 19 September 1953 – 'The first motion picture in CinemaScope. You see it without glasses!'

p. 68   Hedda Hopper: *Los Angeles Times*, 28 December 1952.

p. 68   Burton's life, as reported: 'First Star of 3-D Films', unidentified magazine, 20 March 1953; *Hollywood Citizen-News*, 19 February 1953; by Violet Wolfson in unidentified movie magazine, 26 April 1953; *Look*, 8 September 1953; *New York Herald Tribune*, n.d.

pp. 68–9 *Christian Science Monitor*: July 1953, exact date unknown.

p. 69   *Saturday Evening Post*: 3 October, 1953.

p. 69   Welsh television interviewer: John Morgan, *Panorama*, BBC TV, 12 September 1966.

pp. 69–70 'Seen from close range': Except for the sentence 'Yet the newcomer ...' everything in this paragraph is based on a letter that Burton wrote to a friend in London at the end of April 1953.

CHAPTER SIX: MOVING AWAY

p. 71   Burton's calculation: quoted in *Daily Express*, 16 April 1953.

p. 71   Television interview: by Vincent Kane, BBC, 12 February 1977.

p. 72   'More nerve-racking': *Manchester Guardian*, 18 July 1953.

p. 72   Familiar phrases: (1) Philip Hope-Wallace, *Manchester Guardian*; (2) Cecil Wilson, *Daily Mail*; (3) David Lewin, *Daily Express*. 'Close to hysteria': Elizabeth Frank, unidentified newspaper.

p. 72   'Dead tired': quoted in Richard L. Sterne, *John Gielgud Directs Richard Burton in Hamlet. A journal of rehearsals* (Heinemann, 1968).

p. 73   Burton's Churchill story: the version here is in 'a fascinating private diary, compiled by New York journalist Jimmy Breslin', *Sun*, 15 May 1967.

p. 73   Gielgud's biographer: Ronald Hayman, *John Gielgud* (Heinemann, 1971). His account confirms the 'until you're better' anecdote.

p. 73   Tynan: *Acting in the Sixties*, *op. cit.* 'Inadequate': interviewed by Peter Evans, *Daily Express*, 28 June 1963. 'Raving maniac': interviewed by Lewis Nichols, *New York Times*, 5 April 1964.

p. 73   Burton's second Hamlet: two American actors in the cast of this 1964 production each wrote a book about it. The 'John, dear' remark is in William Redfield, *Letters from an Actor* (Cassell, 1967); 'dreeeam of passion' and 'speaking flatly' in Richard L. Sterne, *op. cit.* The ingenious Sterne hid a tape recorder and emerged with 120 hours of recordings.

pp. 73-4 Hedda Hopper: *Daily News* (New York), 28 September 1953.

p. 74   *Frankie Howerd Show*: written by Ray Galton and Alan Simpson with Eric Sykes. BBC Light Programme, 23 November 1953. BBC Script Library.

p. 74   Approached by Cleverdon: letter beginning 'Dear Richard', 3 December 1953, asking 'Is there any chance of your taking the main narration? This is the part that Dylan would have carried, and I have naturally been thinking over the whole matter with some anxiety.' BBC Written Archives.

pp. 74-5 Burton and Dylan Thomas: Philip Burton told the story of *Two Streets* in the 'Dylan Thomas Memorial Number' of *Adam*, No. 238, 1953; he described the evening with Thomas but didn't mention the phone call. Richard Burton talked about it to the *Evening Standard*, 5 February 1971.

p. 75   Gielgud's forty parts: Richard Findlater, *The Player Kings* (Weidenfeld & Nicolson, 1971).

p. 75   A dozen parts: Ten are listed in the text, *Dark Summer*, *Castle Anna*, *Brassbound*, *The Lady's Not for Burning*, *The Boy with a Cart*, *Henry IV* Parts 1 and 2, *Henry V*, *Legend of Lovers*, *Montserrat*. The other two were brief appearances in another Fry play, *A Phoenix too Frequent*, and in Chekhov's *The Seagull*, outside London.

p. 75   *King John* reviews: quotations are from John Barber, *Daily Express*; *Manchester Guardian*; Ivor Brown, *Observer*.

p. 76   Ten years later: Thelda Victor with Muriel Davidson, 'The drama the cameras missed', *Saturday Evening Post*, 11 July 1964.

p. 76   *Coriolanus* reviews: (1) Cecil Wilson, *Daily Mail*; (2) Felix Barker, *Evening News*, both 24 February 1954. *Sunday Times*, 28 February 1954.

p. 76   'A fine end': Ivor Brown, *Observer*, 18 April 1954.

p. 76   Scribbled comments: USC, folders on *The Prince of Players*.

p. 77 $150,000 fee: Burton quoted in *New York Post*, 25 October 1964.

p. 77   Philip Dunne: in conversation. Dunne, better known as a screen writer, was also responsible for the final draft of *The Robe*; he took it over at the request of Zanuck, but 'had no interest in the picture at all'. His screenplays include *The Rains Came* and *How Green Was My Valley*.

p. 77   Documents in a library: Theatre Collection at the Lincoln Center, New York City. 8-MWEZ x nc 20,765. Folder marked 'Shangri-la Correspondence'.

p. 77   Signed in New York: *Variety*, 24 November 1954.

Christmas in Wales: Burton in *In Town Tonight*, BBC TV, 27 November 1954.

p. 77   'More sex': USC, *Rains of Ranchipur* folders.

p. 78   *Ranchipur* filming: Joe Morella and Edward Z. Epstein, *Lana. The public and private lives of Miss Turner* (Citadel, US, 1971).

p. 78   'Crippling influence ...': *Films and Filming*, October 1962.

p. 78   'Cast of Thousands!': two-page advertisement in *Los Angeles Examiner*, 28 March 1956.

p. 78   Burton on *Alexander*: *Sunday Graphic*, 9 December 1956.

p. 78   Burton on *The Robe* and *Ranchipur*: *Time*, 26 April 1963.

p. 78   *Ranchipur* advertisement: Lincoln Center, MFL nc 1324 (on microfilm).

p. 78   Gregory Peck: quoted in Sheridan Morley, 'Peck still fighting against the old image', *The Times*, 3 July 1980.

p. 79   'Snobbish about films': Olivier to Kenneth Harris, *Observer*, 2 and 9 February 1969.

p. 79   'Too busy': Burton in *In Town Tonight*, BBC TV, 24 December 1955.

p. 79   *Henry V* reviews: (1) Cecil Wilson, *Daily Mail*, 14 December 1955; (2) Tynan, *Observer*, 18 December; (3) *The Times*, 14 December.

p. 79   Tynan on *Othello*: *Observer*, 26 February 1956.

p. 80   'I think I'm afraid': Burton to Margaret Hinxman, *Sunday Telegraph*, 8 June 1969.

p. 80   'Actors from the womb': Burton to Vincent Kane, BBC TV, 12 February 1977.

p. 80   'Look at my contemporaries': Burton to Barry Norman, *Daily Mail*, 20 May 1969.

p. 80   'Acting, the job itself': to Margaret Hinxman, *op. cit.*

p. 80   Tynan's question: *Acting in the Sixties*, op. cit.

p. 80   *Variety*: 8 May 1957.

pp. 80-1 'Indiscreet account': *Evening Standard*, 28 July 1978, quoting an interview with Joan Collins in the *Los Angeles Times*. The autobiography: *Past Imperfect* (W.H. Allen, 1978).

p. 81   What Ifor said: anon, in conversation.

p. 81   The reporter: Robert Robinson, *Sunday Graphic*, 9 December 1956.

p. 81   Television producer: Cynthia Judah, letter to Burton, 14 February 1957. BBC Written Archives.

p. 81   Glib: '... because I'm very glib', to Ludovic Kennedy, BBC TV, 5 December 1977.

p. 81   Celtic blood: to Barry Norman, BBC TV, 1978, 'I get my usual periodic bursts of Welsh Celtic melancholy.'

pp. 81-2 In Tripoli: Ralph Cooper, *Empire News*, 17 March 1957.

pp. 82   Adopting a child: family information.

CHAPTER SEVEN: MARKING TIME

p. 83   *New York Times*: 6 December 1970.

p. 84   Susan Strasberg's account: *Bittersweet* (Putnam, US, 1980).

p. 84   *Ted and Jinx Show*: 3 December 1957.

p. 85   Richard Hubler: *Saturday Evening Post*, 3 October 1953.

p. 86   *Look Back in Anger*: most of the details of the production are from Alexander Walker, *Hollywood, England: The British Film Industry in the Sixties* (Michael Joseph, 1964). Walker interviewed Saltzman.

p. 86   Burton on togas: Tynan interview, *Acting in the Sixties*, op. cit.

p. 87   *Los Angeles Times*: 10 May 1959.

pp. 87-8 Daniel Petrie: in conversation.

p. 88   *Ice Palace*: the figure of $350,000, the memo and production details, USC, misc. Warner files.

pp. 88–9 Vincent Sherman: in conversation.

p. 89   Jim Backus: in conversation.

pp. 89–90 Aled Vaughan: in conversation.

p. 90   Richard Findlater: 'Life with the Swiss Family Burton', *Evening Standard*, 28 December 1959; and in conversation.

p. 90   Roderick Mann: *Sunday Express*, 19 June 1960.

p. 90   Moss Hart suggests Burton: Alan Jay Lerner, *The Street Where I Live* (Hodder & Stoughton, 1978).

p. 90 $4,000 a week: *New York Mirror*, 20 December 1960; John Gold in unidentified British newspaper, quoting Burton, 'I'm getting £1400 for *Camelot* now.'

p. 91   *Scandal and Concern*: BBC Written Archives.

p. 91   'Get that boy!': Burton quoted in *Los Angeles Times*, 1 May 1961.

p. 91   Jack Le Vien: in conversation.

p. 91   'Peter Sellers imitation': *Sunday Express*, 28 January 1962.

p. 92   'They know me as a Welshman': *Los Angeles Times*, 1 May 1961.

p. 92   *Camelot*: details of the production are in Alan Jay Lerner, *op. cit.*

p. 92   'The unfortunate thing ...': Burton to Philip Oakes, BBC radio, 14 July 1963.

p. 92   Burton to Tynan: *Acting in the Sixties*, *op. cit.*

p. 93   Bottle of vodka: *New York Times*, n.d.

p. 93   Father half Jewish etc: Burton quotes are from two interviews, *New York Mirror*, 20 December 1960; *Theatre* (US), May 1961.

CHAPTER EIGHT: CLEOPATRA AND FRIEND

p. 94   The making of *Cleopatra*: besides interviews, the main sources are Jack Brodsky and Nathan Weiss, *The Cleopatra Papers* (Simon & Schuster, US, 1963), and an edited version in *Esquire*, August 1963; Walter Wanger and Joe Hyams, 'Cleopatra. The trials and tribulations of an epic film', *Saturday Evening Post*, 1 June 1963; Kenneth L. Geist, *Pictures Will Talk. The life and films of Joseph L. Mankiewicz* (Scribner's, US, 1978); Rex Harrison, *Rex. An autobiography* (Morrow, US, 1975); Elizabeth Taylor, *Elizabeth Taylor. An informal memoir* (Harper & Row, US, 1964); Sheilah Graham, *Confessions of a Hollywood Columnist*, *op. cit.*; Mel Gussow, *Don't Say Yes Until I Finish Talking*, *op. cit.*

p. 94   'Tits and sander': Vincent Sherman in conversation.

p. 94   Groucho Marx: quoted by Brodsky and Weiss, *op. cit.*

p. 95   Skouras disenchanted: Wanger, *op. cit.*

p. 95   Taylor's earnings: *New York Post*, 20 December 1963. The figures are confirmed in *Variety* (n.d., but about 1964) reporting that a lawsuit had been filed against Taylor and Burton for alleged breach of contract, described by them as 'ludicrous'.

p. 95   Egypt at Pinewood: Geist, *op. cit.*; Wanger, *op. cit.*; *Newsweek*, 25 March 1963.

p. 96   Robin French: in conversation.

p. 97   Buying out Burton: various accounts, including Burton's (interview in *Sunday Express*, 29 January 1962) say it cost $50,000.

p. 97   Buying out Mankiewicz: Geist, *op. cit.*

p. 97   'Miss Tits': Geist, *op. cit.*

p. 97   Burton's $250,000: Geist, *op. cit.*; Wanger, *op. cit.* Burton's $500,000: the undated *Variety* report, above.

p. 97   Doc Merman: in conversation.

p. 98   Late on the set: Geist, *op. cit.*

p. 98   On fire, massaged by handmaidens, leg trouble: Wanger, *op. cit.*

p. 99   'Most public adultery': Brenda Maddox, *Who's Afraid of Elizabeth Taylor?* (Granada, 1977).

p. 99   Brodsky and the publicity chief: in conversation.

p. 99   Denials, counter-denials: Wanger, *op. cit.*; Brodsky and Weiss, *op. cit. Daily Mail*, 21 February 1962.

p. 100   John Heyman: in conversation.

p. 100   'Get away with murder': Taylor's *Memoir*, *op. cit.*

pp. 100–1 Emlyn Williams: in conversation.

p. 101   David Lewin: in conversation.

p. 101fn. Oakes interview: BBC radio, 14 July 1963.

p. 102   'I never felt dirty': Taylor's *Memoir*, *op. cit.*

p. 102   On the yacht: Brodsky and Weiss, *op. cit.*

p. 102   The friend: anon.

p. 103   Mankiewicz on a stretcher: Geist, *op. cit.*

p. 103   Mankiewicz on Zanuck: in *The Movie Moguls*, BBC Radio 4, 11 April 1979.

p. 103   Three and a half hours of film: Geist, *op. cit.*

p. 103   'Roman Jimmy Porter': the Philip Oakes interview, *op. cit.*

p. 103   'Drunk and shouting': Taylor's *Memoir*, *op. cit.*

p. 104   Frost interview: from a transcript of an interview with Burton and Taylor filmed in Budapest and broadcast on Channel 5, New York, 14 March 1972.

p. 104   'Like a French tart': *Saturday Evening Post*, 11 July 1964. 'Burnt-out Welshman': Redfield, *op. cit.*

p. 105   To Elaine Dundy: *Esquire*, December 1965.

p. 105   The Rattigan play and *London Lights*: BBC Written Archives.

p. 106   Burton on the kind gentleman: *News of the World*, 14 February 1962.

p. 106   *The VIPs*: information from anon interviews, Los Angeles and New York.

p. 106   De Grunwald's travels: *Los Angeles Times*, 10 September 1963.

p. 107   Attacked at Paddington: 'Burton Wears an eyeshield', *South Wales Echo*, 21 January 1963; 'Liz Screams! Mob Beats Up Burton', *Photoplay* (US), April 1963.

p. 107   'Street fight': to Barry Norman, BBC TV, 1978.

p. 107   Carrying a knife: Robert Ottaway, unidentified magazine, about 1966.

p. 107   The friend: anon, in conversation.

p. 107   *Time*: 26 April 1963.

p. 108   Romany Bain: 'And so it's ten years "since Scandal Time"', *Cosmopolitan*, n.d. (1972).

p. 108   MGM worried: anon interview in New York.

p. 108   Burton quoted, 1972: Sydney Edwards, *Evening Standard*, 25 February.

p. 108   'Legal separation': *Daily Telegraph*, 11 April 1963.

p. 108   Lewin interview: *Daily Mail*, n.d.

p. 108   'Pulchritudinous': interview in *Sunday People*, n.d., about 1968.

p. 108   'I loved before': *People* interview, above.

p. 109   Magazine article: Francis Wyndham, 'A day with Elizabeth Taylor VIP', unidentified magazine.

p. 109   Zanuck quoted: *Time*, 26 April 1963.

CHAPTER NINE: PICTURES OF SUCCESS

p. 110   Burton quoted: 1970, *New York Times*, 6 December; 1972, *Sunday Times*, 24 September; 1975, *Sunday Mirror*, 8 June, interviewed by David Lewin. On BBC TV, 5 December 1977, Ludovic Kennedy quoted the 'acting is shameful' remark back to Burton, who said, 'Oh no, that's a misquote. At least, I might have said it, but I was probably on the fourth bottle that day.' The 1974 interview: Elizabeth Snowden-Palmer, *The Times*, 19 August.

pp. 110-11   At Pontrhydyfen: filmed interview by Vincent Kane, BBC TV, 12 February 1977.

p. 111   The Train Robbery idea: Burton to Duff Hart-Davis, *Sunday Telegraph*, 18 April 1965.

p. 111   Burton's fee: anon interview in London.

p. 111   Choice of roles: *Sunday Express*, 31 May 1964.

p. 111   Hal Wallis: in conversation.

p. 111   Burton on *Becket*: *Life*, 13 March 1964.

p. 111   Cohen and *Hamlet*: Jack Gaver of UPI, 'How Richard Burton was "bagged" for 20-week "Hamlet" engagement', *Morning Telegraph* (New York), 4 October 1963. Cohen used his desk diary to check dates.

p. 112   Taylor quoted: her *Memoir, op. cit.*

p. 112   Burton's version: an article by Burton, 'A reluctant Hamlet reviews the tale of how it got to be or not to be', *Life*, n.d.

p. 113   *Iguana* earnings: anon interview.

p. 113   Burton gives away £500,000: interviewed by Barry Norman, *Daily Mail*, 12 April 1966.

pp. 113-14   Huston's biographer: Axel Madsen, *John Huston* (Doubleday, US, 1978).

p. 114   Secretary with diary: Thelda Victor. 'The drama the cameras missed' ('with Muriel Davidson'), *Saturday Evening Post*, 11 July 1964.

p. 114   *Hamlet* preparations: Lincoln Center. A folder (8-MWEZ X NC 21,707) titled 'HAMLET – correspondence with Gielgud, Burton and Cohen' has Burton's letter to Cohen, together with other letters and cables.

p. 114   Sheilah Graham: *op. cit.*

p. 115   Burton v Fisher: *Daily Telegraph*, 23 and 24 January 1964.

p. 115   Redfield and Sterne: see Notes to pp. 72 and 73.

p. 116   Burton's review: 'A reluctant Hamlet' etc in *Life*, n.d. (see Note to p. 112).

p. 117   The Burtons reconciled: Philip Burton.

p. 117   Wedding presents: Sterne, *op. cit.*

p. 117   Boston's welcome: Redfield, *op. cit.*; *Daily Telegraph*, 24 March 1964.

p. 117   *New York Times*: 26 June 1964.

p. 118   *Variety*: 12 August 1964.

p. 118   The *Hamlet* film: *The Times*, 26 September 1964; *Observer*, 11 October 1964.

p. 118   New York reviews: one word apiece from *New York Times, New Yorker, Time, Newsweek*.

CHAPTER TEN: MARRIED COUPLE

p. 119   Washing dishes: Romany Bain, 'The truth about our marriage', *Woman's Own*, n.d.

p. 119   Repose at night: David Lewin, *Daily Mail*, 18 May 1971.

pp. 119-20 Taylor quoted: the *Memoir, op. cit.*

p. 120   Beverly Hills woman: anon, in conversation.

p. 120   Nudity, trouser dresses: Romany Bain, *Vanity Fair*, November 1969.

p. 120   Burton on feminists: Fred Robbins, 'Is there life after Liz?', *Playgirl* (US), n.d. 1974.

p. 120   'Arrogant Welsh bastard': David Lewin, above.

pp. 120-1Burton on his daughters: Romany Bain, *Sun*, 3 July 1972.

p. 121   Dalton Trumbo: *Variety*, 15 October 1971.

p. 121fn. Fees and expenses: anon interview.

p. 121   Trumbo's biographer: Bruce Cook, *Dalton Trumbo* (Scribner's, US, 1977).

p. 121   Minnelli: his autobiography ('with Hector Arce'), *I Remember It Well* (Doubleday, US, 1974).

p. 121-2 Taylor quoted: her *Memoir, op. cit.*

pp. 122   Burton quoted: (1) *TV Guide* (US), 18 October 1969; (2) *New York Times*, n.d.; (3) *South Wales Echo*, 13 August 1969.

p. 122   The gold brooch: anon interview in London.

p. 122   *Coriolanus* envisaged: *New York Times*, 18 October 1964.

p. 122   *Observer*: 27 December 1964.

p. 123   Barry Norman: *Daily Mail*, 9 February 1965.

p. 123   *Herald Tribune*: on *Sandpiper* set, Cynthia Grenier, 'The Burtons at work and play', 3 January 1965; in Dublin, Cynthia Grenier, 'Back to the mines for Richard Burton', 30 March 1965.

p. 123   Forty-seven whiskies: to Peter Evans, *Sunday Express*, n.d.

p. 123   Burton's price: anon interview.

p. 123   Burton thanks *Hamlet*: *Evening Standard*, 9 April 1965.

p. 123   *Ice Station Zebra, Goodbye Mr Chips*: anon interview.

pp. 123-4'We did films': to Barry Norman, BBC TV, 1978.

p. 124   Papers about *Who's Afraid of Virginia Woolf*, including correspondence and studio memoranda, are in files deposited by Warner Bros at USC. In the same place, in the Ernest Lehman collection, is material catalogued under the film's title, as 'papers, memos, notes, script revisions, letters, jottings found in the desk of the screenwriter and producer of the film, E.L.'

p. 124   Lehman and Taylor: USC/Lehman.

p. 124   'Too young': Roy Newquist, 'Behind the scenes of a shocking movie', *McCall's*, June 1966.

p. 124   Taylor's campaign: USC/Lehman.

pp. 124-5Burton on the part, and on 'Elizabeth's choice': Newquist, *op. cit.*

p. 125   The moose jokes: C. Robert Jennings, 'All for the love of Mike', *Saturday Evening Post*, 9 October 1965.

p. 125   Sandy Dennis: R̯ex Reed, 'A lotta things I wanted more and didn't get', unidentified newspaper, 1966.

p. 125   Burtons' fees: USC.

p. 126   Filming schedules: USC.

p. 126   Looking after the Burtons: USC.

p. 126   Taylor's timekeeping: USC.

p. 127   Rude words: USC.

p. 127   Roy Newquist, *op. cit.*

p. 127   Offered $100,000: *Evening Standard*, 9 April 1965.

p. 128   'Retiring in 3 years': *Sunday Mirror*, 9 May 1965.

p. 128   *New York Times*: 14 November 1965.

p. 128   Payments waived: USC.

p. 128   Ear-rings and brooch: Sheilah Graham, *op. cit.*

p. 128   'My only concern': C. Robert Jennings, *op. cit.*

p. 128   'That moon-faced chap': *New York Times*, 6 September 1965.

p. 128   'Indifferent': Tynan interview, *Acting in the Sixties*, *op. cit.*

CHAPTER ELEVEN: PARADISE LOST

p. 129   'Homesickness': *News of the World*, 14 February 1965.

p. 129   'I want to go back': *Sunday Express*, 7 February 1965.

p. 129   'I wake up': *Daily Express*, 9 July 1968.

p. 130   Burton quoted: (1) and (2), *Daily Telegraph*, 2 February 1966; (3) *Sun*, 9 February.

p. 130   Reviews quoted: (1) *The Times*; (2) Alan Brien, *Sunday Telegraph*.

p. 130   Coghill complains: Cottrell and Cashin, *op. cit.*

p. 130   'What can I say?': *Sunday Telegraph*, 8 June 1969.

p. 131   'An indoor art': Burton interviewed on BBC radio, 27 September 1966.

p. 131   'Bitterly negotiated': John Heyman.

p. 131   'Mudpie in the face': the radio interview, above.

p. 131   Elizabeth Sweeting: in conversation.

p. 133   Alec Guinness: in conversation.

p. 133   *New York Times*: (magazine), 7 May 1967. © 1967 by the *New York Times* Company. Reprinted by permission.

p. 135   Title changes: *Hollywood Reporter*, 28 August 1967.

p. 135   'The sound of shock': *New York Times*, 13 February 1966.

pp. 135–6 Losey quoted: Richard Roud, 'The reluctant exile', *Sight and Sound*, summer 1979.

p. 136   Tennessee Williams: in his *Memoirs* (W.H. Allen, 1976).

p. 136   'Opportunism': quoted in Alexander Walker, *op. cit.*

p. 136   'Working together': *Sunday Express*, 17 September 1967.

p. 136   *New York Times*: n.d., summer 1967.

p. 137   Television interviewer: Barbara Howar, CBS, 4 January 1977.

p. 137   'Many failures': on BBC TV, 12 February 1977.

p. 137   Stewart Granger: interviewed by Sheridan Morley, *The Times*, 8 July 1978.

p. 138   Elliott Kastner: in conversation.

p. 138   Burton's fee etc: anon interview.

p. 139   'Vivid dreams': to David Lewin, *Photoplay* (US), February 1977.

CHAPTER TWELVE: THE TREADMILL

p. 140   Three television interviews: (1) BBC, 5 December 1977; (2) CBS, 4 January 1977; (3) BBC, 12 February 1977.

p. 140   *New York Times*: 27 February 1966.

p. 141   'Pain and riches': Roger Falk, 'Why Burton wants a baby', *Woman's Own*, 23 November 1974.

p. 141   Burton quoted: *Sunday Mirror*, article © Atticus Productions, 3 November 1968.

p. 141   The English actor: anon, in conversation.

p. 142   'A year's holiday': *Daily Express*, 23 October 1969.

p. 142   Burton on 'young people': *Hollywood Reporter*, 18 March 1970.

p. 142   Frost interview: transcript in *Listener*, 9 September 1970.

p. 142   Soda water: *Evening News*, 5 May 1970.

p. 143   'Chinese gentleman': anon.

p. 143   The critic: Richard Cuskelly, *Herald-Examiner* (Los Angeles), 18 March 1971.

p. 143   Harry Tatelman: in conversation.

p. 143   'Absolute choice': *The Times*, 10 May 1971.

p. 144   'One of those weak fellows': *Look*, 27 June 1967.

p. 144   'Unutterable rubbish': *New York Times*, n.d., 1977.

p. 144   The advertising offer: *Sunday Mirror*, 17 September 1972.

p. 144   *Villain* fees: anon interview.

p. 145   *New York Times*: 6 December 1970.

p. 145   'Knighthood on condition': *Sun*, 24 October 1977, which said Burton was 'offered the title when Ted Heath was Prime Minister'.

pp. 145-6 Interviewed on the set: for a Harlech TV documentary about the making of *Under Milk Wood*.

p. 146   American critic: Stanley Kauffmann, *Critic*, n.d.

p. 146   His drinking: anon interview.

p. 146   *New York Times*: Vincent Canby, 18 June 1971.

p. 146   Drinking and Kate: anon interview.

p. 147   Losey on Burton: Judy Stone, 'Why make a movie about the assassination of Trotsky?', *Saturday Review*, 7 October 1972.

p. 147   *The Fifty Worst Films of All Time* (*and how they got that way*): by Harry Medved with Randy Dreyfuss (Popular Library, CBS Publications, US, 1978).

p. 148   Taylor quoted: *Life*, 25 February 1972.

p. 148   Tomalin's reports: *Sunday Times*, 27 February 1977; *The Times*, 28 February.

p. 148   Victor Spinetti: in conversation.

p. 149   No gift was made: Sir Alec Cairncross, former Master of St Peter's, in conversation.

p. 149   Paddy Donnell: in conversation.

p. 149   London friend: anon, in conversation.

p. 150   Osborne on *Divorce His*: in a letter.

p. 150   Minor executive and visitor: anon, in conversations.

p. 151   Carrie Nye's article: *Daily Mail*, 28 June 1973, reprinted from *Time*.

pp. 151-4 Waris Hussein: in conversation.

pp. 155-6 Keith Baxter: in conversation.

p. 156   The friend: anon, in conversation.

CHAPTER THIRTEEN: FILM STAR AT BAY

p. 157   'The problem ...': *Sunday Mirror*, 8 June 1975.

p. 157   'Battle royal': *Playgirl*, n.d., 1974.

pp. 157-8 Film producer: anon, in conversation.

p. 158   Burton on television: BBC, interviewed by Barry Norman, September 1974.

p. 158   Laurence Harvey: quoted in *Sunday People*, n.d., probably August 1973.

p. 158   Nigel Dempster: *Daily Mail*, 5 July 1973; *Harpers and Queen*, September 1973.

p. 158   'The seventh son': *Variety*, 1 August 1973.

p. 159   The journalist: anon, in conversation.

p. 159   Burton embarrassed: *Playgirl*, n.d., 1974.

p. 159   Jack Le Vien: in conversation.

p. 160   Sydney Edwards: *Evening Standard*, 25 November 1973, and in conversation.

p. 160   'Hello, Lumpy': Romany Bain, '"We were together too much, but we can't live apart"', *Woman's Own*, n.d., 1974.

p. 160   Romany Bain: in *Woman's Own*, above.

p. 161   'Interview a drunk': Robert Kerwin, reporting from the *Klansman* set, *Chicago Tribune Magazine*, 29 September 1974.

p. 161   Burton's answers: Joe Pilcher, 'The slings and arrows of outrageous Burton', *Sunday News* (New York), 14 April 1974.

p. 161   Buying the ring; living on trout: Joe Pilcher, above.

p. 162   Merv Griffin: quotes from the interview were published in *Los Angeles Times*, 14 May 1974.

p. 162   *Playgirl*: July 1974.

p. 163   The night is freezing fast: from *The Collected Poems*. Copyright 1922 by Holt, Rinehart & Winston, Inc., Copyright 1936, 1950 by Barclays Bank Ltd. Copyright © 1964 by Robert E. Symons. Reprinted by permission of The Society of Authors as the literary representative of the Estate of A. E. Housman, and Jonathan Cape Ltd as publishers, and Holt, Rinehart & Winston, Inc.

p. 164   On television, 1977: BBC, 5 December.

p. 164   To David Lewin: *Sunday Mirror*, 8 June 1975.

p. 164   Susan Strasberg: *Bittersweet*, *op. cit.*

p. 165   Herbert Wise: in conversation.

p. 165   Taylor in court: *Daily Telegraph*, *Daily Express*, 27 June 1974.

pp. 165-6 Alan Bridges: in conversation.

p. 166   Cecil Clarke: in conversation.

p. 166   Roger Falk: *Woman's Own*, 23 November 1974, and in conversation.

p. 167   Colin Morris: in a page of letters to the *New York Times* ('Burton berated for attack on Churchill'), 8 December 1974.

p. 168   What Burton told Meelan: Meelan, in conversation.

p. 168   Burton's article: *New York Times*, 24 November 1974.

p. 169   Burton's other article: 'The shock of his presence was like a blow under the heart', *TV Guide*, 23 November 1974.

p. 169   'A bogey man': *Daily Telegraph*, 28 November 1974.

p. 170   London *Times*: 30 November 1974.

p. 170   'All killers': *Playgirl*, n.d., 1974.

p. 170   The Lewin interview: *Sunday Mirror*, 8 June 1975.

p. 171   Taylor on her illness: *Woman*, n.d. (February 1976).

p. 171   Burton at his party: *National Enquirer*, n.d.; *Daily Mail*, 11 November 1975.

p. 172   'Most beautiful woman': Robert Ottaway in unidentified magazine.

p. 172   A choice of women: *Playgirl*, n.d. 1974.

p. 173   CBS TV: 4 January 1977.

pp. 173-4 Alex Harvey: *Sun*, 25 February 1978.

CHAPTER FOURTEEN: THE PAST REVISITED

p. 175   'To discipline myself' etc: BBC TV, 5 December 1977.

p. 175   'I'm not dedicated': *New York Times*, 6 December 1970.

p. 175   'Odd and mystical': Richard Burton, *Life*, 13 March 1964.

p. 175   'A very odd being': *Playbill*, April 1965, quoting from an ABC TV interview.

p. 176   'The mystery of the actor': *McCall's*, June 1966.

p. 176   Dexter on Burton: in a letter.

p. 176   *Lear* plan founders: *New York Times*, 25 April 1978.

p. 177   'Muttering Dysart': *New York Times*, 4 April 1976.

p. 177   Burton on taking the plunge: Mel Gussow, *New York Times*, 27 February 1976.

p. 177   Walter Kerr: 7 March 1976.

p. 177   Clive Barnes: 27 February 1976.

p. 177   Burton paraphrases Barnes: BBC TV, 12 February 1977.

p. 177   *New York Post*: 6 March 1976.

p. 177   On the mirror: Mel Gussow, *New York Times*, above.

p. 177   Marian Seldes: *The Bright Lights. A theatre life* (Houghton Mifflin, US, 1978).

p. 178   'I might be dead': *Daily Express*, 30 July 1980, quoting from a US television interview recorded by Dick Cavett.

p. 178   The film producer: anon, in conversation.

p. 178   'Self-destruction': *Sun*, 25 February 1978.

p. 178   'Susan saved my life': Roderick Mann, 'Richard Burton: back from the brink', *Los Angeles Times*, 19 March 1978.

p. 178   'Profoundly shocked': BBC TV, 12 February 1977.

p. 178   'Lament for a dead Welshman': 11 July 1976.

p. 179   'Unhappy': *Sun*, 25 February 1978.

Richard Burton

p. 179   *Variety*: 17 June 1977.

p. 179   *New York*: 4 July 1977.

p. 179   Boorman quoted: *Wall Street Journal*, 30 June 1977; unidentified newspaper ('by Joseph McBride ... Hollywood'), 29 June.

p. 180   'This is home': *Radio Times*, 13 February 1977.

p. 180   The filmed interview: broadcast 12 February 1977.

p. 181   Jack Gold: in conversation.

pp. 181-2 Romany Bain: in conversation.

p. 182   Euan Lloyd: in conversation.

p. 182   Ludovic Kennedy interview: 5 December 1977.

p. 183   The director: anon, in conversation.

Bibliography

Brodsky, Jack and Weiss, Nathan, *The Cleopatra Papers* (Simon & Schuster, New York, 1963).

Burton, Hal (ed.) *Acting in the Sixties* (BBC, London, 1970).

Burton, P.H., *Early Doors. My Life and the Theatre* (Dial, New York, 1969).

Burton, Richard, *A Christmas Story* (Heinemann, London, 1965).

Collins, Joan, *Past Imperfect* (W.H. Allen, London, 1978).

Cook, Bruce, *Dalton Trumbo* (Scribner's, New York, 1977).

Cottrell, John, *Laurence Olivier* (Weidenfeld & Nicolson, London, 1975).

Cottrell, John and Cashin, Fergus, *Richard Burton ... A biography* (Coronet, London, 1974).

David, Lester and Robbins, Jhan, *Richard & Elizabeth* (Arthur Barker, London, 1977).

Findlater, Richard, *The Player Kings* (Weidenfeld & Nicolson, London, 1971).

Geist, Kenneth L., *Pictures Will Talk: The life and films of Joseph L. Mankiewicz* (Scribner's, New York, 1978).

Graham, Sheilah, *Confessions of a Hollywood Columnist* (William Morrow, New York, 1969).

Gussow, Mel, *Don't Say Yes Until I Finish Talking: A biography of Darryl F. Zanuck* (Doubleday, New York, 1971).

Harrison, Rex, *Rex: An autobiography* (William Morrow, New York, 1975).

Hayman, Ronald, *John Gielgud* (Heinemann, London, 1971).

Hurren, Kenneth, *Theatre Inside Out* (W.H. Allen, London, 1977).

Kass, Judith M., *Olivia de Havilland* (Harvest, New York, 1976).

Lerner, Alan Jay, *The Street Where I Live* (Hodder & Stoughton, London, 1978).

Maddox, Brenda, *Who's Afraid of Elizabeth Taylor?* (Granada, London, 1977).

Madsen, Axel, *John Huston* (Doubleday, New York, 1978).

Medved, Harry, with Dreyfuss, Randy, *The Fifty Worst Films of All Time (and how they got that way)* (Popular Library, CBS Publications, New York, 1978).

Minnelli, Vincente, *I Remember It Well* (Doubleday, New York, 1974).

Morella, Joe and Epstein, Edward Z., *Lana: The public and private lives of Miss Turner* (Citadel, New York, 1971).

Parish, J.R. and Stanke, D.E., *The Leading Ladies* (Arlington House, New York, 1977).

Redfield, William, *Letters from an Actor* (Cassell, London, 1967).

Seldes, Marian, *The Bright Lights: A theatre life* (Houghton Mifflin, Boston, 1978).

Sheppard, Dick, *Elizabeth: The life and career of Elizabeth Taylor* (W.H. Allen, London, 1975).

Shipman, David, *The Great Movie Stars: The international years* (Angus & Robertson, London, 1980).

Richard Burton

Sterne, Richard L., *John Gielgud Directs Richard Burton in Hamlet: A journal of rehearsals* (Heinemann, London, 1968).

Storey, Anthony, *Stanley Baker: Portrait of an actor* (W.H. Allen, London, 1977).

Strasberg, Susan, *Bittersweet* (Putnam's, New York, 1980).

Taylor, Elizabeth, *Elizabeth Taylor: An informal memoir* (Harper & Row, New York, 1964).

Tynan, Kenneth, *A View of the English Stage* (Paladin, London, 1976).

Walker, Alexander, *Hollywood, England: The British film industry in the sixties* Michael Joseph, London, 1974).

Williams, Tennessee, *Memoirs* (W.H. Allen, London, 1976).

Zec, Donald, *Sophia: An intimate biography* (W.H. Allen, London, 1975).

Index

Richard Burton's (RB's) plays and films are listed under a sub-heading of his main entry, and not separately.

Index